THE MARVEL BOOK

THE
MARVEL
BOOK

SENIOR EDITOR
Cefn Ridout

SENIOR DESIGNER
Robert Perry

COPY EDITOR
Kathryn Hill

DESIGNERS
Clive Savage, Jessica Tapolcai

INFOGRAPHIC ILLUSTRATORS
Robert Perry, Jessica Tapolcai,
Clive Savage

PRE-PRODUCTION PRODUCER
Jennifer Murray

SENIOR PRODUCERS
Mary Slater/Jonathan Wakeham

MANAGING EDITOR
Sadie Smith

DESIGN MANAGER
Vicky Short

PUBLISHER
Julie Ferris

ART DIRECTOR
Lisa Lanzarini

PUBLISHING DIRECTOR
Simon Beecroft

DK would like to thank
Brian Overton, Caitlin O'Connell,
Jeff Youngquist, Jeff Christiansen,
Rob London, Mike O'Sullivan,
Jacob Rougemont, and Joe Hochstein
at Marvel for vital help and advice;
Ruth Amos for editorial assistance;
Megan Douglass for proofreading and
Vanessa Bird for creating the index.

First published in Great Britain in 2019 by
Dorling Kindersley Limited
80 Strand, London, WC2R 0RL

Page design copyright © 2019
Dorling Kindersley Limited
A Penguin Random House Company
19 20 21 22 23 10 9 8 7 6 5 4 3 2 1
001 – 311511 – Oct/19

A CIP catalogue record for this book
is available from the British Library.

ISBN: 978-0-24135-765-1

Printed in China.

A WORLD OF IDEAS:
SEE ALL THERE IS TO KNOW
www.dk.com

CONTRIBUTORS

STEPHEN "WIN" WIACEK, AUTHOR

Stephen "Win" Wiacek has worked in all areas of the comics industry for over 30 years, as a writer, artist, editor, and designer. While running his own art and design consultancy, he taught and lectured on comics creation and production, and worked as a journalist and consultant for television and film. From 1997-2007, he was chairman of the UK professional industry body, the Comics Creators Guild.

Currently freelancing as a copywriter and reviewer, Win writes about comics for the *Marvel Fact Files* partworks, and for books such as *Marvel Year By Year: Updated And Expanded*; *The Ultimate Marvel Guide,* and *The Black Panther Ultimate Guide*—all from Dorling Kindersley.

He lives in Kent with his extremely patient wife Miki, and tells people what they should read on his *Now Read This* graphic novel review blog (www.comicsreview.co.uk/nowreadthis).

Dedicated to Stan Lee, Jack Kirby, and Steve Ditko

CONTENTS

SUPER SCIENCE AND TECHNOLOGICAL WONDERS

MAGIC AND THE SUPERNATURAL

COSMIC FORCES AND SPACE ADVENTURES

ALTERNATE WORLDS AND DIVERGENT TIMELINES

INTROD

CTION

The multimedia phenomenon we all know as Marvel began in the Fall of 1961 when comic book editor and writer Stan Lee and his top artist Jack Kirby created the company's first Super Hero comic in six years. The move would revolutionize an industry slowly emerging from a bleak downturn, but which had once enjoyed massive popularity.

Comic books were invented in 1933, but didn't really take off until 1938, with the creation of Super Heroes. Immensely and instantly popular, and generating astounding sales, the innovation galvanized established book and magazine publishers, who clambered aboard the gaudy bandwagon. Soon, dozens of companies had their own contingents of "mystery men."

Publish and be damned!
One such company was Newsstand Publications, owned by Martin Goodman, which offered numerous pulp magazines (prose periodicals) in a range of popular genres: science fiction, westerns, detectives, sports stories, jungle adventures, and more. In 1939, Goodman founded Timely Publications to exploit the Super Hero craze. Outsourcing creative duties to professional writers and cartoonists, he published *Marvel Comics* #1 in October 1939, which introduced the Human Torch and Sub-Mariner to the world. Also included in the anthology were gag pages, prose short stories, and three other comic strip adventures: the western Masked Raider, and two revamped Goodman pulp stars—hard-boiled detective the Angel and jungle lord Ka-Zar the Great.

With a monster hit on his hands, Goodman renamed his hit title *Marvel Mystery Comics,* and began flooding the newsstands with more of the same. In 1941, Timely struck gold a second time when industry innovators Joe Simon and Jack Kirby created Captain America, an icon of the era as the US entered World War II. Success triggered explosive expansion. Goodman stuck with a tried-and-true pulp formula, creating similar patriotic warriors while also developing comics for every conceivable genre, and canceling anything that wasn't an instant success.

In 1947, Timely transformed into Atlas, a major comics player relentlessly following sales trends. Atlas was the name of Goodman's distribution arm, selling not just comics but periodicals, books, and magazines. Comic book readers, however, simply came to recognize the Atlas logo on covers as a mark of quality thanks to many of the industry's greatest names producing impressive, memorable work.

Atlas shrugged
Back in 1939, Goodman had hired his wife's cousin, 17-year-old Stanley Leiber, as a general office assistant. Two years later, after his comic book managing editor Joe Simon quit, the apprentice became the new boss. Barring his war service, Leiber, who later changed his name to Stan Lee,

I was tired of doing monster mags. Joan (my wife) wanted me to make something of myself in the comic-book field. The timing was perfect. The elements were all at hand. Kismet.
Stan Lee

would steer the comics division for decades to come, ultimately changing the face of comic books. In the years before television ownership was widespread, comic books were hugely successful. However, the advent of free entertainment in the home changed everything. Rapid shifts in reading tastes made it hard to repeat the comic book successes of the war years. Readers failed to distinguish one cowboy hero or funny animal from another, and comics began to increasingly rely on licensed stars of film and TV to headline their titles. In the early 1950s, Atlas tried to revive Captain America, Sub-Mariner, and the Human Torch, but the public weren't buying it. Literally.

To make matters far worse, the industry came under concerted fire for corrupting America's youth. The attack was sparked by one Dr. Fredric Wertham, a child psychologist who claimed to have found a causal link between violent comics and juvenile delinquency in his 1954 book *The Seduction of the Innocent*. Seized on by the media, the issue became so heated that it resulted in Senate hearings in 1954. It prompted those publishers that managed to survive the ensuing public scrutiny and censure to

institute a draconian self-regulatory Comics Code Authority to prove they had cleaned up their act. It wasn't enough. In 1957, Atlas distribution foundered and their comic book line imploded, barely hanging on with a skeleton staff, and only publishing 16 titles every other month. Popular genres included teen humor, westerns, and science fiction monsters, however industry leader National Periodicals had just begun reviving Super Heroes for a new space-age generation. This time the kids were on board and sales started slowly rising. Legend has it that Goodman, ever sensitive to trends, told Lee the company had to give Super Heroes another go.

Marvel Tales

When Stan Lee and Jack Kirby launched the Fantastic Four in 1961, they discarded all preconceived notions for costumed crusaders. Rather than being comradely and clean cut, these were almost heroes by accident: raucous, self-absorbed, and argumentative—and they didn't wear costumes! These superhumans were all too human. It was a revelation and an instant hit with a new generation of readers: savvy, college-age kids keenly attuned to a fast-changing world

Marvel Comics—not so much a name as a special state of mind... a mood, a movement...
Stan Lee

and more than ready for relatable stories, mature themes, and complex characters.

Upsetting the status quo became the norm for the newly named publisher Marvel Comics, as Lee and his growing band of cocreators debuted, in swift succession, a range of compelling antiheroes and resplendent Super Heroes. One was a misunderstood, gamma-irradiated monster called the Hulk; another a nerdy teenager whose guilt makes him become the hero Spider-Man; and another who claimed to be a Norse god, stranded on Earth by his father to teach him humility. And none were really trusted by those they saved or the public at large. »

That outcast theme shades all eras of Marvel's output and continues to this day: from mutant outsiders the X-Men and alien gangs such as Guardians of the Galaxy, to crazed vigilantes like the Punisher and the lunatic mass murderer Deadpool, to the satirical comedy relief of Howard the Duck and Squirrel Girl.

In the 1960s, however, Marvel's runaway success took everyone by surprise, bringing with it change. Lee's increasingly limited time and resources, combined with a demanding publishing schedule, led to a new way of working.

Eschewing detailed scripts, which was common practice in the comics industry, veteran illustrators Kirby, Steve Ditko, Don Heck, Bill Everett, Marie Severin, and Lee's brother Larry Lieber would "direct" stories from a plot outline. After pacing, settings, and action were laid down on paper, the story would then be scripted, lettered, and inked. Talented newcomers, who had grown up reading Marvel comics, soon joined the company's expanding ranks, enjoying the creative liberty of collaborative production to push the horizons of

graphic storytelling. The era's climate of social unrest and radicalism also permitted creators to explore themes never tackled before. Innovative, influential writers such as Roy Thomas, Archie Goodwin, Steve Gerber, Don McGregor, Frank Miller, Ann Nocenti, Louise Simonson, and others were matched by the adventurous visual triumphs of Jim Steranko, Neal Adams, Jim Starlin, P. Craig Russell, and more, all striving to push the comics medium forward. The tradition remains strong as ever today with brilliant raconteurs

Inside the Bullpen

In 1961, Stan Lee oversaw a one-room publishing enterprise in mid-town Manhattan, using freelancers for all aspects of comic book production. With Lee handling much of the writing and editing, he was able to call on arguably the best comic artists in America: Jack Kirby (née Jacob Kurtzman) and Steve Ditko, unique stylists and gifted storytellers. Both applied their skills convincingly across a range of genres, with Kirby excelling at action-packed

science fiction, while Ditko's quirky, light touch was perfect for supernatural morality tales. When the Fantastic Four became a hit, the company followed up with an explosion of Super Hero titles, to which the trio quickly turned their collective talents.

As demand increased so did Marvel's offices, becoming the legendary "Bullpen," a creative, collaborative hothouse where many veteran and new artists and writers would create the pioneering Age of Marvels.

like Brian Michael Bendis, Mark Waid, Jason Aaron, G. Willow Wilson, Kelly Sue DeConnick, Jonathan Hickman, Mark Millar, Ed Brubaker, and illustrators like Alex Maleev, Sara Pichelli, Adi Granov, Joe Quesada, Annie Wu, and others, reshaping the Marvel Universe to reflect and challenge modern tastes.

House of ideas

Marvel's other game-changing idea in the early 1960s was simple yet subtle. Where rival companies' heroes joined forces, but largely worked in a vacuum and depended on their own abilities to succeed, at Marvel, everything happened in the same place at the same time. Heroes frequently got in each others' way, clashed over jurisdiction, and often fought each other in one another's titles. This shared continuity is the glue holding the "Marvel Universe" together: adding veracity and authenticity to the mix no matter how far and wide-ranging the universe grows. Equally important was a self-deprecatingly inclusive authorial style. A consummate showman, Lee established a wry rapport with Marvel's readership: jokey banter, conspiratorial asides, and foreshadowing created a sense

of belonging to an exclusive club. Lee also gave talks at college events, establishing brand awareness, and further fostered loyalty via letters pages where fans could communicate with the creators, editors, and each other.

Artists and writers even became characters in Marvel's fictional world and, unlike other publishers, Editor-in-Chief Lee allowed them a measure of recognition by crediting creators in the comics themselves. Moreover, the carefully cultivated intimate relationship with readers afforded creators a platform to address contemporary social issues. How many kids first confronted racism, intolerance, militarism, drug abuse, or ecological crises thanks to a gripping, well-crafted tale in a comic book?

Marvel became the market leader in comic books, but it was when its characters and concepts escaped from two dimensions to animated/live action movies and TV series, and video games that the brand truly became a global force. Yet even the success of these digital and audio-visual incarnations rests on a solid foundation created by the amazing, astounding, and sensational stories in the comics discussed on the following pages.

How to explore this book

The Marvel Book provides an in-depth look at the concepts that underpin the sublimely interconnected Marvel Universe (or more exactly Multiverse), including key events and characters. Supporting the main "in-Multiverse" articles are elements that contribute to the big picture. Introductions frame the subjects being discussed; On the Record boxes offer context and fast facts; infographics and timelines provide clarification and perspective; topic boxes highlight notable people or themes; and quotes give a feel for the characters and narrative texture of the source material. This book isn't a comprehensive examination of Marvel Comics, but an entertaining, insightful guide to a complex and thrilling universe that is best enjoyed in the pages of a comic book. ∎

Nuff said!
Stan Lee

A MULTIVE
MARVELS

RSE OF

The cosmos is infinite, filling an endless universe with wonders beyond imagining. However, even that immeasurable vastness is the merest fraction of the true scope of the Multiverse. Far from hypothetical, this vital crucible of creation abounds with a variety of worlds, shadow dimensions, and voids that sustain life of every description. From the smallest subatomic quanta to the boundaries of physical matter and beyond, this is an arena of Marvels...

A time before time in a region beyond space.

↑

UNKNOWN

Created to entertain him, The First Firmament's Aspirants battle their own creations, the Celestials. The clash sunders the First Firmament, birthing countless universes and driving the First Firmament's consciousness to the Far Shore.

↓

FIRST BIG BANG

Possesses a consciousness derived from the remnants of the Second Cosmos. This second Multiverse has a female aspect and originates the concept of heroism in Lifebringer One.

↑

THIRD COSMOS

FIRST COSMOS

↓

Composed of and comprising mass intelligence, the First Firmament forms, eventually creating life to lessen his loneliness.

SECOND COSMOS

↓

The first Multiverse is born from the scattered remains of the First Firmament. It, too, is a sentient manifestation of all life within it.

FOURTH COSMOS

↓

A Multiverse of questions and mysteries, personified by a now-missing abstract entity referred to as "the Pilgrim."

The totality of reality is an Omniverse composed of endlessly proliferating Multiverses and constituent universes that are kept apart by a highly reactive form of informational space called the Superflow. This barrier medium demarcates each universe while also connecting all living things. From here, sentinels of First Race "The Builders" occasionally bestow the blessing of a "White Event" on sentient races they regard as having reached a threshold of evolutionary advancement. Cosmic protocols then create monitoring "shepherds" from the populace to supervise planetary ascension. When that moment arises for Prime Earth during the Seventh Cosmos, the Superflow malfunctions and the process is corrupted.

Student Kevin Connor is selected by the mechanisms of the White Event to become a shepherd, a planetary protector imbued with infinite power. However, the malfunctioning Superflow attaches the all-powerful Starbrand to Connor without imparting any knowledge of how to control it. Many savants believe the Superflow is a cosmic channel that enables telepathy in sentient life-forms, while also feeding dreams and cognitive inspiration.

Each universe within the Superflow links to, and forms part of, a network of dimensions, subdimensions, and planes made up of fundamental forces that are surrounded by ethereal, largely inaccessible mystical realms. These realms are inhabited by beings able to circumvent the

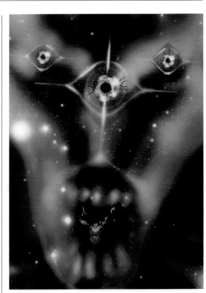

A single mistake In the beginning there was only one universe, the First Firmament, which eternally regrets creating life to allay its solitary existence.

Manifested as the Fourth Multiverse, a reality of magic and illusion.

Primal material Alpha/Omega impacts with Galan of Taa, triggering a Big Bang. Eternity manifests as the embodiment of life's totality. The Seventh Cosmos prematurely ends as alternate universes collide within it as a result of Doctor Doom and Molecule Man's war with extradimensional Beyonders.

When their time is over, all multiversal personifications pass on to a place beyond: the Far Shore. Beyond that lies the unknowable "Next Place."

FIFTH COSMOS

SEVENTH COSMOS

UNKNOWN

SIXTH COSMOS

EIGHTH COSMOS

Instigator of science and builder of the junction to everywhere. When their time ends, the essence of the Sixth Cosmos combines with the last mortal survivor, Galan of Taa, to avoid the encroaching Big Crunch.

Restarted as an almost identical continuation of the Seventh Cosmos, but with some mortal survivors aware of the rebirth and the true nature of reality. The abstract entity Eternity is renewed and maintains the new existence.

natural, rationalistic laws of physical matter. Almost all dimensions, planes, realms, and realities—with the notable exception of Limbo—experience time in a linear fashion.

Altered states

Encompassing the Multiverse are regions generated by the processes of life and populated by higher beings of an abstract or conceptual nature. The notion is difficult for any non-super-genius to grasp, but Prime Earth's transdimensional security force A.R.M.O.R. (Alternate Reality Monitoring and Operational Response) has proposed practical definitions for whenever its agents have to face dimensional breaches. "Parallel Universes" are alternate realities related to Prime Earth that rarely intersect through natural circumstance, but can be artificially manipulated into intersecting. "Perpendicular Universes" are alternate realities naturally crossing over with Earth, generally at a fixed point, such as the Watcher Uatu's home on Earth's Moon. "Wave Universes" are realms and dimensions that converge with Earth for a prescribed period of time, such as reappearances of the fabled city K'un-Lun in the Himalayas every ten years.

None of these rules applies when voyagers access the Nexus of Reality (mostly located in the swamps around Citrusville, Florida) or its sometime guardian Man-Thing. Underspace, Microverse, Macroverse, and Overspace are progressively more singular planes connected to the Multiverse and Superflow, while remaining separate from them. These realms are accessible from any universe within the Multiverse if their inhabitants reach a tipping point of power or possess sufficient cosmic awareness.

Reality is compromised in the dying days of the Seventh Cosmos, when the immensely powerful and curious Beyonders attempt to erase the Multiverse as part of a grand cosmic experiment. Their scheme is hijacked by Earth super-genius mage Victor von Doom who ascends to ultimate power. He turns the last survivors and remnants of various realities into a personal fiefdom where he is the supreme being. His reign ends when Reed Richards and the Molecule Man thwart his schemes and bring about a new Eighth Cosmos, which closely mirrors the destroyed Seventh. ∎

CELESTIAL CONNECTIONS
PARALLEL LIVES

ON THE RECORD

DESIGNATION
Seventh Cosmos

PROPERTIES
Infinite worlds/dimensions, superabundant life, fixed physical laws, magical hacks, quantum links, ascended and abstract beings

STATUS REPORT
Doomed to destruction

The Multiverse is the result of a cyclical process: an endless succession of Big Bangs and Big Crunches, where a mass of super-condensed material explodes, forms galaxies and realities over time, before ultimately collapsing and recondensing to begin the cycle anew. When each new Cosmos emerges from the chaos of explosive creation, the first function is the establishment of natural laws. All universes need constant and immutable physical processes such as speed of light, atomic weights of elements, characteristics of subatomic particles, and definitions of life. When in place, these laws allow creation to progress without constant supervision.

These natural laws can vary greatly—even from region-to-region and plane-to-plane within the greater whole—but once finalized, must be self-regulating. The most critical physical process to form for each reality is the establishment of time: its inherent progression, stability, and responsiveness to outside manipulation, alteration, and divergence. This is crucial as higher beings can circumvent any physical law by utilizing magic: a process of high-energy acts of will operating as the "cheat codes of creation." These uncanny operations bypass the physical laws of reality for personal outcomes.

Although abstract beings and other omnipotents are restrained by ethics and guided by omniscience, lesser beings who gain power are less circumspect. They aspire to the

Gateway guardian A mix of science and magic, Man-Thing is a portal to the Multiverse via the Nexus of Reality.

same exalted positions of power by twisting or circumventing natural laws. At the highest levels, the difference is indistinguishable, but the use of magic comes at a price. Only if the magic wielders possess sufficient reserves of personal power or will, such as the god Loki or

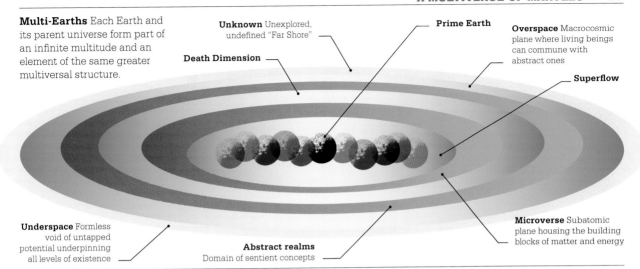

Multi-Earths Each Earth and its parent universe form part of an infinite multitude and an element of the same greater multiversal structure.

Unknown Unexplored, undefined "Far Shore"

Death Dimension

Prime Earth

Overspace Macrocosmic plane where living beings can commune with abstract ones

Superflow

Underspace Formless void of untapped potential underpinning all levels of existence

Abstract realms Domain of sentient concepts

Microverse Subatomic plane housing the building blocks of matter and energy

demon Mephisto, can they hope to avoid damaging physical, mental, and spiritual repercussions.

Quantum entanglements

Life in the Multiverse—from nano-bacteria to gods and greater—runs on the basic principles of evolution and natural selection. These forces work against those systems that are designated to seek balance in all things, and that ongoing conflict resonates throughout all levels of creation. In the elevated realm of abstract beings it manifests as the eternal struggle between Master Order and Lord Chaos. All universes are constructed with parallel and adjacent dimensions as well as a full array of malleable time-strands. History and all possible futures are simply another facet of the universal structure. As life proliferates, a Web of Life and Destiny forms: a psychic and sometimes physical conduit between realities—transferring power, psionic information, and even beings across realities. The Multiverse is buffered by myriad quantum realities, most easily accessed from the material world by shrinking. Countless inhabited universes exist in the Microverse, divided into disparate realms such as Sub-Atomica. Here physical laws differ and the gap between science and magic is much smaller. Similar effects can be found in the Macroverse, which exists "above" multiversal physicality. Beyond these regions exist the higher planes: domains and meeting points for abstract beings and those mortal creatures whose determined efforts have granted them enough might to ascend. ■

See also: Prime Earth, Enchanted source code, Weirdworld and otherworldly realms

Multiversal migrants

Although passage between alternate realities is extremely difficult, it does occur, and at an accelerated rate once the mechanisms underpinning existence begin to malfunction. For unexplained reasons, many unique beings are drawn to Prime Earth such as peace-loving Kree voyager Noh-Varr or hyper-powered "paramedic of the Multiverse" America Chavez, originally from the sublime Utopian Parallel. Many individuals reoccur—albeit minutely altered—in manifold realities. Prime Earth has been home to various iterations of the multi-powered Marcus Milton, aka Hyperion (pictured). An orphaned Eternal and Super Hero on Earth-13034, -712, and -31916, working alongside the Squadron Supreme and Avengers, Milton has also been the atomic fueled villain Zhib-Ran, plucked from the Microverse to serve in the Grandmaster's Squadron Sinister as well as sociopathic world-killer King Hyperion of Earth-4023.

EYE IN THE SKY
THE WATCHERS

ON THE RECORD

POWERS
Beyond comprehension, seemingly limitless

KEY OPERATIVES
Uatu, Aron, Ecce

MISSION
Neutral, noninterventionist observers of all universal events and phenomena

STATUS REPORT
Since the murder of Uatu, Watcher activity has been less apparent in Earth proximity

During the earliest eons of the universe, one species achieves sublime intellectual sophistication. Deeply philosophical, yet extremely curious, this advanced race quickly masters all aspects of science and rationality to become almost godlike in their powers. Following much philosophical debate, these innately benevolent beings opt to share their findings and advancements with other, lesser races and begin traveling in small groups to every outpost of existence in their universe. After teaching simple nuclear technology to an emergent species called the Prosilicans, these proud, cosmic benefactors move on to new worlds, unaware that their well-intentioned gifts will be abused and turned into doomsday weapons. When they return, they find the planet Prosilicus shattered by atomic war and the survivors curse them for their meddling.

This revelation deeply shocks these advanced beings, who vow that from this time on, they will restrict their insatiable desire for knowledge to simply observing all that occurs. Never again will these newly self-appointed

Cosmic convocation Only significant threats to their own kind can compel the Watchers to act together.

Doctrine of noninterference?

Although most Watchers carry out their self-appointed task in isolation, one of them is forever compelled to interact with his subject world. After the Fantastic Four discover his lunar citadel, Uatu inexplicably alerts humanity to impending threats such as the planet-ravaging Galactus, timeline alterations, and even social upheavals such as those wrought by the American Superhuman Registration Act. He warns his favored human heroes of impending dangers and creates an extra-dimensional prison for the all-powerful Molecule Man when he first manifests. After being blackmailed by Kree terrorists into attacking Mar-Vell, Uatu is put on trial by his fellow Watchers. Admitting his guilt and that he has become emotionally invested in the survival of humanity, Uatu pledges to mend his ways and is allowed to resume his station. When Uatu is murdered, his archived secrets are dispersed to random Earthlings with devastating consequences. It is unclear if Uatu remains dead.

> There are worlds beyond... this reality... Worlds not of energy and matter, but of thought and mind.
> **Uatu**

"Watchers" interfere with the development of another species. Dispersing across the universe, the Watchers stand mute and solitary witness to a wealth of natural wonders, triumphs, and tragedies, the travails of intelligent life-forms, and every aspect of the cosmos.

Look, but don't touch

Their mission continues over billions of years, but is not without incident or personal danger. For reasons no mortal may comprehend, Watchers exist in an eternal cold war with the Celestials: interventionist space gods who aggressively manipulate the development of species across creation in contrast to the Watchers' own avowed hands-off approach. For countless eons, the observations of a factional sect of Watchers is transmitted to The One: a supreme living repository of data. Eventually, however, this ultimate Watcher overreaches, seeking to end the current Multiverse before its appointed time and restart reality with the great sin of Prosilicus erased. The scheme is thwarted by the Celestials, whose executioner Exitar destroys The One, postponing universal termination for millennia.

One Watcher who may regret his vow of noninterference is Ecce. In the early evolution of the current Multiverse, he encounters a power-laden artifact that has survived the Big Crunch of the previous Multiverse and the Big Bang that created the current one. This object is a capsule containing the rapidly-evolving being who will become the Devourer of Worlds, Galactus. Despite fearing for the future, Ecce observes passively, rather than destroy it. Ecce's resolve to let fate decide the outcome of his inaction leads to wide scale destruction after Galactus begins consuming planets.

Not all Watchers possess Ecce's self-restraint. Aron, nephew of Prime Earth observer Uatu, grows infatuated with Earth's heroes and villains. He attempts to create a pocket universe to preserve them as his playthings and orchestrates a clash between the Watchers and the Celestials to cover for his actions. For his selfish interventions—which cause the destruction of The One—Aron is stripped of his powers and position. His life energies help create a new version of The One to store the accumulated knowledge of the remaining Watchers. ∎

Power cut For Ecce, the greatest trial is suppressing his power in situations he knows will harm universal life.

THE HUNGER
GALACTUS

ON THE RECORD

REAL NAME
Galen of Taa

ALLEGIANCES
Eternity, Infinity, Eternity Watch, The Ultimates

BASE
Taa II **(starship)**

POWERS
Beyond comprehension, almost limitless

MISSION
Galactus does what Galactus must

STATUS REPORT
After a brief period as a life giver and maker of worlds, Galactus has returned to consuming planets

When the Sixth Multiverse shrinks and dies, it reverts to a primordial state of potential known as the Cosmic Egg. In the last moments of existence, space explorer Galan of Taa drives his starship into the core of the reforming Cosmic Egg—the universe's largest sun—in a final desperate act of defiance against the ending of life and light. As reality expires, Galan is spared oblivion in the impending Big Crunch by the Sixth Cosmos—the personification of the Multiverse's sentience. Donating its essence, the Sixth Cosmos preserves Galan until a new Big Bang begins the cycle of existence.

Following the birth of a new Multiverse, Galan's subtly altered remains—now merged with the Sixth Cosmos—gestate for eons until discovered by Ecce the Watcher who accidentally triggers an astonishing metamorphosis. Galan's vestigial form rockets into space, gathering energy and matter, reconstituting as a colossal incubator for an entirely new and unique being.

Devourer of Worlds

After millennia, something emerges with godlike power and insatiable hunger. Ingesting the life-force of worlds, the being's relentless passage across creation leaves devastation in its wake: toppling ancient civilizations and destroying embryonic planets. Intergalactic races learn to accept losses to their territory or devise strategies and technologies to mask their presence from this embodiment of inescapable doom known as Galactus, Devourer of Worlds. This strange, cosmic colossus must constantly consume to subsist. As time passes, Galactus recruits lesser beings to

True colors Galactus has no true form, but wears armor he has built himself to contain his cosmic energies.

Galactus' heralds

Galactus only consumes worlds containing energies sufficient to sustain life, be it primordial organisms or ancient societies. Rather than wander aimlessly, he creates a succession of heralds to search out these planets. Some, like Silver Surfer Norrin Radd, seek planets devoid of sentient life. However, because of the Devourer's vast appetites, even he is not always able to spare inhabitants from doom. Other heralds such as Morg, Terrax the Tamer

(pictured), or Stardust are chosen for their cruelty and lack of empathy. These intergalactic scouts crave battle and revel in bringing terror and destruction to helpless sentient creatures.

Earth has supplied Galactus with a disproportionate number of heralds, including Mike the Preacher (the Praeter), Cybermancer Suzie Endo, Alison Blaire (the Dazzler), Anti-Man Conner Sims, and Fantastic Four cofounder Johnny Storm.

locate suitable worlds for him. He imbues these heralds with a measure of his incalculable power. When one—the Silver Surfer—leads him to Earth, the unimaginable occurs. Galactus is defeated and driven away by the planet's defenders.

The Earthlings repeatedly repulse Galactus, leading the major empires of the universe to pay attention to this seemingly innocuous, fringe world. At one point, Galactus almost starves to death, but is saved by the Fantastic Four's Reed Richards. The scientist deduces that Galactus is a vital component of vast metaphysical processes that underpin existence, and that all creation would suffer if he were gone. In truth, Galactus is a divinely appointed cosmic agent of balance between Death and Eternity, and is critical to the evolution of life itself.

Although unintentional, Galactus' actions have huge consequences. After he consumes Skrull homeworld Tarnax IV, the empire dissolves into civil war. This leads to a fundamentalist religious revival and the Secret Invasion of Earth by shape-

shifting zealots who believe the world to be their promised land. Having almost destroyed Earth so often, Galactus is eventually targeted by the planet's champions, the Ultimates. Their solution to the Devourer's never-ending threat is to overfeed him. This forcibly evolves him from a creature hungry for planetary energies into a benevolent voyager transforming dead planets into hospitable, life-sustaining worlds. As Lifebringer, Galactus works with the Ultimates to save Eternity from an overwhelming multiversal threat, before being cruelly reverted back to his former world-ravaging state by the all-powerful cosmic entity Logos. ∎

Throughout the cosmos, worlds must die... that Galactus may live!
Galactus

WORLD CENTRAL
PRIME EARTH

ON THE RECORD

DESIGNATION
Earth-616, Terra, Tellus

INHABITANTS
Mortals, gods, demons, Eternals, Deviants, mutants, Inhumans, *Homo mermanus*, extraterrestrials, other races

LOCATION
Sol solar system

MISSION
Supporting varied life under the auspices of Gaea

STATUS REPORT
Currently Eighth Iteration, under constant threat

Earth is the third of eight planets orbiting Sol: a G-type (G2V) star—commonly referred to by humans as a yellow dwarf—in the Milky Way galaxy. Over billions of years, the Sol system has been home to a number of godlike beings and alien travelers. Eternals from Earth have colonized other planetary bodies such as Uranus and Saturn's moon Titan. Over billions of years, Earth has been the breeding ground for countless species, including gods, demons, and many primordial races adept at manipulating—and dependent upon—magical forces. These beings' natural gifts pass down to a fraction of Earth's dominant intelligent life-form, *Homo sapiens.* Mankind has evolved from a hominid species selectively adapted by Celestial gods to create genetically unstable "Deviants" and super-powered "Eternals." This intervention leaves "Latents" to evolve through natural selection.

Earth's dominant simian species is further shaped over eons by numerous spacefaring races such as Fortisquians, Nuwali, Kree, and others. Each intercession results in further divergence of the hominid genome. Kree war-biologists create a super-intellectual offshoot who ultimately alter their own DNA to become Inhuman, while the Fortisquian Caretakers of Arcturus unleash clans of science-based animorphs similar to werewolves and magical Cat People. Other rival species spring from the Deviants' rash genetic experiments, while numerous Moloid subspecies and giant monsters dwell in the vast networks of tunnels and caverns riddling the substrata of the world. The origins of aquatic *Homo mermanus,* however, remain a mystery. This nomadic tribe controls the ocean depths, some 70 percent of the planet. Thankfully, unlike aggressively territorial humans, that seems to be enough for them.

Lucky stars
Earth's location is advantageous to many interstellar civilizations. A natural hyperspace warp is located in the Sol system, used by empires such as Skrull, Kree, and Shi'ar. Positioned midway between the perpetually warring Kree (in the Greater Magellanic Cloud) and Skrulls (Andromeda Galaxy), the

Why is this world always the one upon which the fate of everything hinges?
Silver Surfer

warp is strategically crucial to both, with Earth a desirable springboard for many alien cultures.

Although much of humanity is insular by nature, constant alien invasions, superhuman battles, and magical incursions have created a perceptual and technological imbalance. Residents of major cities such as New York, have little choice but to acknowledge the existence of super-science, otherworldly beings, or even alternate realities, while those insulated by distance, traditional beliefs, and sheer luck do not. There is no market for flying cars, sentient robots, or miraculous resurrections in rural townships or riches enough to attract the attention of super-crooks.

Prime target Earth is the focus of recurring alien invasions, though some media in the big cities seem determined to deny their existence.

Earth is a permanent fixture in every alternate universe of the Multiverse, but not all of these Earths are the same. Prime Earth is a focal point for events of cosmic significance and a magnet for refugees from parallel realities. The planet is linked to countless adjacent dimensions, divine planes, and mystical realms, such as the Ten Realms of Asgard; it is a keystone in celestial mechanisms that underpin the Multiverse. Earth also houses the extraordinary transdimensional Nexus of Reality, linking countless worlds whose inhabitants are sustenance for a vast number of supernatural predator species and parasitical entities like Nightmare and other Fear Lords. ∎

See also: Parallel lives, Asgardians, Weirdworld and otherworldly realms

Multiversal ground zero

Earth is the center of a network of countless interlinked zones of energy and existence, from inhabited worlds, to vast repositories of primal forces.

Alternative universes
Interception and access points to divergent realities and parallel Earths

Force planes Source of exotic transformative energies: Light, Darkforce, Kinetic Energy Dimension

Earth's core
Subterranean realms
Earth's surface

Higher realms
Dimensional conduits to pan-universal realms—Dreams, Nightmare, Dark Dimension, Quadriverse, Limbo, Hells, Heaven—that intersect with alternate worlds; path to Micro- and Macroverses

Weirdworld Geo-stationary dimensional vortex absorbing weaker realms and their inhabitants

Unstable divergent timelines "Temporary" realities created and destroyed through meddling with the time stream

Rational dimensions Adjacent, science-dominant domains such as Fifth Dimension, Mojoverse, Cancerverse, Negative Zone, Sub-Space, Dimension Z

Mystic realms Domicile dimensions home to magical emigrants and cultures from Earth, such as the Seven Capital Cities of Heaven, Otherworld, Olympus, and Asgard's Ten Realms

Metaphysical dimensions Highest, abstract and conceptual levels of reality; beyond Micro- and Macroverses

WAR
AND
PEACE

In every aspect of creation, conflict is a constant. A self-perpetuating struggle for survival and advantage underscores the actions of all sentient creatures. However, where some beings maintain the right to take what they want by any means necessary, others believe they have a duty to protect those weaker than themselves. Their selfless acts of heroism are best enshrined in the mantra: "With great power comes great responsibility."

Earth forms around dying Celestial the Progenitor: a casualty of war between Creation's oldest races.

Cretaceous-Paleogene extinction event ends dinosaurs' dominance. Set banished as Gaea cultivates the world's mammal species.

African humans and proto-gods drive out numerous beast races and establish a pantheon of the Orishas.

War between the Deviants and Celestial Second Host leads to the Great Cataclysm that sinks Atlantis and ushers in the age of barbarism.

Immortal, teenage demi-god Herakles begins a life of monster hunting and villain crushing.

4.5BN YEARS AGO   **C. 66M YEARS AGO**   **C. 1M YEARS AGO**   **C. 20K YEARS AGO**   **1291BCE**

C. 4BN YEARS AGO   **MORE THAN 1M YEARS AGO**   **LESS THAN 1M YEARS AGO**   **2620BCE**

Earth's magic-charged biosphere generates proto-god the Demiurge. Mystically adept life begins... as does war.

The Celestials' First Host creates Latents, Deviants, and Eternals. Deviants battle with Eternals and enslave their human cousins.

Asgardian Odin, human heroes, and mystics unite to destroy the mad Celestial, Zgreb.

Pharaoh Imhotep, En-Sabah Nur, and the Fist of Khonshu defeat a Brood invasion. Imhotep founds the Brotherhood of the Shield and the Spear.

From greater than gods to less than beasts, all inhabitants of every reality operate under one great impulse: fight or die, evolve or fade away. Across the Multiverse, life is a struggle composed of personal survival, the drive to propagate, and—in the case of those organisms that can organize and cooperate—expand and dominate the environment. From clan to tribe, nation to empire, and across all reality, these imperatives repeat almost without exception. In all such struggles, some individuals excel: better warriors, strategists, and survivors. They will come to be known as heroes.

Billions of years ago as gasses and space debris cool and coalesce into the planet Earth, a Celestial infected by horde-parasites dies and is enveloped by the developing

...a season of heroes and Marvels has dawned... To save everything, the heroes have come.
Uatu

landmass of Antarctica. This Progenitor's poisoned life-force contaminates the region and, eventually, the entire evolving biosphere. These deific, mutagenic essences permeate every strata and atom of the planet, rendering it unique in the cosmos. Earth will be a singular world, populated by combative beings. Its inhabiting species—in particular, progressively transformed humans—develop an unparalleled capacity for mutagenesis, superhuman alteration and, paradoxically, violence and compassion in equal measure.

Fight for life

The world fills with indigenous life after its power-charged biosphere spontaneously achieves sentience in the form of the Demiurge, the embodiment of living planetary potential. A global response creates mighty beings: Elder Gods Gaea, Set, Chthon, and countless more. Earth-Mother Gaea joins with the planet's biomass to spawn new, less ethereal life-forms, however, her companions predate upon each

Shield Brotherhood savant Zhang Heng repulses the Celestial Madonna, moving her Celestial Egg from Earth to the Sun.

114ce

Young Asgardian Thor begins adventuring and monster hunting in northern Europe.

c. 9th century ce

Galileo Galilei leads the Brotherhood of the Shield to repel planet-devouring Galactus.

c. 16th century

The advent of costumed Super Heroes is followed by two decades of unsanctioned masked vigilantism.

1914–18ce

1289bce

Fifty empowered heroes and gods band together under mariner Jason to seek the Golden Fleece as Argonauts.

c. 6th century ce

Arthur Pendragon and Merlin found Camelot: a bastion of nobility and heroism in a dark, savage age.

c. 1k years ago

The Celestials' Third Host lands in Peru and defeats a coalition of gods from many pantheons.

c. 1865ce

Two-Gun Kid, Black Rider, and Red Wolf herald a wave of masked vigilantes cleaning up the American west.

1939–45ce

A proliferation of costumed heroes rise to defend liberty from fascism. Their actions lead to the Modern Age of Marvels.

other and her newborn offspring, degenerating into demons. Gaea summons and mates with the Demiurge. The result is primal god Atum who, as the Demogorge, heroically battles and consumes the demons. Eventually, the surviving horrors flee the planet to shelter in distant, inaccessible dimensions.

In the Cretaceous period, the primal champion returns from a sabbatical in the Sun to complete his purge, finally driving serpentine Set into exile and marking the end of reptilian dominance on Earth. Atum spawns new creatures and evolves into the primary deity Ra. The gods he fathers mirror and presage the rise of mammals: especially the primates who will eventually dominate Earth. Primal spider god Omm and others take regional territories, while tribes and families of gods form new

Rock god Primal deity Atum cleanses the developing Earth of demons and dark gods, ready for humanity to flourish.

pantheons such as the aboriginal deities who claim the planet's southernmost lands and flourishing abstract realm the Dreamtime.

Later deific clans spread across the globe as returning Celestials and other races manipulate the evolution of short-lived, potential-filled animal species, steering them, over eons, toward high intelligence and power. Ra becomes Amon Ra, primordial Sun god of Egypt and founder of the Heliopolitan pantheon. His family quarrel and war with each other, establishing a pattern of avarice, ambition, and conflict that will repeat endlessly among various societies of gods and the mortals who worship them.

Numerous races evolve to share the planet: Celestial-designed humanity and its offshoots the Eternals and Deviants; Kree-altered Inhumans, *Homo mermanus,* and other intelligent species. Many die out, but combat strengthens the victors and makes them fit to rule. ∎

A GATHERING OF HEROES
ORDEAL AND TRIUMPH

In a world constantly in conflict, extraordinary individuals inevitably emerge to change the course of battles and the history of empires. For millennia, Earth is clandestinely sheltered from alien assault beneath the warlike mantle of the Brotherhood of the Shield and the Spear, but successive leaders resist the urge to seriously interfere with human progress and hegemony. Extraterrestrial incursions are repelled by secret scientific intercession, and mass gatherings of warriors are reserved to decide the fate of nations.

Brief flowerings of individual heroic endeavor, such as the monster-killing of Olympian, Asgardian, or Eternal stalwarts including Hercules, Thor, and the Forgotten One, gradually decline. The foredoomed utopia of King Arthur's alliance of knights in 8th Century Camelot flourishes then falls—adding to humanity's rich trove of stories and legends, but doing little to improve

Battle world Earth's champions are equally valiant, whether crushing the world's enemies or battling each other.

the lot of mankind's masses. Here improvement comes only gradually; through toil, minor technological innovation, and laborious advances in agriculture. All through these times, extraordinary champions battle mankind's perennial foes

Trial by combat

In a Multiverse that thrives through conflict, the concept of personal clashes and gladiatorial contests repeats endlessly across existence. Some clashes are personal and cerebral, duels of mind and intellect, but most are visceral and violent, measuring the physical prowess of contenders and their appetite for victory. More disturbingly, the prospect of such contests of champions is considered entertainment by most races in existence. The Shi'ar empire's judicial system includes public trial by combat, and worlds like Sakaar (pictured)—and Earth—applaud ruthless battle, whether it be a state-sponsored arena or illegal cage-fighting pit.

Crucially, cosmic heavyweights such as Universal Elders Grandmaster, Challenger, and Champion will decide the fate of entire worlds by the actions of the living playing pieces they pit against each other.

with valor, but in anonymity. The status quo begins to change with the emergence of a new breed of masked adventurers who come to the fore during World War I.

Masked marvels

There have always been heroes who conceal their identities, such as Sir Percy of Scandia who battles for King Arthur as the Black Knight, or lawyer Matt Hawk who seeks justice as the Two-Gun Kid in the American Old West. However, the flamboyantly garbed and nationalistic Freedom's 5 gain public scrutiny in the press and boost morale in the trenches of WWI. The unofficial unit undergoes numerous personnel changes, before quietly retiring when peace returns.

Once conflict ends, nations and governments prefer that masked champions return to seclusion and anonymity. Their disruptive and potentially subversive actions are removed from public sight and their achievements quickly minimized and preferably forgotten as the task of everyday progress and profit resume. However, the genie is out of the bottle and the following 20 years sees recurring outbreaks of masked vigilantes and mystery men combatting a marked rise in both uncanny crimes and common

Blades of glory In holding evil at bay, Black Knight and Valkyrie both favor the use of magic swords.

gangsterism. To the public, however, reports of fantastic heroes, mad scientists, and rampaging monsters remain the fanciful products of fiction. The official stance changes when the Axis alliance of Nazi Germany, fascist Italy, and Imperial Japan begin their war of conquest. The Nazis, especially, have been stockpiling ancient arcane artifacts, funding new scientific methods of cheating death, and experimenting with ways to super-charge human physiology. They have also been seeking alliances with hidden forces most of the world refuse to believe in: wizards, gods, and lost races like the Atlanteans.

This period coincides with a wave of shocking, highly publicized debuts: a super-strong flying merman attacking New York, amazing robots and flaming artificial men, and costumed vigilantes declaring war on criminals everywhere. An age of Marvels has arisen.

When World War II erupts and the Axis begins its seemingly unstoppable conquest of Europe and the East, the US government starts creating its own fringe-science projects. It harnesses its intellectual resources into weaponizing atomic energy as well as its own citizens. Utilizing Nazi defectors and German refugees, the US military seeks to create Super-Soldiers to complement the army of patriotic citizens who come forth to defend the nation as Super Heroes. Again, once peace is declared, the authorities expect the unsanctioned militias to retire, except those they can control or oversee.

The present is a different world. Too much proof exists of the need for Super Heroes. Suppression and cover-ups cannot hide the fact that Earth is threatened by unnatural terrors with which the authorities simply cannot cope. ∎

See also: Captain America, Wartime heroes, Vigilantes and Mystery Men

GODS OF WAKANDA
ORISHAS

ON THE RECORD

KNOWN MEMBERS
Thoth, Bast, Kokou, Mujaji, Ptah, Nyami

ALLEGIANCES
Wakanda, Heliopolitan pantheon

POWERS
Immeasurable strength and longevity, magic fueled by worship, energy manipulation

MISSION
Defending Wakandans, body and soul

STATUS REPORT
Returned to glory after the people sought their help

O ver a million years ago, clans of mystical beast folk—collectively known as the Originators—are driven from East Africa and imprisoned in trans-dimensional nether-realms by migrating humans. Remnants of a vast array of sentient beings spawned by Earth Mother (and Elder God) Gaea and primal deity Atum the Demogorge, the Originators had at first welcomed the human wanderers until competition for resources ignited a brutal war. Although savage and powerful, the Originators prove ultimately helpless against the combined prowess of human warriors, the mystic powers of pre-Wakandan mages, and the worship-fueled might of the humans' hero-gods the Orishas.

During this time of tumultuous transition, a huge meteor crashes in the region, mutating many of the now-dominant humans. These mortal horrors are destroyed by the warrior-cult of charismatic leader Bashenga, who trains his followers to battle the monstrosities created by the mineral mound his descendants will come to call Vibranium.

...We are Wakanda. Change can only multiply our glories.
T'Challa

King of beasts Fearless Bashenga and his descendants prove that Panthers are the true lords of every jungle.

Aligned to both the Orishas and the Heliopolitan pantheon, predator-deity Bast seeks out Bashenga as she requires faithful guardians and a secure repository for sacred secrets. They strike a pact that creates an interventionist, but monotheistic, religion connected to a number of spiritual regions. Among such areas are the Djalia Ancestral Plane—housing the race's every memory—and the Kummandla: Realm of the Remainders, an extension of the human spirit, and an infinite shelter for dead gods and their disciples. The alliance also creates a ghostly council of chiefs residing in Necropolis, the City of the Dead, who offer advice from beyond the grave to generations of Black Panther chiefs. As the people thrive, they divide into 24 warring tribes, but are eventually united under the Black Panthers' rule. Their unified lands would come to be known as Wakanda.

Church and state

Over millennia, Wakanda prospers in total secrecy, a haven of learning kept safe by a dynasty of warrior-kings and a sacrosanct policy of complete obscurity. The self-sufficient nation employs extreme measures to assure that no potential invaders learn of its existence. Thanks to Bast's patronage and Vibranium, Wakanda becomes the most advanced nation on Earth. As civilizations rise, successive Panther kings use spies to infiltrate the outside world and steer colonizing empires in other directions.

However, after King T'Challa brings the nation onto the world stage, chaos, disaster, and even invasion wrack the country and people. Proudly rationalist and forward-thinking, the young king outlaws sorcery in Wakanda, forcing the practice out of his new cities back into the rural regions where it had originated. Yet many Wakandans—

including Queen Mother Ramonda—still consult "witch-men," and eventually circumstances dictate that T'Challa reinstate the works of shamans and wizards.

Following attacks by Atlantis, alien invasions, and a multiversal crisis, civil war further weakens the people's spirit and it seems that the Orishas have forsaken Wakanda. When the ancient Originators return, slaughtering citizens as shock troops of the preternatural predator Sefako the Adversary, the Royal Family discovers how some humans empowered by faith can become gods. With Wakanda reeling from the Originators' brutal assaults, the

Godforsaken Modern Wakandans don't turn to their ancient gods until disaster strikes and prayers go unanswered.

ancient Orishas finally remanifest, battling alongside T'Challa, his sister Shuri, and their foreign allies. As all Wakandans—the *Dora Milaje*, the military, and shamans—resist the incursion, T'Challa's estranged wife—and the country's former queen—Storm joins the fight. So beloved is she by the people that their adoration, hopes, and worship amplify her powers; magnifying her strength until—as a new Wakandan goddess on Earth—Storm routs the Adversary. ∎

Wakanda forever

Primordial Africa is inhabited by numerous tribes and species—the Originators—spawned by Earth mother Gaea. They are driven into exile by nomadic humans and their god-heroes, the Orishas.

Decades later Bashenga leads his tribe in fighting mutant monsters created by raw Vibranium. Bast sponsors Bashenga's people, introducing science and knowledge in return for eternal devotion.

1940s Black Panther Azzuri, Captain America, and Nick Fury's Howling Commandos repel a Nazi invasion of Wakanda. Azzuri provides a sample of Vibranium that forms part of Cap's new shield.

A year later T'Challa joins the Avengers and openly declares Wakanda's hitherto secret existence to the world.

Approx. 1,000,000bce A huge Vibranium meteor crashes to Earth in Wakanda, East Africa.

Centuries later 24 warring local tribes unite as the kingdom of Wakanda and institute a total exclusion policy.

Decades later T'Challa challenges the Fantastic Four, revealing Wakanda's electronic jungle and the nation to outsiders for the first time.

Now T'Challa travels into deep space and discovers the existence of the Intergalactic Empire of Wakanda.

LIVING WITH GODS
ASGARDIANS

ON THE RECORD

LOCATION
Formerly extradimensional; then in the Solar System; currently destroyed

POWERS
Immense strength, durability, and longevity; energy and matter manipulation; magic

MISSION
Defending all life from evil

STATUS REPORT
Having long interacted with humans, Asgardians are worshipped as gods by many in Europe

After the Elder Gods are driven from Earth in antediluvian times, nature spirit Gaea and first god Atum spawn humanity's mortal precursors and semi-ethereal beings of great power. These sublime, yet lesser, gods are aligned with potent cosmic forces, and forge links with humans in various regions of the world. Among these are the Aesir, one of the later pantheons to bond with mankind. Initially a ferocious nomadic warrior

tribe led by their chieftain Bor, the Aesir move to cold northern climes. With territory on Earth curtailed by worshippers of other deities, the Aesir explore adjacent dimensions permanently linked by the branches of the World Tree Yggdrasil, and settle in a dimension they call Asgard. It is connected to Midgard (Earth) and the other seven branches, or realms, by Bifrost, the Rainbow Bridge, and guarded by all-seeing god Heimdal.

Many Aesir, or Asgardians, join primitive heroes of Midgard to battle monsters and alien invaders. When Bor dies, his son Cul, God of Fear, becomes ruling All-Father, but his reign is brutal. He is ousted by his brothers Ve, Vili, and Odin, and imprisoned deep in Earth's ocean. New All-Father Odin seeks to extend Asgardian territories through the dimensional branches of the World Tree. He allies his people with the Dwarves of Nidavellir and the Light Elves of Alfheim, but wages war on the Giants of Jotunheim, the sorcerous Vanir of Vanaheim, the Dark Elves of Svartalfheim, and the Angels of Heven. When the Angels abduct Aldrif, Odin's baby daughter, his retaliation results in the severing of Heven from Yggdrasil and the removal of its inhabitants from the Multiverse.

Can there be anything closer to heaven than to live and die in eternal battle?
Odin Borson

Twilights of the gods
Eventually Odin sees the folly of his actions, turning away from war for its own sake and dedicating his people to fighting injustice. However, his realm is locked in an inescapable 2,000-year cycle of death and rebirth called Ragnarok. Obsessed by unending prophecies of doom and the recurring twilight of the gods, Odin seeks ways to break the cycle. After one such cataclysm, as his pantheon is again reborn, he travels to Midgard and mates with Gaea—in her guise as the giantess Jord—to father a half-human child, Thor. The boy will represent a new generation of champions less attuned to, or constrained by, Asgard.

Epic sagas The inhabitants of the Ten Realms spend eternity in a continual state of intrigue, conflict, and combat.

Thor is raised on Asgard by Odin's wife, Freyja. As he grows, Thor leads his fellow Asgardians into undreamed of exploits. However, Odin's plan is a qualified success: Ragnarok still comes, but the result is not a static rebirth, it is a wholly new outcome. His people even become open to new experiences, especially Earthly science and technology, and after Odin's own death, Asgard breaches the dimensional barrier to materialize over Broxton, Oklahoma.

Asgardians establish regular contact with mortals and are soon enmeshed in Earth's constant wars and political dramas. Tragically that connection also includes Asgard's greatest enemies. Earth is increasingly terrorized by Storm and Frost Giants, various tribes of trolls, dragons, demons, sorcerers, and even Odin's banished brother Cul the Serpent, liberated by the Hammer of Skadi. When King Malekith and his malign Dark Elves invade Midgard, that bond also serves to unite heroes of Earth and Asgard in the all-consuming War of the Realms. ■

The Ten Realms World Tree Yggdrasil is a localized cosmic axis connecting a number of pocket dimensions to Earth. A living symbol of the Asgardian pantheon's belief structures, it links the realms of many races.

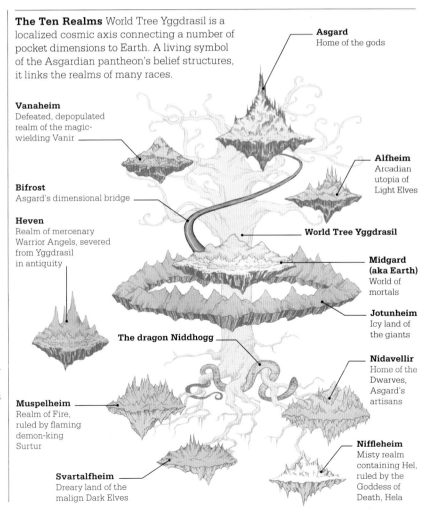

Asgard
Home of the gods

Vanaheim
Defeated, depopulated realm of the magic-wielding Vanir

Alfheim
Arcadian utopia of Light Elves

Bifrost
Asgard's dimensional bridge

World Tree Yggdrasil

Heven
Realm of mercenary Warrior Angels, severed from Yggdrasil in antiquity

Midgard (aka Earth)
World of mortals

Jotunheim
Icy land of the giants

The dragon Niddhogg

Nidavellir
Home of the Dwarves, Asgard's artisans

Muspelheim
Realm of Fire, ruled by flaming demon-king Surtur

Niffleheim
Misty realm containing Hel, ruled by the Goddess of Death, Hela

Svartalfheim
Dreary land of the malign Dark Elves

AS BELOW, SO ABOVE

OLYMPIANS AND OTHER GODS

ON THE RECORD

LOCATION
Extra-dimensional space connected to Mount Olympus in Greece

POWERS
Immeasurable strength, durability, and longevity; energy manipulation; magic

STATUS REPORT
Olympians have ceased contact with humans but maintain covert influence, other pantheons still operate and retain active followers

All Earth's divine pantheons descend from Elder Goddess/Earth Mother Gaea and prime god Atum the Demogorge. Gods draw power from the devotions of humans and their geographical domains are directly connected to the territories of their worshippers. As humanity progresses, many fruitless battles between warring gods end in stalemate as only the conversion of mortal congregations can expand their power bases. Moreover, when

humans convert to other religions, the power and influence of indigenous local gods fade. Many divine tribes simply cut ties and remove themselves to adjacent planes and dimensions.

Responding to the arrival of Celestial space gods in prehistoric times, a Council of Godheads is formed to counter the threat. After resolution, it remains in place to resolve disputes among pantheons, but otherwise the gods keep to themselves as their influence ebbs. One of the earliest pantheons to peak and fade are the Egyptian gods—Heliopolitans—whose worshippers are absorbed first by Greek and then Roman human expansion. Heliopolitans pass into obscurity, but some malcontents seek ways to consolidate and sustain their power.

Divine indulgence

Bast makes a pact with the Wakandans of Africa, becoming an interventionist deity in a secret kingdom. Other revenants like serpent-god Seth strive to maintain relevance by attacking Earth and even other pantheons in their dimensional citadels. This is also the tactic of Hellenic death-god

> Am I unjust? Of course! But I am also utterly necessary!
> **Zeus**

Pluto, who targets Earth and the preserve of Norse gods, Asgard.

Olympians influence human culture and civilization in Greece and Rome between 2500BCE and 500CE before retiring to their hedonistic pursuits as monotheism deprives them of worshippers and strength. The only exception is Poseidon who, as Father Neptune, remains prime deity of the Atlanteans in an arrangement similar to Bast's. On withdrawal from mortal realms, Olympians take with them most of the bizarre beings and beasts that attended or battled them. Soon centaurs and winged horses become the stuff of legend. Zeus bans all contact with

Earth, but later reverses the edict, accepting that some monitoring is necessary. The Olympus Group is formed: an Earthly commercial enterprise designed to watch—and influence—human development.

The Hellenics also reach an agreement with the Celestial-generated race of Eternals. Their scientifically created powers mirror those of the gods, causing centuries of confusion as the wandering immortals are frequently mistaken by humans for actual deities.

Although most pantheons retreat into other realms, some remain fully realized on Earth. The Daevas of Asia still embody a thriving religion, with worshippers around the globe, but choose to act sparingly on Earth. More commonly, ancient gods act through human agents such as Cheyenne divinity Owayodata, who bestows power upon Johnny Wakely and William Talltrees, making them guardian Red Wolves of justice in the 19th and 21st centuries; or Amadeus Cho, who is consecrated the

Partisan pantheons The Council of Godheads includes Inca god Inti, Horus of Egypt, and Japan's Izanagi-No-Mikoto.

Olympians' new Prince of Power following the death of the demi-god Hercules. Recently, however, humans have become increasingly aware of the existence of deities long-described as imaginary and mythical. This is leading to a resurgence of divine interest in Earthly affairs and, inevitably, the potential for more and greater wars of the gods. ∎

Hercules

Born to cleanse the world of monsters and usher in an age of rationality, Herakles is the son of Alcmena of Thebes and Zeus, who took the form of her husband Amphitryon to seduce her. The boy becomes a mighty hero, battling beasts and toppling kings before he is killed through treachery by the centaur, Nessus. Retrieved from Hades by Zeus and then transformed into a powerful, living Olympian god, Herakles —meaning "Glory to Hera"— resumes his activity on Earth.

Throughout his adventures, he is attacked by Hera who hates how a half-human tribute of Zeus' infidelity is more revered than her own son, Ares. In reply, Herakles accepts the Roman form of his name and becomes Hercules. Roaming for many years, the burly, bombastic warrior is the personification of heroism, before being recalled to Olympus. Later, after an innocent clash with dimensionally adrift Thor (Odinson), Zeus despatches Hercules to Earth to investigate a new Age of Heroes.

GUN LAW
OLD WEST HEROES

ON THE RECORD

KEY OPERATIVES
Two-Gun Kid, Rawhide Kid, Apache Kid, Ringo Kid, Night Rider, Black Mask

ALLEGIANCES
Avengers

BASE
American West (1870–1901)

MISSION
Keeping the peace

STATUS REPORT
A host of brave heroes bring law and order to regions that have none

Hands up, owlhoots! This is the Rawhide Kid talkin' at'cha!
Rawhide Kid

As Earth enters an age of rapid technological progress, evil opportunists become ever more ingenious and rapacious. On the frontier of the American West, ordinary bandits and cunning robber-barons compete with uncannily empowered villains to prey on ordinary, law-abiding citizens. They are all opposed by valiant lawmen, misunderstood outlaws, and a new breed of hero: highly skilled gunfighters who mask themselves with fake identities or gaudy costumes. All across the lawless West, mysterious avengers such as Two-Gun Kid (pictured above), Black Mask, and Apache Kid quell the ravages of super-bandits like Dr. Danger, the Raven, Tarantula, and evil speedster, Hurricane.

The already harsh life of settlers is also occasionally threatened by otherworldly and time-displaced perils. Even the skies prove to be harbingers of doom. Kid Colt and the Arizona Girl face their harshest challenge in Wilcox, Oklahoma, where they expose a band of shape-shifting aliens (Skrulls) impersonating valued allies such as Jesse James and the Rawhide Kid.

The greatest manifestation of these unearthly wonders occurs in Tombstone, Texas in 1873. When a Super Hero from the future, Hawkeye, crashes to Earth, he finds the town enslaved by the futuristic despot Kang the Conqueror. Hawkeye's knowledge and skills prove invaluable to a coalition of the Rawhide, Two-Gun, and Ringo Kids, Night Rider (later known as Phantom Rider), and Kid Colt in defeating the invader— as does the last-minute appearance of three apparent gods: Thor, Immortus, and Moondragon. When the dust settles and the time-travelers depart for their home era, Two-Gun Kid goes with them, hungry to see what tomorrow holds for heroes. ∎

Top guns The dauntless Rawhide Kid is equally adept with his twin Colt Single Action Army Peacemaker revolvers.

AGENTS OF FREEDOM
VIGILANTES AND MYSTERY MEN

ON THE RECORD

TEAM NAMES
Freedom's Five, Mystery Men

MISSION
Avenging the wronged, punishing the wicked

STATUS REPORT
Freedom's Five: government-sanctioned operatives active during World War I

Mystery Men: vigilantes active in the US in the 1920s

I don't think any man was meant to wield that kind of power.
The Revenant

The Great War of 1914-1918 spawns a new generation of masked heroes as well as macabre menaces such as the vampire Baron Blood. The Allies' war efforts are bolstered by a loose knit team of human heroes dubbed Freedom's Five: American aviator Phantom Eagle; British warriors Sir Steel and masked commando Union Jack; Silver Squire; and Frenchman Crimson Cavalier.

When the US joins the conflict, Freedom's Five is supplemented by superhuman agents. Although less well-reported, champions such as

Albion (a mystic Pendragon Knight descended from the heroes of Camelot); super-strong, bulletproof John Steele; and the legendary Iron Fist, Orson Randall, all distinguish themselves in battle against the Hun. Randall comes from a centuries-long line of martial artists trained in the mystic city K'un-Lun, who use their powers to anonymously battle injustice. Bearing modern arms and gifted with astonishing physical abilities—including a glowing punch like an exploding howitzer shell—Randall decimates the German forces before vanishing in the last days of the conflict. The constantly fluctuating team even defeat an invasion of

London by Martian tripods at the war's end (pictured).

After the Armistice, the world attempts to move on, but a Pandora's box has been opened. Over the next two decades, stories of occult predators and scientific madmen opposed by valiant bands —such as Randall's Confederates of the Curious—persist. In 1920s United States, history is made when five vigilante "Mystery Men"—the Operative, the Revenant, Achilles, the Surgeon, and the Aviatrix— join forces to successfully repel a supernatural incursion by the demonic Fear Lord, Nox. ■

Mystery Men Separate but interlinked cases briefly bring the vigilante loners together against a threat to all mankind.

SENTINEL OF LIBERTY
CAPTAIN AMERICA

ON THE RECORD

REAL NAME
Steven Grant Rogers

ALLEGIANCES
**Invaders, James (Bucky)
Barnes, Nick Fury and
the Howling Commandos,
United States of America,
Democracy, Freedom**

POWERS
**Chemically-enhanced to
peak physical capacity,
augmented healing system,
extended longevity**

MISSION
**Fiercely patriotic, Rogers
fights tyranny and injustice
on the home front and
around the world**

As the 1930s draw to a close, superhuman menaces and "masked mystery men" begin to appear, adding to fears of another global war. Concerned, US authorities look to establish their own superhuman task force to combat these threats in the form of Project: Rebirth. The critical factor is Dr. Abraham Erskine,

recently extracted from Nazi Germany by US agents Nicholas Fury and Red Hargrove. Erskine's discoveries promise to transform ordinary mortals into physically and intellectually perfect soldiers. Regrettably, the data Erskine was forced to leave behind would form the basis of Project: Nietzsche, the Third Reich's own Super-Soldier program.

A test subject is required, but Erskine's radical procedures seem too dangerous and his colleagues balk at taking the final step. Elsewhere, sickly Steve Rogers has repeatedly been classed as 4-F: too frail to fight. Despite the US's neutral status, the young man's zeal to enlist impresses General Chester Phillips. He pushes Rogers through the Super-Soldier program, and the new recruit becomes the first test subject. However, a Nazi agent infiltrates Project: Rebirth, murdering Erskine and leaving Rogers as the project's only Super-Soldier. Erskine had refused to record key parts of his formula—including crucial radiation therapy—and those details die with him.

Symbol of liberty
With no prospect of being able to replicate the process, the War Department drafts Rogers, training him in every martial art and strategic system. Now a morale-boosting,

Beacon of hope
Cap's costume is designed to project a reassuring example of Truth, Freedom, Decency, and Democracy.

Secret soldier

The details of the Super-Soldier process die with Dr. Erskine, but Colonel Walker Price and Dr. Wilfred Nagel are determined to reconstruct it and give the US a super-army. Unwilling to experiment on white servicemen, they opt to conscript 300 African-American soldiers to their top-secret project, testing various formulations on them until only a handful survive and are relatively operational. These enhanced but mutated survivors are then treated as an expendable commando team on black ops missions, until only Sgt. Isaiah Bradley remains.

In 1943, after Bradley returns from a supposed suicide mission to eliminate the creator of a Nazi Super-Soldier Serum, he is unjustly court-martialed for stealing US government property and going AWOL. He remains imprisoned until 1960, when outgoing President Eisenhower pardons him on condition that he never reveals any detail of the covert Captain America project.

him in every martial art and strategic system. Now a morale-boosting, patriotically clad symbol of US power, Rogers becomes the government-sanctioned adventurer Captain America, whose clashes with saboteurs, spies, gangsters, and costumed villains become part of the army's propaganda machine. Rogers is supported by his intensively trained (but human) partner, James Barnes, aka Bucky. Although vital, their well-publicized exploits provide cover for secret overseas missions that deal crippling blows to the Axis powers after World War II starts. These missions are often carried out alongside specialist units such as Sergeant Nick Fury's Howling Commandos, or spy operatives like Agent Peggy Carter.

As the war proceeds, the Allies face the growing menace of super-scientific and supernatural foes. To engage these threats, Captain America and Bucky are seconded to a new combat unit consisting of the Sub-Mariner, Human Torch, Toro, and the Flaming Kid. Dubbed "The Invaders" by British Prime Minister Winston Churchill, the team takes the fight to the heart of Adolf Hitler's "Fortress Europe." Battling beside

Knight rider Cap was originally issued with a heater-shaped shield and sidearm to take on Nazi spies and saboteurs.

truly superhuman "marvels," Rogers discovers his ability to lead and inspire his comrades to victory.

Captain America and Bucky remain at the forefront of the war, facing soldiers, super-weapons, monsters like Baron Blood, and arch-villains such as the Red Skull. Their downfall comes at the hands of Nazi scientist Baron Heinrich

Zemo. In early 1945, with Germany collapsing, Zemo tricks the heroes into pursuing a drone-missile that explodes over the Atlantic, seemingly killing them both.

President Truman orders the incident to be hushed up, recruiting William Naslund (formerly Super Hero Spirit of '76) and young Fred Davis to impersonate Captain America and Bucky until the war against Japan is concluded. Naslund dies in 1946 facing android conqueror Adam II, and is replaced by another Cap-inspired champion, Jeff Mace, formerly the Patriot. ∎

As long as freedom may be threatened... Captain America must follow his destiny... wherever it may lead!
Captain America

AGE OF MARVELS
WARTIME HEROES

ON THE RECORD

TEAM NAME
The Invaders

KEY MEMBERS
Captain America I and II, Bucky, Human Torch, Toro, Sub-Mariner, Union Jack I and II, Spitfire

BASE
Times Tower, New York City; Clock Tower, Westminster Palace, London

MISSION
Crushing tyranny on home soil and abroad

STATUS REPORT
Most members retire when the war ends

The horrors of another European war and a rising tide of espionage and sabotage in US cities disturbs many Americans who resolve to help in any way they can. Some of these are individuals just discovering unnatural abilities that they have been using to fight crime. Now they turn those gifts to defending their

homeland and wiping out the combined threat of Germany, Italy, and Japan—the "Axis Powers." Others are detectives or adventurers like Tom Halloway, who crushes crime and evil as the Angel.

Across the US, a wave of Super Heroes captivates the public consciousness, risking their lives to confront an upsurge of monsters, madmen, and Super Villains. Fighting beside bizarre beings like Sub-Mariner and the Human Torch, or incredible mechanical miracles

Heroes united An army of costumed champions and empowered individuals arise to battle beside valiant soldiers.

like Elektro and Dynamic Man, are mortal masked sensations such as Captain America and Bucky. Their anti-espionage exploits inspire a legion of Stars and Stripes imitators including the Patriot, Miss America, the Defender and Rusty, Captain Terror, Citizen V, and Spirit of '76. Journalists dub these ever-multiplying mystery men "Marvels."

> Look out, Axis...
> Here we come!
> **The Invaders**

In late December 1941, German spies steal part of Dr. Abraham Erskine's Super-Soldier formula and target visiting British Prime Minister Winston Churchill. Chief agent Krieghund creates Nazi superhuman Master Man for the assault, leading to an impromptu team-up of Captain America, Bucky, Sub-Mariner, the Human Torch, and his junior partner Toro:, resulting in an astounding battle on American soil.

After defeating the plot, the heroes are asked by Churchill to become a specialized taskforce—the Invaders—to tackle Hitler's forces on the European mainland. The squad expands as the years pass. British hero Montgomery Falsworth—World War I's masked commando Union Jack—comes out of retirement to join the team, and when he is crippled battling Nazi vampire Baron Blood (also his brother), his daughter Jacqueline replaces him as super-speedster Spitfire. The group further expands when Jacqueline's brother Brian returns from Germany—where he battled behind the lines as the Mighty Destroyer—to become the second Union Jack.

Home front heroes

The Invaders spend much of the war in Europe and Africa, occasionally returning to the US. One fateful visit results in the creation of a US-based team every bit their equal. Back in the US for a public war-bond tour, the Invaders are brainwashed by the Red Skull, with only "weakest" member Bucky left behind. With FBI assistance, Bucky organizes a Liberty Legion of newer, unaffiliated heroes who unite to crush the threat. They subsequently stay together for the duration, safeguarding US shores.

Liberty Legionnaires Whizzer and Miss America serve overseas with the Invaders and after the war join Namor, Human Torch, and Toro in a short-lived post-war All-Winners Squad. They are joined by replacement Bucky Fred Davis and Captain Americas William Nasland (Spirit of '76) and, following his predecessor's death, former Patriot Jeff Mace. They battle spies, gangsters, deranged nuclear scientists, and an invasion from the future, before acrimoniously splitting up at the end of the 1940s, when costumed crusaders fall out of fashion and fade from public view. ■

See also: Captain America, Bucky/Winter Soldier, Vigilantes and Mystery Men

Where next? With the war over, there is little prospect of adventure for the heroes of the All-Winners Squad.

Mighty Destroyer

The full extent of Nazi atrocities remains unrevealed until the war ends, but their experiments in mysticism and super-science lead to many disasters. Perhaps the worst stems from imprisoning British citizens Brian Falsworth and Roger Aubrey along with US journalist Keen Marlow. Aubrey is transformed into a doll-sized super-man, while Falsworth and Marlow are held in the same concentration camp as Eric Schmitt. The dying chemist had been Abraham Erskine's assistant and had created his own Super-Soldier Serum. To keep it from his captors, Schmitt gives the serum to his cellmates. It turns them into human weapons who escape and jointly sabotage the Nazis behind enemy lines, both assuming the codename Mighty Destroyer to confuse the enemy.

When Falsworth eventually joins the Invaders, his now-revived lover Aubrey joins Marlow as another fearsome Destroyer (pictured), terrorizing the German occupiers until the war's end and beyond as a member of the anti-fascist secret society V-Battalion.

BROTHER IN ARMS

BUCKY/WINTER SOLDIER

ON THE RECORD

REAL NAME
James Buchanan "Bucky" Barnes

ALLEGIANCES
Invaders, Young Allies (WWII), New Avengers

POWERS
Peak martial artist and marksman, bionic left arm

MISSION
Defending liberty and democracy

STATUS REPORT
Seeks redemption after years as a mindless weapon of tyranny

Installed by army chiefs as Captain America's partner, orphaned army brat "Bucky" Barnes is intensively trained to undertake black ops duties deemed unseemly for the nation's symbolic figurehead. He is designed as an inspirational American counter to the Hitlerjugend (Hitler Youth). Serving valiantly at home and abroad as one of the Invaders, Bucky also

Abiding allies Forged in the heat of battle during WWII, Cap and Bucky's friendship is an enduring, unbreakable bond.

organizes other Super Hero teams: the adult Liberty Legion and juvenile squads Kid Commandos and Young Allies. In early 1945, he and Captain America are reported killed in action battling Baron Zemo. In fact, Bucky's maimed body is recovered from the North Atlantic by a Russian submarine. In the Kremlin, Soviet scientists seek to extract the Super-Soldier Serum from his blood, but on discovering he is merely human, place him in cryostasis.

In 1954, Bucky is revived, brainwashed, and code named the Winter Soldier. Fitted with a bionic arm and with his memories suppressed, Barnes' skills are exploited to assassinate enemies

of the state. Between missions, he is returned to hibernation, aging mere months over several decades. When the Soviet Union collapses, the Red Skull acquires the Winter Soldier and, while battling Captain America, Barnes' memories are restored. After Steve Rogers is apparently killed, Bucky becomes a new Captain America, but reassumes his Winter Soldier role when the original returns.

Torn by a need to atone and the knowledge that freedom comes at a cost, Barnes roams the world righting wrongs until Nick Fury Sr. is transformed into the Unseen. Assuming Fury's role, Barnes becomes the latest Man on the Wall, covertly and tirelessly safeguarding others from all manner of menaces. ∎

You did your part,
now let me do mine!
Bucky

SKY'S THE LIMIT
THE FALCON

ON THE RECORD

REAL NAME
Samuel Thomas Wilson

ALLEGIANCES
Avengers, S.H.I.E.L.D., New Invaders, Heroes for Hire

POWERS
Peak martial artist, psychic affinity with birds, mechanically assisted flight

MISSION
Saving lives and redeeming the repentant

STATUS REPORT
Currently fighting street crime and social issues

Son of a Harlem Minister, Sam Wilson loses his parents to street violence and rejects his father's faith. He becomes a social worker, but his life is forever changed after the Red Skull transforms him into a secret weapon against Captain America. His memories altered by a reality-warping Cosmic Cube, Wilson is marooned with Steve Rogers on Skull's Exile Island. Believing himself to be a reformed gangster, Wilson is trained by the Super-Soldier, exploiting a (cosmic cube-induced) psychic link with his pet hawk Redwing to become fledgling Super Hero the Falcon.

With the Skull defeated, Wilson returns to Harlem as a heroic role model. However, working with the Star-Spangled Avenger leaves him lost in the veteran hero's shadow. Even with the addition of Wakandan-built wings enabling him to fly, and despite numerous solo-successes against thugs, Super Villains, and world-shaking threats, Falcon feels under-appreciated. This view is confirmed when National Security chief Henry Peter Gyrich seconds him to the Avengers to fill a government racial-integration quota.

The Falcon fights on, confirming his A-List status as a costumed hero, while his alter ego Sam Wilson advocates for his community. When the age-inhibiting Super-Soldier Serum malfunctions and Steve Rogers suddenly becomes a frail old man, Wilson is chosen to be the next Captain America. He is more than equal to the challenge, but the choice is controversial and feeds civic unrest covertly instigated by Hydra. This allows the secret society to polarize public opinion

American eagle Sam Wilson's role as a new, socially-active Captain America brings him into conflict with government authorities, including S.H.I.E.L.D.

and seize control of America. After Hydra's "Secret Empire" is overthrown, a recovered Rogers resumes his position as Captain America and a reinvigorated Falcon takes to the skies again, tackling street crime and aiding society's most beleaguered. ∎

SOLDIER, SPY
NICK FURY

ON THE RECORD

REAL NAME
Nicholas Joseph Fury

ALLEGIANCES
US Army, CIA, S.H.I.E.L.D., Secret Warriors

POWERS
Peak physical, tactical and strategic abilities; enhanced health and longevity; army of android doubles

MISSION
Fury is willing to make hard choices to preserve humanity

STATUS REPORT
Forcibly installed as new Watcher on the Moon

Son of a World War I pilot, Nicholas Fury is born during the Great Depression and grows up in poverty alongside his two younger siblings in Hell's Kitchen, New York. A compulsive thrill-seeker, Nick and his best friend Red Hargrove work as agents for master tactician "Happy Sam" Sawyer in the years before World War II. They bring Abraham Erskine to the US and meet superhuman John Steele: a captive of German scientists since 1918. Foreseeing their country's involvement in another war, the two friends enlist. When Red dies at Pearl Harbor, Fury transfers to the US Army Rangers, and undertakes many missions, often beside Captain America and the Invaders. They face Nazi terror-weapons and operatives such as Baron Zemo, Wolfgang von Strucker, and the Red Skull. Fury later moves to the Office of Strategic Services.

Secrets and lies

Knowing only combat and intrigue, Fury remains in military intelligence. In 1954, he joins the CIA. Active in Korea, Indo-China, Europe, and Central/South America, Fury's opponents include terrorist societies such as Strucker's Hydra, Soviet spies, and resurgent Neo-Nazi groups. Unable to trust others, Fury keeps many secrets. Refusing to delegate dangerous missions to others, Fury is hands-on, even when his recruits are super-powered such as the "Avengers" he uses in 1959 to

Max firepower Army veteran Fury is not afraid to bring out the big guns on S.H.I.E.L.D. missions.

Howling Commandos

In the army, Fury quickly rises to the rank of sergeant and is given command of a US Ranger unit. Able Company, First Attack Squad is a highly unorthodox, multidisciplinary, multiethnic task force dubbed the "Howling Commandos" because of its members' flamboyant battle cry. Stationed in England, these specialists are dispatched all over the globe on "unwinnable" suicide missions. During their period of service, they achieve stunning victories against German, Japanese, and Italian forces, facing Desert Fox Erwin Rommel, mad scientist Baron Heinrich Zemo, the Red Skull, and other lesser enemies. The team's explosive sorties take them to atomic research facilities, jet aircraft factories, secret weapons plants, and even concentration camps such as Treblinka in occupied Poland.

After the war, the surviving squad members go their separate ways, but reunite for a key mission during the Korean War. Later, many former teammates come out of retirement to lend their expertise to Fury when he becomes director of S.H.I.E.L.D.

I'm runnin' this show. So just keep yer eyes peeled... and your yapper shut!
Nick Fury

hunt Nazi war criminals and thwart a demonic incursion. Fury's greatest secret is the Infinity Formula: a serum he is first given in WWII that rapidly heals near-fatal wounds. The drug's creator, Professor Berthold Sternberg, reveals it will maintain Fury's peak fitness and retard aging. In return for annual top-up doses, Sternberg demands pay-offs for decades until his death, when Fury confiscates the formula for S.H.I.E.L.D.

In the 1950s, Fury is caught in another conspiracy that shapes the rest of his life. In Kansas he meets Woody McCord and war-associate Howard Stark. They belong to an ancient cult, the Men on the Wall: a fellowship of humans clandestinely combating otherworldly threats. When McCord is killed by Tribellian invaders, Fury becomes sole Man on the Wall. Using Stark's gadgets and weapons, he continues this work in complete anonymity for many years.

As Hydra's growth threatens the UN, Fury is invited to lead high-tech intelligence agency S.H.I.E.L.D. His highly-publicized triumphs against Advanced Idea Mechanics, Zodiac,

The Unseen Being a helpless observer is the greatest punishment man-of-action Fury could ever imagine.

and others, make him the world's most famous secret agent and a regular ally of the new Super Heroes emerging across the US. During this period, he also begins extensively using android duplicates—Life Model Decoys—to take his place on official missions while he works undercover. Fury's contentious methods eventually lead to his removal as S.H.I.E.L.D.'s director, forcing him to go rogue. Unable to create more Infinity Formula and with time finally catching up to his body, Fury works with a personally vetted team of Secret Warriors to keep Earth safe according to his own uncompromising views on security.

This resolute certainty brings about his greatest folly, murdering the omniscient Watcher Uatu for refusing to share his observations, which triggers a superhuman crisis. For his crime, other Watchers transform Fury into the Unseen, a being afflicted with cosmic awareness and sentenced to witness all events in the Multiverse without interfering. He later assuages this burden by forming a trans-dimensional team of Exiles to police the time stream on his behalf. ∎

COLD WAR WARRIORS
SUPERHUMAN POLITICAL THREATS

ON THE RECORD

OPERATIVES
Mandarin, Plan Chu, Zheng Zu, Red Skull (II), Electro

ALLEGIANCES
The Communist State

BASES
Behind the iron and bamboo curtains

MISSION
Destroy freedom, democracy, and the West

STATUS REPORT
Eternal vigilance required

I am all powerful!
Your new Master!
Mandarin

With World War II ended, clandestine consolidation and expansion for nations and their ancient secret societies begins, sparking an insecure era of widespread espionage. Superhuman operatives are scarce, and their exploits frequently suppressed by governments. The defeat of the Axis powers leaves the US as de facto leading nation on Earth, but a rapid amassing of power by Soviet Russia's annexation of Warsaw Pact countries is matched by a rise of communist-leaning dictatorships in Asia.

The upheaval caused by China's fall to Mao Zedong leads to the prominence of three separate counter-revolutionary imperialist factions—each claiming descent from Genghis Khan. Utilizing archaic alchemy, mysticism, and alien science, these rivals seek to restore the lost empire of their ancestor. The Mandarin (pictured above), Zheng Zu, and Plan Chu (aka Golden Claw)—the latter two having bedevilled the occupying British Empire—plan global conquest. Apparently allying with the Peoples' Republic, they run campaigns of terror against the West, trialing scientifically devised monsters and magical atrocities.

Russian expansionism spreads to Africa, where jungle champions Jann, Lorna, Leopard Girl, and others battle seditious Socialist encroachment, even as Europe becomes an armed camp divided by an iron curtain. The Kremlin finds uses for suitably programmed pawns such as Red Room graduate Black Widow, brainwashed assassin Winter Soldier, lightning-wielding Ivan Kronov (aka Electro), and communist spy chief Albert Malik. Malik steals the guise of the Nazi's greatest operative to become a new Red Skull, destabilizing the West in secret and attacking the United Nations in high profile strikes. ∎

Red scare Soviet impostor Malik later hides from the real Red Skull who seeks revenge for the theft of his reputation.

AGE OF PARANOIA
MARVEL BOY AND THE AGENTS OF ATLAS

ON THE RECORD

TEAM MEMBERS
Marvel Boy, Jimmy Woo, Namora, Living Robot M-11, Gorilla Man, Venus, 3-D Man

ALLEGIANCES
US government, FBI, Atlas Foundation

BASE
Temple of Atlas beneath San Francisco, California

MISSION
Safeguarding democracy

STATUS REPORT
After decades in retirement, a revived team operates in the 21st century

As the Cold War intensifies, superhuman activity goes undercover. Mystery men fade from memory, but paranoia and global tensions remain. Extraordinary adversaries still clash, however, their battles are kept from the public by control-obsessed governments. While paranormal activity increases exponentially, reports of such events are suppressed or belittled to avoid panic in a world that is on the brink of atomic annihilation. Canadian agent James "Logan" Howlett's missions are permanently classified and the astonishing true adventures of Uranus-raised Bob Grayson are dismissed as fiction after the release of his autobiographical comic book *Marvel Boy*.

The US permits no appetite for freaks or heroes, but as the decade progresses, numerous alien incursions threaten the enforced calm. In Russia, former intelligence agent Peggy Carter encounters alien-hunting Woody McCord and Howard Stark, ultimately sharing the secrets of these "Men on the Wall."

Escalating inexplicable events prompt undercover Eternal Makkari to form a band of Monster Hunters. Immortal beast-killer Ulysses Bloodstone, expatriate Wakandan warrior Zawadi, and paranormal investigator Dr. Anthony Druid are later joined by Sub-Mariner's cousin Namora. The latter has a long history of covert adventure, having worked with Marvel Boy, Gorilla Man, Human Robot M-11, the goddess Venus, and FBI handler Jimmy Woo rescuing President Eisenhower from Plan Chu. The team, supplemented by Skrull-created hero 3-D Man,

Secret services Combining cutting-edge science, magic, and super-powers, the Monster Hunters keep secret their uncanny encounters in the atomic age.

is active for six months, repeatedly saving the world until it is ordered to disband to prevent public disquiet. Fifty years later, the group would reunite as the Agents of Atlas. In 1959, CIA agent Nick Fury brings Namora into his black ops Secret Avengers Initiative. She vanishes, following the demise of undercover super-team First Line, who all perish while thwarting a Skrull invasion. ∎

HIDDEN AGENDAS
BLUE MARVEL

ON THE RECORD

REAL NAME
Adam Brashear

ALLEGIANCES
The Ultimates, Avengers, Alpha Flight

POWERS
Super-genius, flight, extended lifespan, immeasurable strength and durability

MISSION
Learning everything and saving the universe

STATUS REPORT
Working for Earth's space force Alpha Flight

Adam Brashear is one of the most brilliant and heroic men of his time. The college sports star and decorated Korean War veteran also holds doctorates in theoretical physics and electrical engineering. As lead researcher in a project to develop clean energy power sources, he is caught in the explosion of a prototype "Negative Reactor" connected to an antimatter universe

> I'd do whatever is right...
> I wouldn't care what
> anyone thinks.
> **Blue Marvel**

(the Negative Zone). Brashear is transfigured into a stable antimatter reactor in human form. His friend, Conner Sims, is reduced to sentient energy, becoming Anti-Man.

   Possessing incredible powers, Brashear dons all-concealing armor to combat disasters as the Blue Marvel. His spectacular career is cut short in 1962, while battling the now-insane Sims. When his helmet is destroyed, Blue Marvel is revealed to be an African American. Fearing harm to the growing Civil Rights movement, President Kennedy privately awards him a Presidential Medal of Honor and asks him to retire. Fading into relative obscurity, Brashear pursues scientific research.

He befriends Uatu the Watcher and occasionally uses his powers covertly for global emergencies: during an alien invasion, he allows S.H.I.E.L.D. to fake his death. Marrying his S.H.I.E.L.D. liaison Marlene Frazier, Brashear settles into retirement and raises a family. On Marlene's death and with escalating crises besieging Earth, the seemingly immortal Brashear is drawn back into active Super Hero service by Iron Man and Reed Richards, serving as an Avenger and later with cosmic troubleshooters the Ultimates. ∎

Ultimate armor Blue Marvel must wear quantum-probability regulating exploration armor in the Neutral Zone.

THE MAN THAT TIME FORGOT
SENTRY

ON THE RECORD

REAL NAME
Robert "Bob" Reynolds

ALLEGIANCES
New Avengers, Dark Avengers

BASE
The Watchtower, New York

POWERS
Super-strength, flight, invulnerability, matter and energy manipulation, psionic abilities, teleportation

MISSION
Being a hero

STATUS REPORT
Convinced he is his own worst enemy

In 1947, Canada's Department K and the US' Operation: Rebirth combine resources to rediscover and improve the Erskine Super-Soldier Serum that created Captain America. As the Cold War intensifies, the joint operation diversifies into hundreds of autonomous projects. With the help of captured Nazi scientists, and led by "Professor Cornelius," Project: Sentry succeeds beyond the military's wildest dreams. In 1957, the Golden Sentry Serum—which bestows incalculable power—is stolen by drug addict Bob Reynolds. It transforms Reynolds into an indestructible, godlike paragon of solar-fueled force, capable of any feat imaginable. Known as the Sentry, Reynolds becomes Earth's greatest Super Hero, eventually mentoring new marvels such as Spider-Man as they join his relentless crusade against evil.

The serum, however, also creates a malicious counter-personality within him. Dubbed the Void, it is permanently and sadistically at war with Reynolds' noble side and determined to destroy all reality. When Reynolds finally realizes the true nature of his foe, he makes the ultimate sacrifice, ending the existence of Sentry and negating the threat of the Void. Uniting with super-genius Reed Richards and mystic savant Doctor Stephen

Solitary sentinel While waiting for Sentry's return, the Watchtower stood unnoticed for years in New York City.

Strange, Reynolds devises a way to remove all knowledge of his existence from human memory. The scheme works and humanity forgets, but not even the Sentry can erase all evidence of his stellar career. Years later, aging failure Bob Reynolds again becomes Sentry and his greatest Super Hero allies fight with him against the returned Void. Now wildly unpredictable, he is eventually killed by Thor, but has recently been resurrected. ∎

FIRST FAMILY
FANTASTIC FOUR

ON THE RECORD

FOUNDING MEMBERS
Reed Richards (Mister Fantastic), Susan Storm-Richards (Invisible Woman), Johnny Storm (Human Torch), Benjamin Grimm (Thing)

KEY AFFILIATE MEMBERS
Spider-Man, Ant-Man, Black Panther, Medusa, Dinosaur, Moon Girl, She-Hulk, Storm

ALLEGIANCES
Avengers, Inhumans, Future Foundation, S.H.I.E.L.D.

MISSION
Learn everything, solve everything

STATUS REPORT
Returned to active duty

After foiling an alien invasion, super-genius Reed Richards realizes the urgent need for humanity to master space travel. He devotes his own fortune and intellect to building a starship, but, on its completion, he is ousted from the project by his fellow financial backers and the US military.

We had to do it...
We had to be the first!
Reed Richards

Impulsively, Richards convinces three friends to help him steal the starship. With his college buddy and former pilot Ben Grimm at the controls, and accompanied by Reed's girlfriend Sue Storm and her teenage brother Johnny, they fly the prototype craft into space. However, it has poor shielding and the four are bombarded by cosmic radiation, losing control of the ship. Surviving the resulting crash, they each develop astounding powers. The induced mutations result in Richards' body becoming as elastic as his mind, while stalwart, diffident Sue commands energies that can render herself and other objects invisible and project psionic forcefields. Impetuous Johnny can transform at will into a being of

flaming plasma and capable of flight, but poor Ben Grimm permanently morphs into an orange-hued, rocky brute of immense strength and durability. Together they pledge to use their fantastic abilities to battle injustice, push back the frontiers of knowledge, and benefit mankind.

Over time, the Fantastic Four become paramount amongst Earth's Super Heroes. At heart, they remain more a family of explorers than a team of crime fighters. Constantly bickering, they split up or take on new members, but invariably reunite. Despite their dangerous lifestyles, Reed and Sue have two children. Mutated by his parents' cosmic irradiation, the eldest child, Franklin, can reshape reality. His interference with the time stream leads to the birth of his super-smart sister Valeria. Eschewing secret identities, the "FF" go public, battling aliens and villains such as the Mole Man and Doctor Doom. They even form Fantastic Four, Inc. to handle their business affairs and administer the patents and royalties from Reed's constant flow of inventions.

The team's highly publicized actions ignite a wave of Super Hero debuts and their initial role fighting super-criminals, marauding aliens,

Negative Zone

Reed Richards's attempts to master star travel lead to his most dangerous discovery. Exploring subspace, he locates an anti-matter universe beset with a hyper-fast time differential, which is rapidly contracting to a cosmic Big Crunch. This Negative Zone is home to predatory beings of immense power, such as Blastaar and Annihilus, who devote all their efforts to escaping their doomed reality and conquering the positive matter universe.

Richards initially uses the region as a dumping ground for menaces like Super-Adaptoid and even Galactus. Later, during the first Super Hero civil war, he helps construct a vast prison, Project 42, for superhuman dissenters, before its inmates and the harsh environment inevitably destroy the jail.

and uncanny monsters gradually gives way to Richards' primary goal: exploration and research. However, his probing of the cosmos, sub-space, the microverse, and parallel dimensions unleashes new threats such as Psycho-Man and anti-matter alien the Ebon Seeker. The team meet Uatu the Watcher on an early Moon voyage and the omniscient observer bends his oath of isolation many times to warn them of looming disaster. Moreover, former defeated foes such as Namor, the Sub-Mariner and Puppet Master—as well as aggrieved lesser villains such as the Wizard, Mad Thinker, and Red Ghost—constantly attack the team.

Future Foundation

Despite their hectic, often dangerous lives, the FF are uncomplicated folk: Johnny loves fast cars and partying; Ben wants to settle down and raise his own family; Sue is forced to look after not only her children, but also her often childish teammates; while

Doom's day The Fantastic Four's greatest foe Doctor Doom holds an abiding personal grudge against former college roommate Reed Richards.

Reed, concerned about the low standards of scientific and ethical education, creates his own school to nurture tomorrow's greatest minds.

The Future Foundation is Richards' attempt to cultivate free-thinking individuals, training them to assess Earth's problems, and equipping them to find solutions. The first intake includes his children Franklin and Valeria, Super Hero Alex Power, pacifist android Dragon-Man, as well as the cream of the world's young super-brains from Wakanda to ancient Atlantis, the subterranean Moloids, and a clone of the villainous Wizard. Intellectually brilliant and socially diverse guest tutors include reformed high-tech burglar Ant-Man, Spider-Man, arch-foe Doctor Doom,and even Reed's own father, the time- and

dimensional-traveling adventurer Nathaniel Richards.

Throughout successive planetary crises, Super Hero wars, and extinction events, the Fantastic Four—singly or in unison—provide unfailing support to humanity and other species throughout the Multiverse. They remain a crusading force for good while continually expanding knowledge and fostering scientific cooperation. ∎

IRON TYRANT
DOCTOR DOOM

ON THE RECORD

REAL NAME
Victor von Doom

ALLEGIANCES
Zefiro Romani clan, Black Swans, Parliament of Doom, the Cabal

BASE
Undisclosed bunker, formerly Castle Doom, Latveria

POWERS
Master sorcerer and scientist, high-tech battle armor

MISSION
Controlling the universe

STATUS REPORT
After finally liberating his mother, becoming a god and a hero, Doom is reassessing his priorities

Quintessential tyrant Victor von Doom is a self-made autocrat. His brilliance and supreme self-belief enables him to compete with the greatest forces in the universe while confirming his conviction that he is lord of all

he surveys. Utterly amoral, his uniquely inventive mind; sorcerous expertise; tactical genius; and continuous, calculated reinventions of himself make Doom the most dangerous man in existence.

The only person he drives harder than those around him, is himself. His parents—a Zefiro Romani healer and a witch who sold her soul to demon-lord Mephisto—were killed from the persecutions of Latverian aristocrat Baron (later King) Vladimir. A fierce and solitary child, Victor proves equally adept at magic and every discipline of science. Vain and proud, he makes a devil's bargain with Mephisto. Every midsummer's eve, Doom will battle all Hell's forces to liberate his mother from infernal torment. The pact shapes his life as much as his need to assert dominance over everything.

Accepting American military sponsors and a scholarship to New York State University, a teenage Doom spurns overtures of friendship from fellow young super-genius Reed Richards. Eventually, he will declare Richards his only admitted intellectual equal. Using the unlimited resources of his US military paymasters, Doom perfects humanoid robots, but his genuine

> My vast and supreme will shall be done!
> **Victor von Doom**

programming breakthroughs he keeps to himself. These will go on to form the basis for his deadly Doombots. The same is true for the time-travel prototype he constructs, which Doom will later upgrade into his infallible Time Platform.

Similarly misappropriating college equipment, Doom builds an interdimensional engine to rescue his mother, but rushes his calculations. When it explodes, scarring him forever, Doom travels to Tibet where mystic monks regard him as their long-awaited Chosen One. Learning all their secrets of blending magic and technology, Doom forges a metal mask and armor to hide his shame. Returning to Latveria, he ousts King Vladimir

Doom's world

Victor von Doom's inventiveness and diabolical cunning have taken him to the level of divinity many times. When Galactus first exiles his herald, Silver Surfer, to Earth, the iron despot devises a way to siphon off the Silver Surfer's Power Cosmic. Doom nearly conquers humanity, but is thwarted by Reed Richards, who creates a way to avert Doomsday, defeat the usurper, and restore order.

Doom repeats the ploy years later, when Earth's heroes and villains are abducted to a composite planet to battle each other for the entertainment of the godlike being the Beyonder. Doom's incredible technology transfers seemingly unlimited power to his body, but with all he has ever wanted within his grasp, the seemingly omnipotent Doctor Doom is once more stripped of his might and defeated.

Men of iron After losing his rule over all reality, Doom reforms and briefly replaces Stark as a heroic new Iron Man.

and reigns as absolute monarch of his homeland. His weapons technology secures tiny Latveria from all outside threats, and he begins accruing more power, subsequently clashing with the Fantastic Four, Iron Man, and many other Super Heroes.

The Great Destroyer

Ruling with an iron fist and through sheer terror, Doom is shielded from retribution by diplomatic immunity. He takes what he wants and repeatedly attempts to conquer the planet, always avoiding political repercussions by deviously playing-off rival governments against

each other. After years of turmoil, intrigue, and failures, Doom learns of the imminent erasure of the Multiverse through the machinations of the overdimensional Beyonders. Using time travel, he inserts himself at the distant start of the crisis.

As the Great Destroyer Rabum Alal, Doom creates a cult of devoted zealots—the Black Swans—to counteract the Beyonders' actions: subtly setting in motion a grand scheme to survive and conquer all that remains after reality ends. Success turns him into the sole god of a Battleworld containing all that remains of the once-infinite Multiverse. When his despised rival Reed Richards and a band of Super Heroes reverse

the destruction and restore the universe, Doom is forced to rethink his life. Seeking atonement, Doom replaces coma-stricken Tony Stark as a new Iron Man. However, the flaws in his character seem certain to draw him back to his old ways. ∎

Walking arsenal
Doom's armor blends magical wards and weapons with cutting-edge sensor-suites.

GREEN GOLIATH
HULK

ON THE RECORD

REAL NAME
Robert Bruce Banner

ALLEGIANCES
Avengers, Defenders,
S.H.I.E.L.D., the Warbound

POWERS
Immeasurable strength,
virtual invulnerability

MISSION
Doing no harm, staying free,
making amends

STATUS REPORT
Banner is reported dead, but
immortal Hulk is at large

Young Bruce Banner endures appalling abuse at the hands of his alcoholic father. His only respite is the summer vacations spent with his cousin Jennifer Walters. When his mother is murdered by her violent husband, the trauma triggers Dissociative Identity Disorder in Bruce. This condition manifests years later after the brilliant physicist is caught in the detonation of the gamma bomb he has built for the US military.

Bruce had been trying to save teenager Rick Jones who had drifted into ground zero as the bomb was counting down.

The blast initially transforms Banner into an aggressive, gray-skinned monstrosity, but the condition progresses and his coloration shifts to green while his mind diminishes to infantile levels. A fugitive since his accident, Banner becomes like a fractious, short-tempered child whenever he is angry or scared—an eight-foot tall, indestructible, tantrum-throwing child, able to punch through steel and leap miles in a single bound.

Banner wanders for years, seeking a cure while his alter ego alternatively causes massive destruction or inadvertently saves the world from monsters, aliens, and Super Villains such as gamma-spawned tyrant the Leader. Hulk even wins super-allies, originally as a founding Avenger, and later as the backbone of the unofficial group the Defenders. The Hulk's mind seemingly waxes

and wanes, and psychologist Leonard Samson diagnoses a personality disorder, suggesting Banner's suppressed traumas are being actualized in varying Hulk forms that match a different aspect of his battered and bruised psyche.

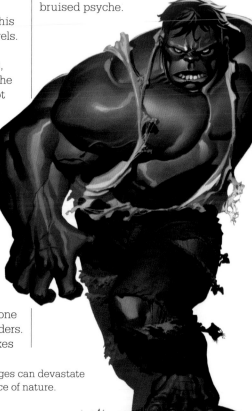

Unnatural disaster Hulk's rampages can devastate cities more completely than any force of nature.

The Maestro

Bruce Banner long believes that his gamma-irradiated form might be immortal: a hypothesis he confirms after meeting a possible future self. When the contemporary Hulk is abducted through time by Rick Jones' granddaughter, he arrives on a dystopian Earth where all Super Heroes have been murdered by a vicious, brutal despot. The monster holds the power of life and death, reveling in the misery of all around him. He was once Bruce Banner, but now calls himself the Maestro.

In this form, the green giant has twice the Hulk's strength and power, Banner's vast intellect, and a sadistic personality that Bruce fears is the inescapable influence of his own murderous father. Although Banner and his human allies eventually overthrow the Maestro, the Multiverse is filled with similar versions and Banner is haunted by the fear that he may one day become one of them.

Attempts to integrate Banner's warring personas result in a more brutal, uncontrollable monster, compelling his friends—secret star chamber the Illuminati—to exile him to a distant planet. Their plan hugely misfires, with disastrous consequences, as Hulk crashes on barbarian world Sakaar. Here he finds love with Caiera the Oldstrong, becomes Sakaar's king, and has a son, Skaar. When Caiera and most of his subjects are killed by Hulk's malfunctioning shuttle, he leads a punitive force of survivors—collectively known as the Warbound—back to Earth, seeking vengeance against those who betrayed him.

> The angrier I get the stronger I get! I'm the strongest one there is! Hulk Smash!
> **Hulk**

Gamma gladiator Avenging the death of his wife and subjects, Hulk takes up arms against the Illuminati and humanity.

Nuclear proliferation

In a pitiless campaign of terror designated "World War Hulk," his forces scourge humanity before the vengeful monster is beaten and Banner taken into custody. While incarcerated, a new Red Hulk terrorizes civilians and Super Heroes, sparking a multi-hued explosion of Hulks and gamma-transformed individuals including Rick Jones (A-Bomb), Red She-Hulk, and Skaar. When Banner escapes, he resolves to counteract the harm his alter ego has caused, working for S.H.I.E.L.D. in both identities and rejoining the Avengers.

After Banner's assistant—an acolyte of clandestine planetary-defense cult the Ancient Order of the Shield—shoots him in the head, Tony Stark saves his comrade by injecting him with the body-modifying Extremis virus. As a result, a new personality forms. Super-Hulk Doc Green is far smarter than Banner and decides to rid the world of gamma freaks. He devises Adamantium-sheathed nanites to absorb radiation as it builds in the body, preventing critical mass transformations, and begins forcibly curing Hulks. He loses his own powers attempting to absorb a meltdown of Kiber radiation that threatens Africa. Hulk's young protégé, Amadeus Cho, draws all the radiation—including gamma—from Banner's cells and becomes in turn a new Totally Awesome Hulk.

After years of running, Bruce Banner retires, but when a second superhuman civil war breaks out, he is executed by Hawkeye. Months before, he had begged the archer to kill him if the Hulk ever began manifesting again. Banner even gave Hawkeye the murder weapon: a lethal gamma-toxin. Hulk is later resurrected by Elder of the Universe, Challenger, and remains at large. ∎

SMALL WONDERS
ANT-MAN AND THE WASP

Leading the way Janet Van Dyne grows from sidekick to being a role model for a new generation of Super Heroes.

ON THE RECORD

REAL NAMES
Henry "Hank" Jonathan Pym and Janet Van Dyne

ALLEGIANCES
Avengers

POWERS
Size-and-mass-shifting, bioelectric stings, flight, control of insects

MISSION
Crime fighting

STATUS REPORT
Early romance devolves into a controlling relationship and eventual separation

Biochemist Dr. Henry "Hank" Pym uses his scientific brilliance to become a succession of size-shifting heroes, but is never truly comfortable as a costumed adventurer. Unable to cope with the unrelenting, but self-imposed, pressure of competing with others, Pym's discoveries and achievements are tragically overshadowed by his mental instability, hostility, and jealousy.

A troubled prodigy, teenage Pym is unable to work under the strictures of corporately funded research and toils alone at the fringes of the scientific community. After his Hungarian wife Maria Trovaya is apparently murdered by enemy agents, Pym experiences his first breakdown. During his recovery he swears to aid humanity and avenge injustice however he can.

Soon after, he manages to isolate subatomic particles capable of altering physical dimensions and mass. In his first test, Pym is trapped in an anthill and becomes fascinated with insects. Regaining his regular size, he devises cybernetic systems to communicate with, and control, insects. He couples this breakthrough with "shrinking gas" (a delivery medium for Pym Particles) as the costumed hero Ant-Man.

Clashing with crooks, enemy agents, the radiation-mutated insect tyrant Scarlet Beetle, and his nemesis Elihas "Egghead" Starr, Pym's life changes forever after he is asked to solve the murder of a colleague. When Janet Van Dyne's father, Vernon, is killed by a transdimensional invader, she seeks revenge and convinces Pym to experiment on her. Using gene-

I can give you wings, antennae. I can make you a human wasp!
Ant-Man

Growing legacy

Hank Pym's subatomic particles have enabled many to follow in his variably sized footsteps. Some co-opt his insect-control techniques, too, as well as his many code names. Clint Barton forsakes his Hawkeye role to be a new Goliath, and when he returns to being a bowman, Pym's former lab partner Bill Foster acts as Goliath and Giant-Man. When Foster dies during the first superhuman civil war, his son, Tom, inherits the role and his father's mission.

Pym's Yellowjacket gear is stolen by Rita DeMara, but her criminal schemes end after she rediscovers her conscience and becomes a Super Hero. His Ant-Man outfit is also swiped—for a good cause—so Pym gifts it to reformed thief Scott Lang, whose daughter Cassie also operates as size-shifting hero Stature. Lang eventually carves out a career as the new Ant-Man, singly and alongside Pym's daughter Nadia, the new Wasp (both pictured), something Eric O'Grady never achieves after he steals size-altering armor from S.H.I.E.L.D. The latest Giant-Man Raz Malhotra uses another cast-off Pym suit to make a big difference to the world.

splicing he gives Van Dyne wings and antennae that engage when she uses his particles to shrink and become the Wasp. Together with Ant-Man, she destroys the Creature from Kosmos who took her father's life, and convinces Pym they should remain crime-fighting partners.

Avenging duo

When the diminutive duo join Thor, Iron Man, and the Hulk as the first wave of mighty Avengers, the Wasp is set on a path that will result in her becoming one of the most effective leaders in the team's history. Strong bonds of codependence develop as Pym and Van Dyne become media darlings, lovers, and eventually a married couple. As years pass, however, Van Dyne grows more confident and capable, while Pym becomes increasingly frustrated, afraid his triumphs are all behind him. Later upgrades give Van Dyne control over insects, natural size-changing powers, and bioelectric stings. Experience polishes her greatest gifts: amazing bravery, organizational skills, and a canny knack for combat tactics and

strategy. Pym's road is far rockier. Always judging himself a failure beside other super-geniuses like Reed Richards, and weak compared to living gods and futuristic knights in armor, Pym pushes the limits of

Search for self
Despite his genius, Pym can't decide who he really is or wants to be.

his body by becoming Giant-Man. Physical traumas caused by size-altering mask his mental disorder as Pym incessantly refines his powers through many different identities—Goliath, Yellowjacket, Dr. Pym: Scientific Adventurer, and, when Van Dyne is seemingly killed, the Wasp. During one period of overwork, competitive stress, and insecurity, Pym dabbles in robotics and AI, unwittingly creating organic life's greatest enemy: Ultron. The robot constantly bedevils his "father," attacking all his achievements and targeting his friends before finally bringing about his maker's downfall.

Pym's greatest victory is one he never learns of. His first wife Maria was not killed as he thought, but remained a Hungarian prisoner until she delivered a baby girl. That child—Nadia—is raised in the Russian deep-programming facility the Red Room. Assassin-trained and schooled in science, Nadia escapes to the US to become a new Wasp, continuing her father's legacy of experimentation and heroism. ∎

GOD OF THUNDER
THOR

ON THE RECORD

REAL NAME
Thor Odinson

ALLEGIANCES
Asgardia, Avengers,
League of Realms

POWERS
Asgardian god; super-strong,
extremely durable, and
immortal; mystic control of
enchanted hammer Mjölnir

MISSION
Protect the weak

STATUS REPORT
Returned to glory after period
of disgrace when Mjölnir
deemed him unworthy

For uncounted centuries, Thor of Asgard has slain monsters, giants, and devils: evil of every description all over the universe. However, he regards the indomitable mortals of Midgard (Earth) his most precious charges, and their greatest heroes his foremost allies and comrades. Born of Odin the All-Father and Elder Goddess Gaea, Thor Odinson grows up with adopted brother Loki, reared by Odin's wife, Freyja. In a society burdened by prophecies of doom and inescapable Ragnarok, the prince is consumed with tales of valor, performing ever-more glorious deeds to earn the mystic hammer Mjölnir he believes is his by divine right.

Asgardian gods are a bellicose, boastful, and boisterous race—and young Thor is among the most powerful and prideful. He wanders the cosmos having adventures and spends much time on Midgard, fighting, carousing, and enjoying the worship of mortals. During these earthly revels, he uses lethal mystic axe Jarnbjorn, or "Iron Bear, the Wrecker of Worlds," which is blessed by his own spilled blood.

If he be worthy...
Gradually, Thor begins fighting for others rather than to please himself. After saving young goddess Sif from the clutches of deathly Hela, he finally

Heavy metal Clad in dwarven armor and wearing Megingjord, the Belt of Strength, Thor is prepared for battle.

proves worthy to wield the mighty Mjölnir. His feats and conquests intensify, as does his arrogance. Odin judges his son to be lacking in godly graces and exiles him to Midgard, transforming Thor into a frail, disabled medical student, "Don Blake." As a doctor, the Thunder God learns humility and fulfilment caring for others. Years later, vacationing in Norway, the medic stumbles upon an alien invasion and the final stage of Odin's plan for his son. Trapped in a cave, Blake finds a wooden walking stick which, when struck, transforms him into a living god.

> For Asgard and honor eternal!
> **Thor**

Moonstruck Unable to lift Mjölnir from the lunar surface, the bereft Odinson realizes he has been judged unworthy.

Before long, the returned Thor—with some memory loss—is at the forefront of a Super Hero resurgence. Battling aliens, mythical terrors, and superhuman villains on Earth, across the universe, through time, and eventually in the Ten Realms, he is reacquainted with old Asgardian comrades. He also encounters heroic mighty mortals in a team he cofounds: the Avengers.

After years of glorious triumphs, Thor's downfall comes with a whispered word. While investigating the murder of the Watcher Uatu, Thor confronts Nick Fury who utters a dark secret in his ear. This causes Mjölnir to reject its master. Deprived of the totem which gives him validation, he witnesses another hero assume his role and powers. After some soul-searching, "the Odinson" resolves to be the best hero he can be—without the hammer's blessing.

His trials are great and painful. Having lost his identity to another hero, his arm is cut off by the vile Dark Elf Malekith. However, he strives on with a new limb forged from mystical Uru metal. When the god-slaying Mangog returns, Odinson joins with the new Mighty Thor—Jane Foster—to defeat the monster. The struggle costs Thor her life and Mjölnir is destroyed. Her dying wish is that Odinson reclaims the name he once again deserves and of which he is worthy. Renewed and humbled, Thor Odinson continues fighting evil and injustice, armed with an arsenal of lesser hammers built for him by the Dwarf smiths of Nidavellir. ∎

Jane Foster, Mighty Thor

Jane Foster is Don Blake's nurse and sometime lover while the Thunder God is in human form. This relationship infuriates Odin, who tries all he can to thwart the affair. When the relationship ends, Jane becomes a doctor. The fates once again conspire to draw her and Thor together, this time as friends. After Odinson loses Mjölnir's trust, the hammer seeks out Foster. It imbues her with Thor's powers, using the spell Odin locked into the hammer. The same forces allow other worthy souls to become Thors over the succeeding centuries.

However, Foster is dying from cancer and every time she turns into Thor the magic undoes all the benefits of the chemotherapy she receives on Earth. Despite this, she fervently believes that the world needs a Thunder God to fight for it and resolutely continues in the role. Battling Roxxon's invasions of the Ten Realms and trying to stop genocide instigated by Malekith, she gives her life to save Asgard from the Mangog. Foster is resurrected by a reinstated Thor, Odin, and the mystic God Tempest, the soul that was confined within Mjölnir.

ARMORED AVENGER
IRON MAN

ON THE RECORD

REAL NAME
Anthony "Tony" Edward Stark

ALLEGIANCES
Stark Unlimited, Avengers, S.H.I.E.L.D.

POWERS
Constantly upgraded brain, ARC power source in chest

MISSION
Saving humanity and inventing tomorrow

STATUS REPORT
Back in armor and action after months in a coma

Son of industrial weapons-designer Howard Stark, Tony Stark is reviewing munitions in Afghanistan when he triggers a hidden landmine. Gravely injured, he is captured by terrorist warlord Wong Chu, who promises medical aid in return for Stark building them a super-weapon. Instead, Stark—assisted by fellow captive Professor Ho Yinsen—creates a robotic bodysuit to keep him alive.

Knowing they cannot trust their captors, the hostages equip it with offensive armaments that Stark uses to rout the terrorists. He finally makes his way back to the US, but at the cost of Ho's life.

Despite having shrapnel lodged near his heart—held in place by a permanently fixed metal chest-plate—Stark cannot resist using the armor to battle enemy agents, super-criminals, and scientific tyrants like the Mandarin. To explain the metal hero's regular appearances at Stark Industries, he claims Iron Man is his bodyguard. In truth, Stark is addicted to adventure. When the Hulk goes on a rampage, Iron Man meets other Super Heroes for the first time. Realizing the potential of a crisis-combat team, Stark subsequently throws his financial resources and contacts into funding a new super-team: the Avengers. Although his company abandons weapons manufacture, Stark's greatest innovations, such as ARC energy and

Power dressing Although Stark's armors constantly change, the message is the same: "beware the power of Iron Man!"

Repulsor Technology, are always first incorporated into the Iron Man armor. However, his technology rapidly outstrips his physicality, and Stark starts modifying his body to match that of the suit's: reaction-time enhancement, cybernetic and

Armor Model 1
Original model cobbled together by fellow captives Tony Stark and Ho Yinsen to keep Stark's heart beating. The armor is equipped with assorted non-lethal gadgets, but is also hugely energy-intensive.

Armor Model 2
Stark's first purpose-built combat model provides enhanced protection, strength, and firepower, but is slow and ponderous, like a walking battleship. The enormous power drain also constantly taxes Stark's damaged heart.

Armor Model 3
A lighter, compact suit that offers greater speed and maneuverability with negligible loss of firepower. Looking and functioning more like a humanoid fighter jet than a knight's war-gear, this armor provides the template for subsequent, highly modified suits.

Armored and dangerous
Originally devised to keep Tony Stark alive, the Iron Man is a continually upgraded mobile weapons platform: the most sophisticated and powerful in the world. Providing complete bodily protection, the suit also grants immense strength, speed, and flight, and houses a host of offensive systems, and task-specific modules.

Armor Model 11 (War Machine Armor)
With Stark incapacitated, James Rhodes runs his company and assumes the role of Iron Man in a suit designed for a trained soldier. It is equipped with standard weapons and technology plus a Gatling gun, rocket launcher, and energy blasters.

Armor Model 31 (Hulkbuster Argonaut)
A rare failure, the Hulkbuster drone gives increased strength, ablative protection, and advanced armaments. However, after being electronically hijacked by Ho Yinsen's son, Stark, in his regular armor, is forced to destroy it.

psychic interfaces, and AI co-pilots. Eventually he uses the organic mutation virus Extremis to integrate his armor and flesh into a unified operating system. He even begins regularly backing up his memories to counter any future catastrophes.

Inner demons
After years of playboy excess and unrelenting pressure in both identities, Iron Man is framed for murder, plunging Stark into a trap crafted by rival industrialist Justin Hammer. The scheme's success is aided by Stark himself, who refuses to acknowledge his alcohol addiction.

Everything I've done... I'll ever do, I do to protect this world.
Tony Stark

While foiling Hammer's scheme, Stark's drinking intensifies, and he alienates his friends and allies, until girlfriend Bethany Cabe forces him to confront his demons and face his greatest enemy—the bottle. During his lost months he had surrendered control of his company and patents, and, when back in control, has to hunt down and destroy unauthorized and immoral users of Stark tech in a succession of Armor Wars.

Stark endures paralysis, bodily collapses, and even death, but he overcomes them all with unfailing ingenuity. However, he almost destroys himself after discovering he was adopted: an anonymous foundling used to divert attention from Howard Stark's true son, Arno.

Only human Stark's reboot also revives Jim Rhodes, but War Machine's pilot struggles to resume his Super Hero career.

This boy was born with genetic defects and raised in secret with the aid of stolen alien technology. With his usual take-charge approach, Tony Stark relentlessly investigates, eventually learning he is the child of S.H.I.E.L.D. agents Amanda Armstrong and "Jude." Unfortunately, his birth father turns out to be a Hydra double agent and is still very much alive.

Tony Stark initially creates the Iron Man armor to prolong his life. Driven to upgrade and repurpose it, continuously adding new weapons and technology, he becomes one of Earth's most powerful Super Heroes. His work is a legacy that endures in a new generation of armored heroes such as Rescue, Ironheart, and War Machine. After lying in a months-long coma, Stark's shattered body has rebooted itself, resurrecting him in human form to face whatever challenges tomorrow brings. ∎

MONARCH OF ATLANTIS
NAMOR, THE SUB-MARINER

ON THE RECORD

REAL NAME
Namor McKenzie

ALLEGIANCES
Invaders, Defenders, The Cabal, Avengers, Illuminati

BASE
Atlantis

POWERS
Superhuman strength, speed, durability; flight; bio-electrical generation

MISSION
Balancing surface world interests with the duties of rebuilding Atlantis

STATUS REPORT
Namor is constantly pulled between his surface and subsea ancestries

> Thus shall it be! Imperius Rex!
> **Namor**

Regarded as the modern age's first mutant, King Namor of Atlantis is one of Earth's most powerful beings. Defying categorization, he is monarch, villain, statesman, outcast, and hero. Rejecting all such labels, Namor considers himself dutiful and pragmatic, doing whatever is necessary for his subjects, his planet, as well as his fellow mutants.

In 1915, a boy is born of a union between American polar explorer Leonard McKenzie and water-breathing Princess Fen of Atlantis.

Possessing extraordinary powers, the child can breathe water and air, although a circulatory oxygen-imbalance triggered by prolonged periods in dry and wet worlds causes violent mood swings, until finally diagnosed and corrected.

Reared by his grandfather Emperor Thakorr to despise surface-worlders, Namor single-handedly attacks New York City in 1939, causing great destruction and battling the android Super Hero, the first Human Torch. A scourge of mankind, his stance softens after meeting policewoman Betty Dean. When Nazis depth-charge Antarctic

Elemental rivalry In one of many battles, Namor fights flaming hero the Human Torch with water-born fury.

Lost Kingdom of Atlantis

Former continent of Atlantis Home of advanced human civilization established over 22,000 years ago. Geologically destabilized and sunk to the ocean floor 21,000 years ago. Namor's realm once extended from the north Atlantic south to Antarctica.

Greenland

North America

Europe

Asia

Capital city Founded 8,000 years ago by nomadic water-breathing *Homo mermanus* and built on the ruins of primeval Atlantis.

Africa

South America

Atlantic Ocean

Reunion site After years of amnesia, Namor recovers his memory and finds his people. He sets about rebuilding a new mid-Atlantic capital city.

Savage Land (formerly Pangea) Colonized by air-breathing Atlanteans 22,000 years ago, magical beasts and extinct dinosaurs thrive in this region.

City of Tha-Korr Following geological upheavals and repeated attacks by barbarian hordes, Thakorr relocates Atlantis nearer the South pole. It is destroyed by Nazis in 1943.

Savage Land

Antarctica

Atlantis, the vengeful Sub-Mariner turns all his anger upon them, serving with the Allies for the duration of World War II, before vanishing from public view. Back in Atlantis, Namor's memories are cruelly suppressed by psionic villain Destiny and he becomes a derelict, haunting New York for decades until revived from this amnesiac state by the second Human Torch, Johnny Storm.

Finding his people scattered and Atlantis destroyed by nuclear tests, Namor declares war on humanity, repeatedly battling Super Heroes such as the Avengers, Fantastic Four, and Daredevil. After reuniting his surviving subjects, Namor concentrates on rebuilding Atlantis. He is regarded by surface dwellers as both a threat and a savior: safeguarding Earth's oceans and denizens, and—when interests overlap—saving humanity from deadly threats and its own stupidity.

Atlantis abides

Apparently ageless, immeasurably powerful, and the absolute sovereign of a technologically advanced, mystically adept nation, Namor never compromises. His right to rule is divinely ordained by Olympian deity Neptune and, despite serving with various surface Super Hero teams, the Sub-Mariner always puts his own opinions and his people's welfare above all else. This stance is bolstered by his greatest advantage. Thanks to his marine explorations, Namor salvages vast wealth from sunken wrecks and uses it to create surface-world conglomerate Oracle Industries, clandestinely furthering his goals in many nations.

Namor's sense of entitlement leads to many clashes with close comrades, as well as alliances with despots and terrorists such as Doctor Doom and Magneto. He feels a special kinship with fellow rulers

and superior individuals: an attitude that leads him to join covert super-powered think tank the Illuminati. He acts with typical ruthlessness when they contemplate thwarting the destruction of the Multiverse by destroying entire worlds. But when the Illuminati find that they must eradicate an alternate Earth to save their own, none in the group can bring themselves to detonate the antimatter bomb. Despising his weak, ethical allies, Namor triggers the device, killing billions to save his own subjects and the world they inhabit. The shock shatters his spirit.

When the Multiverse dies and is restored, the Sub-Mariner is executed by the Squadron Supreme—vengeful survivors of other Earths destroyed by the Illuminati. However, he is later resurrected through accidental manipulation of the time stream to once again defend the newest Atlantis from all threats. ■

Dressed to kill In line with his new anti-surface world political stance, Namor resorts to Atlantean battle armor.

LIVING LEGEND
CAPTAIN AMERICA RETURNS

ON THE RECORD

REAL NAME
Steven Grant Rogers

ALLEGIANCES
**Avengers, S.H.I.E.L.D.
Illuminati, New Invaders**

POWERS
**Chemically enhanced to
peak physical capacity,
augmented healing system,
extended longevity**

MISSION
**Upholding the nation's ideals
while defending life and
liberty**

STATUS REPORT
**A hero out of time trying to
reconcile his old-fashioned
beliefs with an increasingly
divided populace**

Lost in the dying days of World War II, the original Captain America is found decades later, recovered from the north Atlantic Ocean by newly formed super-team the Avengers. Thanks to the Super-Soldier Serum, the sole success of Project: Rebirth has been perfectly preserved in a slab of ice.

Invited to join the Avengers, the Sentinel of Liberty throws himself into this strange new world, spearheading the team after its first roster change when Thor, Iron Man, Giant-Man, and the Wasp take leaves of absence.

Despite large gaps in his memory—he fails to recognize his former Invader ally Sub-Mariner when they clash—the future-shocked hero is tormented by the loss of his partner Bucky and constantly seeks solace in battle or further service. This leads to him contacting Nick Fury and working with S.H.I.E.L.D. Eventually he rises to the position of the organization's director and US Chief of Security. Universally accepted as the public face and de facto leader of the Avengers, Captain America is the ultimate hero, acclaimed by ordinary citizens and fellow Super Heroes as invincible. He is one of a few worthy enough to lift Thor's mystic hammer, Mjölnir.

Fighting the good fight
Over many years, the revived veteran defeats hundreds of villains and monsters, including fellow World War II survivor the evil Red Skull, saving the world from terrorism,

Oldie but goodie A returned Cap quickly learns that evil never dies, but his old-fashioned tactics still work against foes.

My duty to my country comes first. No matter the cost!
Captain America

tyranny, and subversion. However, duty and service come at the cost of love, family, and a personal life for Steve Rogers. Worse still is a gradual eroding of his ideals as the modern United States fragments into warring social ideologies and political factions. Increasingly aware he cannot represent all Americans, Captain America resigns, following the exposure of high-level corruption in the White House. Still resolved to fight for justice, Steve Rogers briefly becomes Nomad, Man Without a Country, before again taking up the mantle of Captain America to save the nation from the Red Skull.

Greater than his enhanced physical abilities or cutting-edge ordnance and defenses supplied by US military technicians is Rogers' unflagging spirit. In combat, Cap's split-second strategic decisions and tactical ingenuity make him a match for any foe, but his drive to succeed and inability to quit are what truly enable him to overcome all odds. These qualities also make him the perfect teacher: he has trained dozens of heroes from Hawkeye to Iron Man and USAgent, while mentoring many partners such as Demolition Man, Jack Flag, Free Spirit, and a succession of Nomads. Some, such as Falcon (Sam Wilson) and Bucky, have even inherited the role of Captain America when

Rogers has been unable to fulfill his duties. His example even reforms some Super Villains such as the mercenary Diamondback (Rachel Leighton) and Mechano-Marauder Fabian Stankiewicz.

Foremost defender of Freedom, Democracy, and American Values, Captain America is humanity's most ardent and inspirational protector. However, his greatest challenge comes when his very history is subverted by a reality-warping Cosmic Cube, and he becomes fascist leader of Hydra and conqueror of the US. Yet even here, his innate sense of morality triumphs and he defeats his evil double, leaving Captain America with the toughest battle of his career: winning back the trust of the American people. ∎

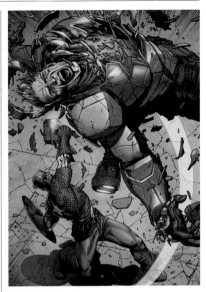

Righteous victory Not even Captain America's Hydra doppelgänger could withstand Mjölnir's mighty judgment.

Best defense From 1941, Captain America's emblematic shield has gone through a range of shapes and chemical compositions, each featuring a dominant white star and red, white, and blue stripes.

Original heater-shaped shield
Cap's first 1941 tempered steel shield is designed to resemble the shield on the Seal of the United States.

Second heater-shaped shield
Now with a scalloped top edge, the second shield is also made from high-grade tempered steel.

First disc shield
A lab accident produces Cap's iconic disc-shaped shield, made from Vibranium, steel, and a proto-Adamantium alloy.

Replacement shield
When Cap and his shield go missing during WWII, his 1950s replacements use copies made from government-issue steel.

Tempered steel shield After being revived, Cap uses a new shield equipped with Tony Stark's magnetic repulsor tech.

Energy shield
When Cap loses his shield, S.H.I.E.L.D. gives him a photonic energy one generated by his gauntlets.

Triangular shield
Used by the Hydra Cap, the shield can split in two, and features an energy blade projectile deployed from its base.

Original Vibranium shield Virtually indestructible, Cap's badge of office is repainted to resemble his post-war shield.

FACE OF EVIL
RED SKULL

ON THE RECORD

REAL NAME
Johann Shmidt

ALLEGIANCES
The Third Reich; A.I.M., Hydra, New World Order, Axis Mundi

POWERS
Malign consciousness for numerous cloned bodies; accomplished martial artist and weapons master

MISSION
Subjugating humanity to his fascist ideology

STATUS REPORT
Believed dead, but rumors of other clone bodies persist

In 1930s Germany, as the Nazi party comes to power, uneducated bellboy Johann Shmidt is singled out by the new Chancellor Adolf Hitler. The Führer is convinced Nazi values can produce an all-conquering super-man. After his Gestapo fail to see the potential in Shmidt and provide him with inadequate training, Hitler personally supervises the transformation of the hate-filled cadet into a chilling symbol of Aryan supremacy. Unleashed to spread terror, the Red Skull commits atrocities across Europe and sets up an espionage network in the US, long before it enters World War II. In Germany, he establishes an organization loyal only to him inside the Wehrmacht, seizing exotic technology and occult artifacts, while secretly eliminating rivals until he is second only to Hitler in the Nazi hierarchy.

Super-Soldier Captain America is democracy's answer to the Red Skull. The symbols clash many times during the war, culminating in Berlin in 1945. Captain America fights the Skull deep beneath the bomb-shattered city during an Allied air raid and the paragon of hatred and his deputies are seemingly buried forever in a massive explosion.

Tomorrow belongs to me
The detonation releases gases that preserve the Nazis in suspended animation. They are revived decades later by agents of T.H.E.M.— a subdivision of Hydra. A master manipulator, the Skull subverts the scientific terrorists, taking over the organization before launching a wave of attacks against the modern world. Devoted to the cause of Aryan supremacy, his reign of terror

Red devil Embracing fascist ideals, the Skull will stop at nothing to control humanity.

Cosmic Cube

Cosmic Cubes are reality-reshaping devices that have been repeatedly discovered throughout the cosmos. Made by an advanced species, they are containment devices for exotic energies, able to alter matter, contravene physical laws, and even rearrange time. Very few beings realize that these energies originate in the overdimensional realm of the Beyonders.

Although shapes may vary, all Cosmic Cubes are matrices of embryonic energy that gradually evolve into self-aware beings of immeasurable power.

Capable of vast universal manipulation, these entities are conditioned by their external environment and imprinted with the personality of the creatures who use them. A Cube wielded by a deranged and aggressive Skrull Emperor destroys half a galaxy on reaching autonomous sentience, before reforming as the omnipotent Shaper of Worlds. Earth's first Cosmic Cube—created by A.I.M. and operated by the Red Skull (pictured), Sub-Mariner, Thanos, and others—eventually shatters before achieving ascension as celestial wanderer Kubik.

is guided by his own perverse ideology. The Red Skull's first targets are peacekeeping agency S.H.I.E.L.D., and wartime enemies Nick Fury and Captain America. He breaks ties with science terrorist group A.I.M. (Advanced Ideas Mechanic) after stealing its greatest discovery: a "Cosmic Cube" able to rewrite reality and grant any wish. Yet, even with this ultimate weapon, he cannot defeat Cap, although he does escape to return many times.

Cruel and diabolically ingenious, the Red Skull constantly attacks the Free World. Even death cannot stop him. Thanks to his old comrade—Nazi geneticist Arnim Zola—the

The world will yet be mine!
Red Skull

Skull's personality is transferred into a series of clones, and even a robot body. These clones are created from Steve Rogers' Super-Soldier Serum transformed flesh, making the Red Skull at last his greatest enemy's physical equal. When not actively attacking democratic countries or his enemies, the Skull patiently expands his own fascist organization. As well as creating an army of Super Villains, he also funds a network of neo-Nazi groups to infiltrate and undermine society, furthering his dream of a National Socialist empire.

To ensure his legacy, the Red Skull fathers a child to succeed him, but is appalled to find he has a daughter, Sinthea, not the son he craved. He despises her, but is persuaded to let her live and she grows up to become lethal terrorist Sin. She even becomes a new Red Skull after he dies again, but only until her father returns in another clone body.

The Red Skull's hunger for power and absolute control is almost attained after the mutant telepath Charles Xavier dies. Despite regarding the X-Men leader as

Reich-hand woman Trained in combat, munitions expert Sinthea will commit any atrocity to win her father's approval.

"sub-human," the Skull steals Xavier's brain and has it grafted onto his own, gaining the abilities of Earth's most potent telepath. Launching devastating attacks on the US and the Avengers, the Skull eventually falls in battle against Magneto. However, thanks to contingency planning, the everlasting villain remains an all-too credible threat. ∎

WARRIOR KING
BLACK PANTHER

ON THE RECORD

REAL NAME
T'Challa

ALLEGIANCES
Royal Council of Ancestors, Avengers, Fantastic Four, the Crew, Ultimates, Illuminati

LOCATION
Wakanda, East Africa

POWERS
Super-genius; enhanced strength, speed, agility, and senses; brilliant strategist and tactician

MISSION
Preserving Wakandans and, by extension, all humanity

STATUS REPORT
Seeks to extend Wakandan influence and human survival to the stars

Since the time of Bashenga, all Wakandan kings have been Black Panthers. The warrior king devised sacred robes in Bast's honor to be proudly worn by all his descendants, each tailored to the current chieftain's specific strengths. Bashenga carves out a mighty, yet secret, kingdom in the heart of Africa, and joins Asgardian Odin, Sorcerer Supreme Agamotto, life avatar Lady Phoenix, demon-tainted Ghost Rider, the first Iron Fist, and planetary protector Star Brand as a team of primordial Avengers to battle a deranged Celestial threatening Earth.

For eons, Wakanda prospers in splendid isolation, but with Europe's Industrial Revolution, humanity's hunger for raw materials brings unrest. During World War II, incursions by both American and Nazi forces are ruthlessly repelled, but years later, raids by terrorist group Hydra force reigning Black Panther T'Chaka into a protocol-shattering alliance with US technologist Howard Stark and his newly formed S.H.I.E.L.D. security agency. After King T'Chaka's wife Queen N'Yami dies giving birth to a son, T'Challa, T'Chaka sinks into despair, ill-prepared for another crisis. When T'Challa is ten, foreign mercenary Ulysses Klaw murders the king during a bloody raid to steal Wakanda's greatest resource: Vibranium ore. A vengeful T'Challa drives off the invaders and years later—after extensive overseas education and surviving Wakanda's Sacred Challenge Rites—becomes the greatest Black Panther of all.

Techno warrior T'Challa's Vibranium uniform conceals advanced weapons and systems attuned to his fighting style.

Orphan King

Despite enhanced physical abilities bestowed by Bast's Heart-Shaped Herb, T'Challa's greatest strengths are his formidable intellect and strategic insights. The embodiment of traditions stretching into prehistory and a devout Champion of the People, he is also an impatient iconoclast. Seeing the world rapidly changing and fearing the rise of superhuman beings, he undertakes a radical redefinition of Wakanda. Dubbed Haramu-Fal (Orphan King) because of his parents' early deaths, T'Challa brings Wakanda into the UN. With Vibranium as a strictly controlled medium of exchange, he turns the

> I am a king... a warrior... but still a man.
> **T'Challa**

nation into an electronic utopia. Through his own inventions and those of national think tank Wakanda Design Group, he ensures that his country is a technological powerhouse to be feared and respected. He becomes a global Super Hero; masking an intelligence gathering mission as his quest to help humanity. Like Bashenga fighting alongside the heroes of 1,000,000BCE, T'Challa becomes a warrior against evil: an Avenger.

Although small, Wakanda is supremely well-armed and equipped. The nation's warrior spirit imbues every weapon T'Challa has commissioned, designed, or built. The Wakanda Design Group is a pioneer in aviation and spaceship innovation: providing interplanetary and extra-galactic vessels for the Avengers and Fantastic Four, while keeping them from rival governments. The only exception is for the UN-sponsored Ultimates. With Earth itself at stake, these cosmic troubleshooters have access to all T'Challa's resources. After surviving an assassination attempt by Doctor Doom and escaping from the Realm of Death, T'Challa returns to the

Panther's wish King T'Challa dreams of a spiritually traditional, scientifically forward-looking, and secure Wakanda.

living lands to find his sister, Shuri, is Black Panther, while he inherits a far rarer role. He becomes King of the Dead and speaker for the Royal Council of Ancestors, a forum of deceased kings advising their living descendants. Relocated to the city Necropolis and its Wall of Knowledge, T'Challa rescinds his youthful prohibitions against magic, while masterminding Earth's response to a series of global and multiversal crises. Eventually reclaiming Wakanda's throne, T'Challa guides his people to their next phase: equal participants in a modern democratic state. ∎

Shuri, the Ancient Future

Princess Shuri is the child of T'Chaka and his second wife, Ramonda. A brilliant, wayward scientific prodigy, she yearns to be Black Panther. She only achieves this after accepting the true responsibility of leadership, the heavy burden of knowledge, and that the people's wishes overrule her own. With T'Challa gravely wounded by Doctor Doom, Shuri petitions Bast to succeed him, but is deemed unworthy and returns to her regular duties. Eventually earning her god's blessing and the throne by forsaking ambition and risking her life for Wakanda, Shuri governs through the nation's darkest hours, and perishes heroically when the Titan Thanos' Cabal invades.

Resurrected by T'Challa, Shuri returns as a mystically empowered avatar, carrying the knowledge of all Wakandans since Bashenga. Her grasp of history and human nature enable Shuri—now the "Aja-Adanna" or Ancient Future—to forge a new democratic leadership for all the fractured factions of Wakanda to unite around.

EARTH'S MIGHTIEST
AVENGERS

ON THE RECORD

ALLEGIANCES:
Fantastic Four, Defenders, S.H.I.E.L.D., UN, Guardians of the Galaxy, Kree, Shi'ar

FOUNDING MEMBERS
Iron Man, Thor, Ant-Man/ Giant-Man, Wasp, Hulk, Captain America

BASE
Avengers Mountain, North Pole (current)

MISSION
Defend Earth and the universe from all threats

STATUS REPORT
Although rosters change, the tradition remains steadfast

There have always been Avengers. Throughout history, monumental crises bring together extraordinary individuals in defense of the planet. A million years ago, warriors united to save Earth from Celestials. Similar brief alliances form down the ages, as heroes fight together and separate when their task is accomplished.

The status quo, however, changes forever after a new Age of Marvels begins in modern times.

Imprisoned in Asgard, but out to bedevil his stepbrother Thor, Loki mystically creates a disaster incriminating the Hulk. With the man-monster seemingly amok, his friend Rick Jones contacts the Fantastic Four, but trickster Loki diverts the transmission. Smugly awaiting the great battle that must follow, Loki reels as Iron Man, Ant-Man, and Wasp also receive the redirected SOS intended for Thor. Converging in southwestern US, the Super Heroes realize Hulk has been framed and confront their real enemy. Triumphant, they remain together as the Avengers, tackling threats beyond the scope of everyday authorities.

Although the volatile Hulk quits, he is soon replaced by

Ready for everything
Combining combat experience, magic, scientific ingenuity, and raw power, the Avengers face any threat to Earth.

legendary World War II hero Captain America, revived after decades of frozen hibernation. The team prospers, thanks to industrialist billionaire Tony Stark's backing, and the Avengers gain Federal and UN accreditation as a unique, global peacekeeping force. However, the

Masters of Evil

Originally drafted by Nazi war criminal Baron Heinrich Zemo, the Masters of Evil are former foes of individual Avengers: Melter (Iron Man), Radioactive Man (Thor), and Black Knight (Giant-Man and the Wasp). When they fail, Zemo allies with Asgardian Enchantress and Executioner to further plague the heroes.

Melter and Radioactive Man join sonic being Klaw in Ultron-5's Masters of Evil, but are betrayed after foolishly recruiting new, heroic Black Knight Dane Whitman, and quickly defeated. Zemo's son, Helmut, gathers together a veritable army of antagonists, including Absorbing Man, Blackout, Black Mamba, Fixer, Grey Gargoyle, Mr. Hyde, Tiger Shark, Moonstone, Wrecker, Bulldozer, and Yellowjacket. They defeat the Avengers, before being routed themselves. The survivors form the basis of Zemo's next team: imposter heroes the Thunderbolts.

> Avengers assemble!
> **Captain America**

stress of leading three lives—secret identities, solo Super Hero careers, and Avengers business—eventually compels some of the founders to take sabbaticals, leaving Captain America to train a new rookie squad. Cap's crew includes Hawkeye, Scarlet Witch, and Quicksilver, former villains seeking redemption. Soon Giant-Man (renamed Goliath) and Wasp return, beginning a period of constant expansion and change. Over the years, several Super Villains, aliens, and almost every costumed US hero serves with the Avengers.

A law unto themselves

Controversial roster choices put the team at odds with the US government, as does their tendency to act first and ask permission later, especially when aiding the country's enemies, such as Russia, or attacking diplomatic allies like Latverian despot Doctor Doom. The creation of a West Coast branch draws heavy Federal scrutiny and the unwanted insertion of government representatives USAgent and Spider-Woman Julia Carpenter. After years combating super-criminal conspiracies, space invasions, and universal Armageddon—as when cyborg god Korvac almost reorders reality—the Avengers are believed destroyed by mutant menace Onslaught. Humanity mourns their loss and is overjoyed when the heroes return from the pocket-dimension in which they had been trapped. Their restoration sparks renewed growth and the induction of many young heroes, culminating with the reversal of time lord Kang's subjugation of Earth.

The Avengers' downfall comes after Scarlet Witch—deranged by her powers and the loss of her magically created children—"disassembles" the team from within by killing her friends Hawkeye, Ant-Man, and former husband Vision. Within months, Steve Rogers and Tony Stark

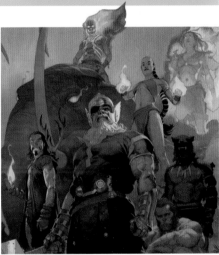

First Avengers Even before the dawn of history, Earth is guarded by gods, demons, monsters, sorcerors, and heroes.

form the New Avengers: loners and hardliners who could never have fitted within the formal structure of previous incarnations. The squad is highly effective, but splits when the government tries to register all superhumans. Through social unrest and Norman Osborn's Dark Reign as US Security Overlord, the Avengers soldier on, albeit at odds with each other and diversified into specialist units like Avengers Unity Division or US-Avengers, but always reunite into an unstoppable force when needed. »

Cosmic Avengers

In the decades before the Avengers are founded, Earth is increasingly visited by universal civilizations. Their second official case involves a shape-shifting "space phantom," and weeks later, while seeking a surgeon to operate on an injured Wasp, the team averts a battle between warring alien races close to Earth that would have eradicated humanity. The Avengers thwart many hostile expeditions and invasions—such as the incursion of android Ultroids—but inevitably a time comes when the heroes are forced to leave their world to fight under alien suns.

War between the Kree and Skrull begins with the shape-shifters infiltrating the US government and forcing the Avengers to disband. The Skrulls reignite intergalactic conflict by kidnapping the Avengers and stealing a Kree Omni-wave Projector. In Skrull hands, this communications array can become a tool of mass annihilation. With Earth potentially cosmic collateral damage, the Avengers board a S.H.I.E.L.D. ship: taking the war to

Deceit and duty Avenger ally Mar-Vell's greatest triumphs are forever tainted by the Supremor's genocidal machinations.

Kree homeworld Hala, and scattering a Skrull armada on the way. Their actions secure Earth's interplanetary boundaries for years to come. They also expose how the ruthless Kree Supreme Intelligence (aka Supremor) plans to kickstart his people's stalled

evolution by inflicting disaster on his own subjects. The Supremor's ambitions and interest in humanity's untapped genetic potential will coincide many times over the years. It results in bitter success after the Supremor orchestrates war between the Kree and Shi'ar empires. Operation Galactic Storm again takes the Avengers into space, but this time they fail to prevent the extermination of billions of Kree across the galaxy when a Shi'ar Nega-Bomb detonates. The survivors are seeded with mutagenic abilities as Supremor had schemed all along.

Earning their stars

Before this tragedy, the Avengers had earned the respect of many intergalactic races by foiling the Mad Titan Thanos' schemes to become a god and extinguish the stars. With their space credentials established, select teams rescue other worlds from subjugation and form the dedicated squad Avengers: Infinity. One mission deters vast, other-dimensional Infinites from erasing galaxies to improve the flow of energy through the Multiverse,

Interstellar Avengers

Earth's mightiest Super Heroes have proudly counted star-born and space-bound champions among their ranks. Steadfast regulars include half-Kree Captain Marvel Carol Danvers, Noh-Varr the Protector, galactic terraformer Ex Nihilo, and human/Contraxian hybrid Jack of Hearts.

Earth natives Heather Douglas and the anonymous daughter of Super Villain Libra both find their destinies beyond Earth. Trained from infancy by the pacifist Priests of Pama, Moondragon and Mantis develop astounding mental and physical

gifts to aid the Avengers: Infinity squad (pictured) in their ongoing interstellar exploits. After facing cosmic Armageddon beside Kree Captain Mar-Vell, the Avengers welcome his Titan ally Eros onto the team. As Starfox, he is a trusted off-world resource, just like the extradimensional, extraterrestrial Hyperion, and even ferocious Shi'ar outcast Deathcry. When the Avenger Quasar becomes Protector of the Universe, he relocates to the stars, but still finds the need to muster teams from his homeworld, and even commandeer aid from the omnipotent Eternity.

while another operation liberates Celestial Madonna Mantis and her son Sequoia from Thanos.

The Avengers face catastrophe at home, however, when a council of star empires judge humanity to be dangerous and quarantine Earth. The council dumps cosmic menaces and criminals on the planet to keep the population occupied and out of intergalactic affairs. Later, when war breaks out between X-Men and Avengers, another away-team is dispatched to deep space in futile attempts to prevent the all-powerful Phoenix Force from returning to Earth and wreaking havoc. As the planet recovers from the crisis, Steve Rogers and Tony Stark rethink the concept: enlisting an army of superhuman soldiers geared up to protect Earth and its inhabitants.

Drawing members from every version of the team—from mutant/human Avengers Unity Division to ultra-secret Illuminati—the ever-fluctuating battalion assembles as required to counter imminent cosmic annihilations. They also deploy for subtler missions, with espionage specialists Black Widow or Shang-Chi applying their skills where powerhouses like Star Brand or the Hulk cannot operate. As interstellar tensions escalate, the Avengers battle alien terra-formers, evil alternate universe counterparts, and their most implacable archenemy, Ultron, who attacks through time,

We take the fight to them… (we) stand with other worlds!
Captain America

instigating an apocalyptic, reality-warped Age of Ultron.

When primordial aliens the Builders discover the Multiverse is fatally unraveling, they deem Earth responsible and send a vast fleet to destroy it and everything in their path. As the Avengers join a coalition of alien races, which includes many former foes and would-be conquerors, to confront the horde, Thanos takes advantage and invades Earth again. With the

Above and beyond Earth's peace and security often require the Avengers to take the fight beyond their own planet.

majority of Avengers off-world, Luke Cage musters remaining Super Heroes into his Mighty Avengers to aid ordinary citizens through his street-level storefront operation, ensuring Earth always remains an Avengers World. ∎

See also: Captain America returns, Super Heroes at war, Infinity Gauntlet

STRAIGHT SHOOTER
HAWKEYE

ON THE RECORD

REAL NAME
Clinton Francis "Clint" Barton

ALLEGIANCES
Avengers, Defenders, Thunderbolts, S.H.I.E.L.D., Avengers West Coast

POWERS
Top-level martial artist and weapons master

MISSION
Grass roots hero helping those least able to help themselves

STATUS REPORT
Exploring the US, aiding ordinary people with extraordinary problems

After Barney Barton's parents die in a car crash, the boy and his younger brother, Clint, go into Iowa's foster care system. Fleeing an abusive foster father, they join the Carson Carnival of Traveling Wonders. Here young Clint is singled out by star-performer Jacques Duquesne —the Swordsman. He recognizes Clint's untapped gifts,

training him with a bow until he is "the world's greatest marksman." Duquesne dubs him Hawkeye. The show is a hotbed of criminality and Barney soon succumbs to the lure of easy money, starting on the path to becoming a mob boss and, eventually, Super Villain Trickshot.

Clint's inherent honesty is frequently tested over the years. When he catches Swordsman robbing the show, master and student clash and Clint is left for dead. When Barney learns that his brother stupidly refused a quick payday, he abandons him.

I fought the law
Years later, Clint performs as Hawkeye the Marksman at Coney Island and witnesses Iron Man preventing a disaster. Headstrong Clint realizes his own gifts, a fancy costume, and some mechanical gimmicks could make him rich and famous, too. However, his first foray ends in disaster. Apprehending a robber, he is accused of theft by the police, and flees. Running into Russian spy Natasha Romanoff and dazzled by her beauty, Clint aids her in her vendetta against Iron Man.

Following numerous battles and believing Black Widow dead,

I'm the greatest marksman the world has ever seen!
Hawkeye

Hawkeye reevaluates his own life. With Iron Man's support, a reformed Hawkeye joins the Avengers when all the founding members take a leave of absence. Alongside fellow former fugitives Quicksilver and the Scarlet Witch—and trained by team leader Captain America—Hawkeye develops into the quintessential Super Hero: capable, competent, and indomitable. He masks his accomplishments under a façade of brusque, cynical insolence and rebellion, but learns everything necessary to eventually lead his own team. Always seeking to improve his capabilities, Clint briefly uses Henry Pym's growth serum to become a new Goliath, but when his powers fade while

Going straight

Hawkeye's isn't the only hero to start on the wrong side of the law. He joins the Avengers alongside former members of the Brotherhood of Evil Mutants: Quicksilver and Scarlet Witch. Over time, the twins' loyalties are severely tested by humanity's intolerance to mutants. Similar pressures affect Sandman, the Swordsman, and Red Hulk when they try to reform. Hawkeye's lover Black Widow becomes a force for good after throwing off Soviet Red Room brainwashing, and Serpent Society mercenary Diamondback turns hero simply to impress Captain America.

Super-thief Black Cat battles against—and then alongside—Spider-Man while enjoying a romantic relationship, but her good deeds become irrelevant after they split. Black Cat returns to crime with a vengeance… and a broken heart. A recent turncoat is Deadly Nightshade, who, thanks to Hawkeye, abandons super-crime to fight injustice as vigilante Nighthawk (pictured).

saving Earth from a Skrull invasion, Hawkeye reverts to the tools and weapons that have never failed him.

Hawkeye finds he is torn between leading teams such as Avengers West Coast and the glory of solo stardom. Despite being traumatized by the apparent death of his wife, Mockingbird, and his own death and resurrection, Clint strives to make his mark in an increasingly dangerous world. Hawkeye's most painful act of loyalty comes when fellow Avenger Bruce Banner makes him swear to kill the apparently cured scientist if the Hulk ever again manifests. The sorrowful duty is performed with arrows tipped in a gamma-toxin provided by Banner himself. Clint is tried for murder, but cleared, and finds himself world-famous at last, but for what he considers the worst deed he has ever committed.

Weary of the Super Hero spotlight, he becomes a grassroots Avenger: saving lives and fighting injustice at street level, both singly and with trusted companions such as Red Wolf and Kate Bishop. Kate, a teenage archer and polymath, assumes Hawkeye's role while Clint is dead and shares his code name after he returns as Ronin. Hawkeye is currently wandering the US, ready for anything. ■

Take a bow
Fellow Hawkeye Kate Bishop respects the talents of non-super-powered human, Clint.

Hawkeye's top trick arrows

Sonic Arrow
Emits a high-pitched 95 decibel sound two seconds after release.

Electro Arrow
Delivers variable-intensity electric shocks that can stun or paralyze.

Cable Arrow
Arrowhead is coupled with grapples to bind foes or swing from buildings.

Acid Arrow
Swiftly burns through solid surfaces, including Iron Man's armor.

Explosive Arrow
Delivers detonations of varying intensity.

Smoke/Tear Gas Arrow
Fires assorted, compressed riot-control vapors.

Putty Arrow
Rapidly expanding sticky-polymer immobilizes foes harmlessly.

Bola Arrow
Releases three small, heavy balls on 18 inch cables to entwine target.

Flare Arrow
Contains magnesium/iron powder flare that lights 5 seconds after release.

LETHAL WEAPON
BLACK WIDOW

ON THE RECORD

REAL NAME
Natasha Alianovna Romanova

ALLEGIANCES
Russian Intelligence, Avengers, Champions, S.H.I.E.L.D., Thunderbolts

POWERS
Peak human augmented by life-extending physical and chemical enhancements

MISSION
After years of indefensible actions, Black Widow seeks to atone by saving lives and punishing evildoers

STATUS REPORT
Reported dead but unverified sightings persist

As befits a master spy, the true origins of the Black Widow are shrouded in mystery and disinformation. The truth has been obscured for decades in a web of meticulously layered back-up and cover stories. The most consistent reports state that Natasha Romanova was born in Russia in the 1920s, as the Soviets consolidated their hold on the country and began to export their revolution to other nations.

One of 28 orphan girls selected for certain aptitudes, Romanova becomes part of the Red Room project: physically altered and augmented while being intensively schooled in every aspect of espionage and assassination. Specialist guest tutors include Canadian agent Logan (James Howlett) and master-assassin Winter Soldier (James "Bucky" Barnes), with whom she pursues

Agent provocateur Despite acquitting herself as a formidable Super Hero, Black Widow was born to be a super-spy.

You have no idea what
I'm capable of.
Black Widow

an unsanctioned affair. After numerous missions for the KGB, Romanova is ordered to marry Alexi Shostakov—trained as the Red Guardian to be Russia's answer to Captain America. When he is reported killed, she assumes the code name Black Widow for her future missions

With the US experiencing a wave of superhuman incidents and the birth of a new generation of Marvels, Romanova is dispatched to steal secrets from munitions inventor Tony Stark, but suffers humiliating defeats at the hands of Iron Man. Calling herself Natasha Romanoff, she seduces emergent hero Hawkeye into being her weapon against Stark. Failing repeatedly, she is recalled to the Kremlin, brainwashed, "re-educated," and armed with mechanical devices that enable her to compete with Super Heroes on their own terms.

After developing real feelings for Hawkeye, Black Widow defects to the West, beginning a long association with the Avengers and S.H.I.E.L.D. Her relationship with the idealistic archer—and later Daredevil— seemingly counteract much of her early Red Room programming and,

as both an intelligence operative and Super Hero, the Widow seeks to make a new life for herself.

Asset management

Conflict and isolation remain major parts of her life, especially as suppressed memories and evidence of her old life continually resurface. Weighing her past deeds against her current morality, Black Widow decides she has too much blood on her hands and resolves to balance the scales by helping the innocent and punishing the guilty.

Black Widow's gifts and training make her one of the most capable fighters and strategists on Earth, and after leading the short-lived super-team Champions of Los Angeles, she renews ties with the Avengers. Her ability to make hard decisions also makes her indispensable to S.H.I.E.L.D., where Nick Fury gives her freedom to handle the dirty, difficult problems Super Heroes are ill-suited to.

Although a loyal and dedicated member of many teams, the Widow's training and temperament prevent her from ever truly trusting anybody or accepting any final judgment but her own. This includes her readiness

Love hurts Former lovers Black Widow and Hawkeye maintain a complicated relationship for years.

to keep killing as a necessary option for neutralizing her opponents. During the climactic battle against Hydra's Secret Empire, when Black Widow and a group of teenage heroes strive to liberate Washington, D.C., she prevents young Spider-Man (Miles Morales) from murdering Supreme Hydra Steve Rogers, determined that no innocents should carry the burden of being a killer. ∎

Widow makers

After Natasha Romanoff defects to the West, survivors of the Red Room program activate a replacement Black Widow: Yelena Belova. Although a worthy substitute, this new agent also proves noncompliant and eventually goes rogue, battling both beside and against her predecessor. Belova briefly retires, but is lured back to espionage work by S.H.I.E.L.D. and is transformed by Hydra into a power-duplicating Super-Adaptoid, before becoming

Minister of State in Super Villain-controlled Bagalia.

She is reported killed by Romanoff, but a Red Room protocol to store fully trained and suitably indoctrinated clones of their most effective agents suggests that an unspecified number of counterfeit Black Widows are still at large in the world. It might also provide the answer to the question: who is carrying on in Natasha Romanoff's name, following her reputed death fighting Hydra in Washington, D.C.?

SHOULDER TO SHOULDER
SUPER HERO TEAMS

ON THE RECORD

ALLEGIANCES
Temporary and inclusive: even extraterrestrials, Super Villains, and civilians

RESOURCES
Mission-specific coalitions of the willing

MISSION
Saving everything

STATUS REPORT
Ready and waiting

Earth is a world plagued by extraordinary events and singular crises, and where a large section of the population are super-beings of one sort or another. Sadly, for every individual eager to help others, there are dozens who prefer to help themselves. In the face of overwhelming odds that no lone hero can hope to successfully defend against, it is no surprise Super Heroes tend to join forces.

Some, such as the Fantastic Four and ClanDestine, develop from family associations, while others, like the New Warriors, are recruited with specific goals. Nations follow

suit: recruiting extraordinary agents for publicly acceptable teams, such as Great Britain's Excalibur, China's People's Defense Force, and Russia's Winter Guard. This policy is not the same as the covert superhumans all governments employ, such as the various incarnations of Weapon X, or deep-cover unit Nextwave. Other groups—such as X-Men or Agents of Atlas—are purpose-built: designed to act cooperatively from the start

A-Force for good Nico Minoru, Dazzler, She-Hulk, Captain Marvel, Medusa, and Singularity form a formidable, no-nonsense, all-female team.

with specific goals, but still suffering from "mission-creep" as the paramount need to save lives often clashes with their agendas.

The most common Super Hero associations are gatherings of similarly inclined individuals banding together: the Avengers, original and new Champions, and arcane-specific groups like the Midnight Sons or Legion of Monsters. This approach is preferred by a few young Super Heroes who lack the experience for forward planning, but most follow specific rules of engagement and understand their role in the bigger picture of Super Hero endeavors. Some teams keep their activities loose-knit and act as first responders, while the Avengers—in all its incarnations and subdivisions—follow tightly organized procedures and a carefully designed charter with full Federal and international backing, and secure, long-term financing.

Defend us from evil
However, the most persistent, varied, and arguably effective grouping is not actually a team at all. Calling themselves the Defenders, these champions from society's fringes reluctantly convene

Alpha Flight

Canada's Department of National Defense forms Dept. H in response to a proliferation of superhumans and uncanny events such as magical or alien invasions. Project leader James McDonald Hudson assembles three "flights" of empowered agents: Alpha (combat-ready), Beta (intermediate), and Gamma (trainee). First choice of Alpha Flight field-leader is Wolverine, but when he defects to the X-Men, Hudson dons a high-tech battlesuit as Weapon X (later Guardian), commanding mutants Aurora and Northstar, mystic Shaman, gamma ray/ magic monster Sasquatch, Arctic goddess Snowbird, acrobat Puck, and amphibious alien Marrina.

Despite years of devoted service, the squad suffers dire loss of personnel and constant government manipulation. They eventually quit to become independent operatives, before being recruited again by later administrations. Following even more casualties, the project fails, with Puck, Sasquatch, and Aurora seconded to the pan-national Alpha Flight Low-Orbit Space Station. Led by Captain Marvel (Carol Danvers), they are Earth's first line of defense.

when the planet or universe are menaced. The ad hoc alliance first forms after Doctor Strange falls battling the imminent invasion of the primordial Undying Ones.

He is (almost accidentally) rescued when the demons subsequently target Namor the Sub-Mariner, and the Hulk. Some months later, Namor asks the Hulk and Silver Surfer to help him stop an American weather experiment that Atlantean scientists predict will end in atomic Armageddon. The proud prince only seeks allies because Earth is endangered and the project is guarded by the patriotic, blithely unaware Avengers. Despite disliking each other, the antiheroes often reunite when a situation demands: eventually working with almost every hero (and

Non-team-up All kinds of superhumans ally with Defenders Silver Surfer, Iron Fist, Doctor Strange, Namor, and Red She-Hulk to protect Earth.

a few villains). These Defenders regard themselves as a "non-team," even though frequent collaborators Nighthawk and displaced Asgardian warrior Valkyrie continually agitate to formalize the arrangement. After the "founders" eventually go their separate ways, one iteration eventually achieves that aim, but the X-Men-heavy New Defenders ultimately split up, too.

Doctor Strange later orchestrates a fluctuating roster of magically selected Secret Defenders to avert specific disasters and, over the years, repeatedly reunites with Namor, Hulk, and the Surfer as universal perils warrant. Other teams Strange works with also co-opt the Defenders' name for brief periods and their own team projects. For a time, it is the appellation used by Luke Cage, Jessica Jones, Iron Fist, and Daredevil as they seek to clean up the streets of New York.

Whether wearing a uniform and following a formal code of conduct, or just hanging out as a gang of like-minded loners, forming a united force to face threats to Earth is the ultimate Super Hero goal. ■

WEBBED WONDER
SPIDER-MAN

ON THE RECORD

REAL NAME
Peter Benjamin Parker

ALLEGIANCES
Avengers, Fantastic Four, Future Foundation

POWERS
Enhanced speed, strength, agility, and stamina; rapid healing; precognitive danger sense; genius intellect

MISSION
Driven by an acute sense of responsibility, Parker obsessively defends anyone at risk of harm

After being bitten by a radioactive spider at a science exhibition, scientifically brilliant high-schooler Peter Parker discovers he has developed astonishing arachnoid abilities. Stronger, faster, psychically aware of incoming dangers, and able to stick to walls, the lonely, bullied orphan decides to cash in on his abilities by becoming a performer. Sewing a flashy, all-concealing costume, Parker also devises an artificial adhesive and powered wrist-shooter units to fire his "webbing."

Keeping his identity secret, the 15-year-old quickly becomes a TV sensation, but wealth and fame turn his head. When a thief races past him at the studio, he does nothing. Later, that same robber kills Parker's beloved Uncle Ben in a home-invasion. Ben and his wife May had cared for Peter ever since his parents—both CIA agents—vanished on a mission when he was a baby. After the traumatized teenager brings the killer to justice, he vows to always use his gifts to help others.

Throughout his school and college years, Parker continually sacrifices his needs to help those around him, whether it's battling world-threatening menaces, super-thugs, and petty crooks as the amazing Spider-Man, or financially supporting his widowed Aunt May by selling

Web-shooter The adhesive fluid Spider-Man fires out can form swing-lines or webs.

J. Jonah Jameson

John Jonah Jameson comes from a wealthy military family, but devotes his life to journalism as owner and publisher of the New York newspaper the *Daily Bugle*. Shrewd, tenacious, and dedicated to the truth, he finally allows profit to dictate editorial policy after becoming obsessed with costumed "vigilantes" such as Spider-Man, whom he persecutes in his publications. He funds many schemes to bring the web-slinger to justice, including backing the villain Mysterio and sponsoring the transformation of private detective Mac Gargan into the super-powered Scorpion.

After losing the *Bugle* to rival publisher Dexter Bennett, Jameson enters politics, becoming Mayor of New York. He resigns after a scandal when the city is overrun by the Goblin Nation and returns to reporting, first for TV news outlet Fact Channel and then radio show *Get to Work!*, where he atones for years of prejudice by vigorously supporting Spider-Man.

on-the-scene photos of his web-slinging alter ego to *Daily Bugle* publisher J. Jonah Jameson. Parker even allows the demonic Mephisto to mystically erase his years of happy marriage to Mary Jane Watson and reset his existence in exchange for the hell-lord preventing Aunt May from being killed. The wall-crawler's fantastic exploits take him from dark alleys to distant worlds, different eras, and magical dimensions. Yet, even when overwhelmed, the ever ebullient Spider-Man invariably responds with a snappy quip that masks his resolute determination. His crusade also sees him fight alongside nearly every Super Hero on Earth and many of the universe's greatest champions. They all learn to respect the indomitable masked hero, if not his incessant, jokey banter.

Spider-Man's courageous efforts often come at great personal cost. His first great love, Gwen Stacy, dies at the hands of arch-maniac Green Goblin and Gwen's father is killed by Doctor Octopus. Even Aunt May and Parker's friends, Harry Osborn and Flash Thompson, are regularly targeted by his foes.

Neighborhood hero

Parker constantly struggles to make ends meet thanks to his low-paying work as a photojournalist and school teacher, but his fortunes turn around after arguably his greatest enemy kills him! When Otto Octavius takes control of the hero's body, overriding his mind and personality to become Superior Spider-Man, Doctor Octopus' vanity will not allow Parker to remain a nobody. He upgrades Spider-Man's costume into a high-tech battle suit, goes back to college as Peter, subsequently receives a doctorate, and starts technology company Parker Industries.

By the time Peter regains control of his body and ousts Octavius, Parker Industries is a world-leading international brand, rivaling Tony Stark's financial empire. Once again, however, the needs of the innocent soon outweigh Parker's own. When Doctor Octopus returns during terrorist organization Hydra's conquest of the US, Parker destroys his suit, his technology, and his company to thwart the Secret Empire. He would rather start from scratch than allow his discoveries to benefit criminals and threaten ordinary people. ∎

Have no fear.
Spidey is here!
Spider-Man

Web of lies Parker spends years hiding his identity from Aunt May; fearful that her anxiety over his safety might kill her.

DEADLIER THAN THE MALE
SPIDER-WOMAN

ON THE RECORD

REAL NAME
Jessica Miriam Drew

ALLEGIANCES
Avengers, S.H.I.E.L.D., S.W.O.R.D., Hydra

POWERS
Super-strong, fast, and durable; enhanced senses and rapid healing; sticks to surfaces; bio-electric venom-blast; flight

MISSION
Fighting for justice and teaching her son to be a hero

STATUS REPORT
Balancing family life with being a Super Hero

After years regarding herself an outsider from the human race due to her biology, Spider-Woman is a ferociously adept survivor, determined to do the right thing whatever the cost to herself. Jessica Drew grows up in Transia in the High Evolutionary's Wundagore Mountain citadel where her father Jonathan works with the maverick geneticist. When the child contracts radiation sickness, Dr. Drew doses her with serums extracted from spider blood and seals her in a genetic accelerator.

Drew awakens decades later to find her parents missing. The High Evolutionary tells her she is the product of his experiments: an evolved spider rather than a modified human with arachnid abilities. She becomes convinced that she is cursed to harm all around her, a view bolstered by a cruel fact of her altered biology, as she emits pheromones that attract men and repel women. When the High Evolutionary abandons Earth, she is left behind. After finding work in Transia, her powers malfunction and Drew accidentally kills her boyfriend. A terrified fugitive, she falls under the influence of Hydra chief Otto Vermis who recognizes her deadly potential. Through brainwashing and pretense of friendship he makes her accept her mistaken beliefs of being a hyper-evolved spider in human form, before training her as an assassin.

Clad in an outfit allowing limited flight, Drew is dispatched to kill Nick Fury, but cannot bring herself to take another life. Rejecting Hydra's

Dark angel Spider-Woman's original outfit is designed by Hydra to enhance her powers and allows limited flight.

Silk

For years, Peter Parker remains unaware that the radioactive spider that gave him his powers also bit another student at the science show. As the arachnid's second victim, Korean-American student Cindy Moon gains similar spider-powers, including the ability to generate webs from her own body. However, she is intercepted by mystic spider-totem Ezekiel Sims who convinces Moon's parents to lock her in a vault for nearly a decade, lest her presence attract the extradimensional predator Morlun to feast on her spider-essence.

When she is finally freed, Moon takes the costumed identity Silk and works with Spider-Man until Morlun and his family, the Inheritors, attack. This situation precipitates an interdimensional crisis, as an army of alternate Earth Spider-Heroes converge from across the Spider-Verse to defeat a swarm of totem eaters. When the fight is concluded, Silk decides to make her own way in the world.

conditioning she flees, becoming an aimless wanderer, and encountering other Super Heroes such as the Thing and Invisible Woman.

Free agent

Moving to California, Drew is mentored by ancient wizard Magnus. Reluctantly becoming a Super Hero, she clashes with bizarre foes, and is drawn into Magnus' centuries-long struggle with sorceress Morgan Le Fay. When Magnus dies, she becomes a super-powered bounty hunter, before relocating to San Francisco and setting up a Private Detective agency. When Le Fay attacks again, Spider-Woman destroys her, but is removed from

From now on Spider-Woman fights back!
Jessica Drew

Baby's on board With baby Gerry inheriting his mother's powers, Jessica Drew's life becomes ever more complex.

reality afterwards. Rescued and returned to the world by the Avengers—but without her powers—Drew relocates to the piratical rogue state, Madripoor.

Her abilities gradually return, but are unstable and keep fading away. During her absence, a number of other heroes appropriate Drew's codename, including the US government-created operative Julia Carpenter and teenager Mattie Franklin. When all three Spider-Women are targeted by Charlotte Witter—using abilities bestowed by Doctor Octopus to absorb their powers—Witter becomes a new, cannibalistic Spider-Woman. She is eventually defeated by her victims, Spider-Man, and Madame Web. Sometime later, another villain takes Drew's identity when she is replaced by Skrull Queen Veranke as a prelude to the Skrull's Secret Invasion. The impostor continues to act as a triple-agent for S.H.I.E.L.D., Hydra, and the Avengers until she is killed. Newly liberated, Drew resumes her role as Spider-Woman, joining extraterrestrial watchdog agency S.W.O.R.D., and working with the Avengers to ensure the planet is kept safe.

Spy, private investigator, bounty hunter, and truth-seeker, Drew eventually returns to freelance detective work. In time, she makes the biggest decision of her life and has a baby. She tries to carve out a normal family life with journalist Ben Urich and reformed criminal Roger "the Porcupine" Gocking—who go from being her crime-fighting associates to devoted family members. Drew even manages to occasionally go adventuring with Ghost-Spider and Silk. ∎

MALEVOLENT MANIPULATOR
NORMAN OSBORN

ON THE RECORD

REAL NAME
Norman Virgil Osborn

ALLEGIANCES
**Oscorp, Goblin Army,
Dark Avengers, The Cabal,
H.A.M.M.E.R., Thunderbolts**

BASE
New York City

POWERS
**Enhanced strength, speed,
reflexes, and durability;
genius intellect**

MISSION
**Attain and maintain
dominance at all costs**

STATUS REPORT
**Seeking to regain physical
power and mental focus to
match his financial muscle**

Cunning, devious New York City entrepreneur Norman Osborn double-crosses his partner Mendel Stromm. Claiming the inventor's numerous discoveries as his own, Osborn's tinkering causes an explosion that grants him enhanced physical capabilities and reckless aggression. Whether the accidentally created "goblin serum" drives him mad or accentuates his inherent instability is impossible to determine. His abusive behavior forces his wife, Emily, to fake her own death, leaving their son, Harry, with the increasingly aloof and driven businessman. Living dual lives, Osborn appears to be a philanthropic financier, efficiently running his powerful tech company, Oscorp, while secretly building bases and safehouses for his macabre alter ego, Green Goblin.

Modifying an Oscorp prototype military battlesuit, he embarks on a brutal, but ill-conceived, campaign of conquest, employing Stromm's gadgets and weapons pilfered from his own labs. His early schemes involve controlling New York's gangs, but successive defeats by teen Super Hero Spider-Man obsess Osborn and

Air raider Riding his jet-powered, low altitude Goblin Glider, Osborn—as the Green Goblin—aims his trademark high-explosive Pumpkin bomb.

he devotes himself to destroying his arachnid archenemy. When he discovers his foe is Peter Parker—friend and classmate of his own weak, hated son Harry—his next clash with Spider-Man results in a full psychotic breakdown and the amnesiac suppression of his malign alter ego. The cure is not permanent, and the Goblin returns often to haunt Parker and Harry. His only real victory against Spider-Man is the murder of Peter's innocent girlfriend, Gwen Stacy: a cruel and devastating act he brags about whenever the two engage in battle.

Faking his own death, Osborn goes into hiding while planning an all-consuming revenge. He contents himself with sponsoring others to plague Spider-Man in ever more complex plots while he searches for ultimate power. This includes seeking alliances with European secret societies and even obtaining magical power, but—afflicted with a liberating madness he thinks is essential to his survival—these avenues are all ultimately denied him. He is either too arrogant, impatient, or dangerously ambitious to follow any advice or teachings. In the interim, upstart impostors utilize his salvaged safehouses and weapons to become a succession of new Green Goblins and Osborn's eventual rival, Hobgoblin.

All these years Spider-Man (has) dealt with a giggling lunatic... You've never faced the real Norman Osborn!
Norman Osborn

Control freak

Despite being exposed by the *Daily Bugle*, Osborn whitewashes his reputation through punitive lawsuits and a bestselling autobiography that admits to mental illness, but denies any criminal activity. True power then comes through wealth and political influence, as the redeemed businessman becomes director of the US government's Thunderbolts program, leveraging himself into the post of US Chief of Superhuman Security following a global attack by Skrulls.

Replacing S.H.I.E.L.D. with the paramilitary force H.A.M.M.E.R., which is personally loyal to him, Osborn targets Super Heroes with his "Dark Reign," leading his own team of Dark Avengers as the Iron Patriot. He is only stopped when his madness compels him to declare war on Asgardia and the American public turn on him. Overthrown and imprisoned, he escapes, converting criminals into an underground cult dubbed the Goblin Nation.

Osborn's undoing comes during another scheme to accrue power and destroy Spider-Man, when he allows the alien Carnage symbiote to merge with him. The resulting deranged creature is more powerful than anything Osborn ever imagined. However, the villain's inherent weaknesses—pride, arrogance, insecurity, and a twisted notion of family fidelity—are also intensified. This enables Peter Parker to induce a psychological conflict that splits the symbiote from Osborn, wiping his memories in the process—but not before the lethal lunatic manages to infect his own grandson Normie with the symbiote seed of the Red Goblin.

Despite his many reversals and setbacks, and whether he is super-powered or reduced to a mere human, Osborn remains a cunning and compelling monster: a potent threat to all who live. ∎

Osborn's Thunderbolts

The original Thunderbolts are a gang of super-criminals assembled by Baron Helmut Zemo who pretend to be Super Heroes to fool the public. The US government appropriates their name for a controversial program in which convicted superhuman felons perform covert missions in return for reductions in their sentences.

After apparently being cured of his psychoses, Norman Osborn is appointed as director of the project during the implementation of the Superhuman Registration Act. He immediately begins using the team to facilitate his own schemes.

When the Skrull Secret Invasion occurs, Osborn leads the Thunderbolts to New York, where, after a climactic final battle, he executes Skrull Queen Veranke on live TV. This ruthless act generates a global wave of public support that Osborn parlays into a place on the Commission on Superhuman Activities committee and eventually control of US security forces.

THE MAN WITHOUT FEAR
DAREDEVIL

ON THE RECORD

REAL NAME
Matthew Michael Murdock

ALLEGIANCES
Avengers, Defenders,
Marvel Knights, S.H.I.E.L.D.

BASE
Hell's Kitchen, Manhattan

POWERS
Blind with hyper-amplified
senses, extreme martial
artist and acrobat

MISSION
Devout hero driven to
counter the law's failings
through vigilantism

STATUS REPORT
Murdock battles divided
beliefs: law vs justice,
forgiveness vs punishment

Matt Murdock is raised in Hell's Kitchen, New York City. His father, former boxer "Battlin' Jack," works for gangster Roscoe "the Fixer" Sweeney, but turns his life around when Murdock's mother Maggie abandons them to become a nun.

As his remarkably smart son grows up, Jack tells Murdock she died, urging the boy to study and make something of his life. A devout Catholic, Murdock is drawn to the certainty of the law, and its promise to treat everyone equally. A natural athlete with an inclination for fighting, Murdock is bullied by other kids, who mock his scholarly pursuits by calling him "Daredevil." Promising his father never to fight or waste time with sports, Murdock trains secretly, honing his body for his own satisfaction. These skills serve him well when he valiantly saves an old man from a runaway truck. It costs Murdock his sight as the vehicle's contents—radioactive waste—hits his face.

Wages of sin
In hospital, Murdock discovers his other senses are hyper-amplified and he now constantly projects a "radar" pulse that maps his surroundings more accurately than eyes ever could. As his father begins a boxing

Baton rouge Disguised as a cane, Daredevil's billy club has an extendible cable hook for swinging from rooftops and can be utilized with deadly accuracy as a throwing baton.

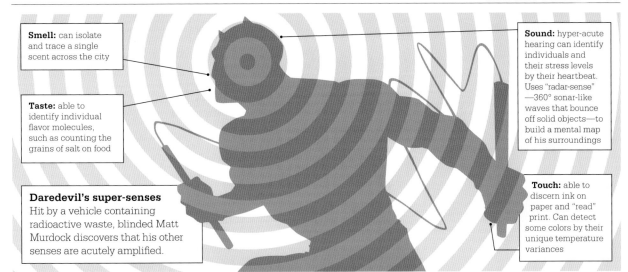

Smell: can isolate and trace a single scent across the city

Sound: hyper-acute hearing can identify individuals and their stress levels by their heartbeat. Uses "radar-sense" —360° sonar-like waves that bounce off solid objects—to build a mental map of his surroundings

Taste: able to identify individual flavor molecules, such as counting the grains of salt on food

Touch: able to discern ink on paper and "read" print. Can detect some colors by their unique temperature variances

Daredevil's super-senses
Hit by a vehicle containing radioactive waste, blinded Matt Murdock discovers that his other senses are acutely amplified.

comeback under Sweeney's management, Murdock almost succumbs to madness brought on by sensory overload. He is saved by blind sensei Stick, who trains him, refining his senses and channeling his natural aggression. Engaged in a centuries-long war against ninja clan The Hand, Stick needs recruits for his warrior-sect the Chaste. He similarly reshapes the lives of Murdock's unstable and tormented first love Elektra Natchios.

When Murdock wins a law scholarship to Columbia, his father Jack emerges as a heavyweight championship contender, but it's simply a long con to manipulate betting odds. When Jack refuses to take a dive and wins his bout, the

> I'm not afraid of you. I'm the man without fear.
> **Daredevil**

Blind faith Matt's strict sensei, Stick, uses every kind of combat training as occupational therapy for his student.

Fixer has him killed. The police fail to arrest Sweeney and Murdock, disguised as a costumed vigilante, seeks extralegal justice. Mission accomplished, he continues his secret crusade while also working as a defense lawyer with best friend Franklin "Foggy" Nelson. Realizing he can target crooks hiding behind the law or beyond its reach, Murdock adopts his childhood nickname Daredevil for his costumed persona.

For years, Daredevil combats criminals and Super Villains, even occasionally saving the world using his acrobatic skills, super-senses, and a modified billy club. Although

based primarily in Hell's Kitchen and usually working solo, Daredevil frequently acts with a small, trusted band of like-minded heroes who prioritize helping the downtrodden over beating crazed Super Villains and invading monsters.

Murdock's religious beliefs are constantly tested as he loves—and tragically loses—a succession of women he loves, including Karen Page, Heather Glenn, Elektra, and Black Widow. He undertakes an obsessive vendetta against seemingly untouchable crime boss Wilson Fisk and insane assassin Bullseye. Murdock's prolonged war against them leads to the loss of his law license and his identity becomes public knowledge until he devises a way to restore his anonymity.

Now a prosecutor, he convicts criminals and advocates for Super Heroes, while training a new generation of champions. Chinese immigrant Samuel Chung becomes his apprentice Blindspot, combining martial arts and an invisibility suit to protect Chinatown, just as Daredevil safeguards Hell's Kitchen. During his twin careers, Murdock is forever driven to protect the innocent, redeem the repentant, and punish the guilty. ∎

LORD OF CRIME
KINGPIN

ON THE RECORD

REAL NAME
Wilson Grant Fisk

ALLEGIANCES
The Hand, Emissaries of Evil, Thunderbolts, Hydra

POWERS
Peak human strength and durability, genius intellect, expert martial artist

MISSION
Obsessive hunger for control

STATUS REPORT
Fisk dominates through manipulation, maintained by successfully massaging his public image

Abused at home and bullied at school, young Wilson Fisk improves his mind through reading and study, and his body through intense exercise and martial arts. Soon he runs a gang in Hell's Kitchen, Manhattan, and comes to the attention of local crime lord Don Rigoletto. Rising to the position of chief enforcer, Fisk learns every aspect of mob business.

The ambitious underling then makes his move, murdering his patron and assuming control of his empire. Fisk's ambition is unquenchable, but his plan to unite and rule New York's underworld is foiled by an unprecedented alliance among his enemies. The Maggia and Hydra join forces to defeat him, and Fisk heads to Japan.

Working as a spice importer, Fisk rebuilds his organization while training in Japanese martial arts to become an even more lethal opponent. Returning to New York, he is unstoppable, uniting warring gangs and only failing after Spider-Man intervenes. Although exposed, Fisk avoids criminal charges and emerges with a clean record. To the world he seems a smart, ruthless businessman, but working below the radar, Fisk knows when to make showy, bloody examples of his rivals.

Profit and loss

Despite maintaining his mask of respectability, Spider-Man, Captain America, and the Punisher continually thwart Fisk's covert criminal enterprises. Frequent clashes with Daredevil eventually shatter Fisk's financial empire and,

reduced to penury, he is forced to rebuild from the ground up. Repeated high-profile and unprofitable battles with Super Heroes and an ill-judged alliance with mystic ninja clan, The Hand, results in Fisk's overthrow by his own subordinates. A prime cause of dissent in his gangs is Fisk's over reliance on "costumed crazies" rather than his own human forces. Despite despising attention-seeking superhumans, he surrounds himself with empowered enforcers and assassins such as Bullseye, Typhoid Mary, and others. Fisk believes they represent the best counter to his costumed persecutors.

Call me what you will, but I never pretended to be anything other than what I am.
Kingpin

rival gang lord the Schemer and, later, the Rose, in misguided attempts to win his father's approval. He even conspires with childhood friend and Kingpin employee, Sammy Silke, to assassinate Fisk. When the plot fails, Vanessa is forced to kill her son: an act of revenge from which she never recovers. Even after bereavement, public exposure, and imprisonment, Fisk remains indomitable and insatiable. Returning to basics in Hell's Kitchen, he rebuilds his empire with extreme brutality, using the second superhuman civil war as cover and regaining much of his former veneer of respectability.

Hiring respected journalist/ghost writer Sarah Dewey, he further massages his image with a tell-all biography *The Life and Times of Wilson Fisk*, and protects New York when it is captured by Hydra during the Secret Empire crisis. These acts lead to a grateful populace electing him Mayor, but this newfound and long-sought preeminence only makes him an even more prominent target for his enemies. ∎

Having barely survived an assassination attempt, Kingpin endures prison and exile from the US, but his determination and cunning lead him into plea bargains and alliances with American law-enforcement agencies, enabling the former crime lord to buy his way home with a clean record.

The personal cost of his hunger for power is terrifying. It destroys the honor and sanity of his beloved wife Vanessa and eventually ends her life. Their son Richard becomes

Hell's Kitchen

In New York City, poverty and privilege continually rub shoulders. Wealth and security abound mere feet away from privation and extreme violence. Clinton and Midtown West—comprising 34th through to 57th Street, and from 8th Avenue to the Hudson River—abuts some of Manhattan's most valuable real estate. This area has been called Hell's Kitchen since 1881, when a *New York Times* reporter wrote of the many murders in its immigrant slums.

Although gentrification is making inroads, the dilapidated streets and alleyways remain a vibrant melting pot of cultures and a crime hotspot that local hero Daredevil strives daily to combat. The docks have always attracted criminal enterprises and sleazy watering hole Josie's Bar has been a vital conduit of illicit deals since the crime-fighting Angel used it in WW II. Notable people born in Hell's Kitchen" include super-spy Nick Fury, and prominent lawyer Matt Murdock.

POINT BLANK
BULLSEYE AND OTHER KILLERS FOR HIRE

ON THE RECORD

REAL NAME
Lester (last name unknown)

ALLEGIANCES
Dark Avengers, Thunderbolts, H.A.M.M.E.R., The Hand, National Security Agency

POWERS
Infallible aim, Adamantium-laced bones, extreme martial artist and weapons master

MISSION
Killing for fun or profit

STATUS REPORT
Currently at large

Some killers work for money because it's a job suited to their skills, training, and temperament. Others inflict death or torture for sheer gratification. The worst combine fun with profit and, especially if they possess superhuman abilities, their notoriety is often as great as their bodycounts. These individuals are a precious asset and Earth's most malicious masterminds and many government agencies have them on speed dial.

Possessing infallible aim and an uncanny gift for calculating trajectories, gleeful fiend Bullseye enjoys killing as much as playing deadly games with his victims. He has ended lives with a thrown paperclip, playing cards, and even one of his own dislodged teeth. Defeated and arrested many times, he always manages to escape. It is significant that he only does so when guaranteed a horrified audience and fresh bodies to add to his tally of homicides.

A master of disinformation, Bullseye creates a stream of contradictory origins for himself whenever he is interrogated by police. His many aliases include Benjamin Poindexter, Lester Jangles, and Leonard McClain. He cites previous professions as varied as a failed baseball player and a government-trained assassin with family connections to the CIA. His abilities and martial arts training have allowed him to successfully imitate both Daredevil and—when Norman Osborn assembles a team of counterfeit "Dark Avengers"—master marksman Hawkeye. As the

team's replacement archer, he acts as Osborn's personal hitman.

In the course of his death-dealing career, Bullseye has been rendered paraplegic and deprived of all his senses. He has also been slain and resurrected by Hand ninja techniques—thanks to his devoted

Death dealer Bullseye is never unarmed as long as he has everyday objects at hand and a clear line of sight.

Noble ninjas

Not all hired killers are corrupt. Medieval Ninjutsu's shady disciplines—espionage, guerilla warfare, and assassination—were used by Japan's leaders to maintain power, before the shadowy agents became vagrant samurai for hire. Such dark arts are employed by modern Ninjutsu proponents to benefit, not bedevil, mankind.

Focussing on spiritual and combat tenets, Stick—of the Chaste—trains troubled souls Matt Murdock (Daredevil) and Elektra Natchios, seeking warriors for his never-ending battle against demon-infested ninja cult The Hand. Elsewhere, Michiyo Watanabe's Shinto priestess mother is murdered by a snow vampire, Yiki Onna. To kill it, the child trains in the old ninja ways, subsequently facing the ultimate vampire, Dracula.

After Japan's defeat in 1945, heroic ninjas resolve to prevent ultra-nationalist crime syndicates Sunrise Society and Eternal Sun from re-waging the conflict in the US. Trained by aging sensei Shigeru Ezaki, the mercenary Shadowmasters (pictured) use ancient combat methods and modern weapons to crush the evil warmongers.

admirer and envious fellow assassin, Lady Bullseye. As lawyer Maki Matsumoto, she witnesses Bullseye effortlessly slaughter an entire gang of Yakuza, and from that moment dedicates her life to emulating the sinister warrior.

His skeleton now reinforced with Adamantium, Bullseye remains an unrepentant lifetaker, dedicated to earning a living by tormenting his enemies and boosting his bodycount.

Assassin nation

Assassins have always been an inevitable and invaluable tool of the rich, ruthless, and powerful. However, with a growing profusion of powered individuals and a wealth of secret societies, true talent for slaughter has never been in greater demand—even if only to thin the herd of competitors or deliver object lessons to future victims and current foes. Gangsters such as Kingpin Wilson Fisk—who mask criminal activities behind a veneer of respectability—frequently employ both the most quietly efficient and flamboyantly attention-grabbing killers to punish, maintain order through terror, and intimidate competitors.

Fuss-free operatives such as Eric Slaughter, Spymaster, or Foreigner operate in secret and anonymously. They only come to public attention when a mission goes wrong, usually after a Super Hero stumbles across and opposes one of their assignments. Flashy costumed psycho-killers, on the other hand, rely on reputation-building through media attention. These include assassins such as Arcade (master of the murder maze), Taskmaster, and Typhoid Mary. The latter possesses lethal martial arts skills and psychic powers, even beguiling her main employer Kingpin. Suffering from dissociative identity disorder, she battles and becomes an occasional lover of Super Hero Daredevil. While Mary is driven by personal demons as much as profit, others of her ilk, such as Elektra, Crossbones, and John Wraith adhere to their own resolute personal code, driven by ideology, faith, or a warped sense of honor. ∎

Bullseye never misses!
Bullseye

Flaming femme fatale Pyrokinetic, telekinetic, and telepathic, Typhoid Mary's multiple personalities drive her to torture and kill victims for money.

UNBREAKABLE
LUKE CAGE

ON THE RECORD

REAL NAME
Luke Cage, legally changed from Carl Lucas

ALLEGIANCES
Heroes for Hire, Defenders, Avengers, the Crew, Fantastic Four

BASE
New York City

POWERS
Enhanced strength, steel-hard skin, rapid healing

MISSION
Defending society's most disadvantaged

STATUS REPORT
Trying to balance being a hero with being a husband and father

Framed for drug dealing, Carl Lucas is incarcerated at Seagate Prison, Georgia. Brutalized by both guards and inmates, Carl volunteers for unsanctioned cellular regeneration experiments conducted by new prison doctor Noah Burnstein. When corrupt guards try to kill Lucas by sabotaging the process, the convict develops incredible strength and muscle density, which he uses to escape. Unknown to all, Burnstein is the son of one of the Nazi researchers tasked with recreating the Super-Soldier Serum that created Captain America, and is determined to finish his father's work.

Returning to New York, Lucas, now a fugitive, hides in plain sight. He assumes the alias Luke Cage and codename Power Man, operating as a Hero-for-Hire while working to clear his name. He finally succeeds after meeting multi-millionaire martial arts Super Hero Iron Fist, and the unlikely duo become firm friends and crime-fighting partners. A free man at last, Cage rededicates himself to cases involving common folk with extraordinary troubles. A solid, no-nonsense problem-solver with his heart firmly set on helping people, Cage has no illusions about fame, reward, or the presumed infallibility of the US justice system. He soon becomes regarded as a true advocate of the "little guy" in a world increasingly controlled by the wealthy and/or the super-powered.

Men at work Blasé New Yorkers are quite used to seeing Cage and Iron Fist keeping the streets clear of crooks.

Family values
After becoming an Avenger, Luke and his girlfriend Jessica Jones have a baby, Danielle. Both are superhuman private detectives and Cage continues risking his life as a Super Hero, adventurer, bodyguard, and community leader. Opposing the US Government's Superhuman Registration Act, Luke becomes a key figure in the subsequent first superhuman civil war, serving with Captain America's Secret Avengers

The Crew

The Crew is a loose band of Super Heroes—comprising Luke Cage, Storm, Australian teleporter and reality-shaper Manifold, cyborg detective Misty Knight, and the Black Panther—tackling problems affecting their communities and cultures. They first act together when Misty joins Storm and T'Challa in investigating the death in custody of community activist Ezra Keith.

As the Lynx, Keith ran his own "Crew" of local Super Heroes in 1970s Harlem.

Far from public gaze, these unremembered champions aided oppressed minorities, but Keith is forced to disappear for years after discovering the Crew's backer is terrorist group Hydra. He later returns, but his secrets become exposed as modern Harlem reels from the extreme policing methods of Hydra's Americops. Keith's protégé Cage leads an updated Crew to seek the truth.

The team later aids King T'Challa of Wakanda as he fights a civil war, fomented in part by rogue billionaire, Ezekiel Stane.

after sending Jessica and baby Danielle to safety in Canada. It is a foretaste of things to come. When his family returns, Danielle is held hostage by Skrulls during their Secret Invasion of Earth and again imperiled when Norman Osborn becomes US security chief in the aftermath.

Instituting a "Dark Reign" of oppression, Osborn declares war on Super Heroes and Cage is once again reduced to the role of outlaw. When Osborn is ousted, Cage, Jessica, and

Conflict resolution Cage's serious attitude is enough to warn troublemakers to think again.

> 66
> I figured I was a new man... time for a new life.
> **Luke Cage**
> 99

Danielle resume a normal life, but between leading a street-level version of the Mighty Avengers and running his own private investigation and personal security company, Cage finds that peace and quiet are very rare commodities. Eventually, Jessica gives in to Luke's persistent marriage proposals. Yet even when they finally wed, danger invariably finds them, and the ceremony is almost ruined when they are attacked by a robotic Adaptoid.

Luke Cage is one of the toughest men alive and deals with every problem head on. Seemingly brash and confrontational, he prefers friends and foes to think of him as rash, impetuous, and not very bright. In truth, Cage is a shrewd warrior, determined to defend the weak and punish the wicked. He is also a fiercely protective father who will do anything for his loved ones. Strong, smart, and resolute, he has seen both sides of the justice system and is always ready to defend society's weakest members from injustice and deal harshly with bad guys wanting to hurt others. ∎

SUPER SLEUTH
JESSICA JONES

ON THE RECORD

REAL NAME
Jessica Campbell Jones Cage

ALLEGIANCES
Alias Investigations, *Daily Bugle*, Avengers, Defenders

BASE
Harlem, New York City

POWERS
Super-strength and durability, limited flight

MISSION
Making a living, supporting her family, helping others

STATUS REPORT
Trouble finds her however hard she tries to avoid it

Even with uncanny powers, some people just aren't cut out to be Super Heroes. That doesn't mean they can't do good, though. Jessica Jones survives an empowering accident to become the kind of champion regular folks need and deserve.

As a young girl, Jessica Campbell has a crush on classmate Peter Parker, but misses her chance to talk with him when he his bitten by an irradiated spider. However fate quickly catches up with the avowed Super Hero fan when Jessica herself is caught up in a radioactive chemical spill. Tragically, she is in a car arguing with her brother at the time and the collision with a military convoy carrying contaminated materials kills her entire family and plunges Jessica into a coma. She begins to come around just as Galactus attacks Earth for the first time and his unearthly energies permeate the city. Remanded to an orphanage, Jessica is soon adopted by the Jones family and takes their name. Discovering she has super-powers, Jessica Jones naturally becomes a Super Hero,

Dress code Not every street-fighting hero needs a flashy costume to get their message across: "don't push your luck!"

but her stint as the crime fighter "Jewel" is only a limited success. Failing to shine over four years, she fades from public view. Nobody realizes she has actually been enslaved by Zebediah Killgrave, the mind-controlling Purple Man. For eight months Jewel is his puppet enforcer, compelled to perform horrific acts before being accidentally liberated by the Avengers after Killgrave orders her to kill Daredevil and his friends. During her recovery, she is invited to join the Avengers and S.H.I.E.L.D., and briefly operates as the savage vigilante Knightress.

After meeting Luke Cage, Jones realizes she would rather protect the innocent than waste time and energy chasing bad guys or fighting costumed idiots. Qualifying for a Private Detective

Uncanny detectives

Even in a world where mind-readers, time machines, and magic are commonplace, people in trouble always need discreet specialists for problems that cops or Super Heroes won't touch. However, to make their mark, freelance detectives have to be truly exceptional... or at least have a solid schtick.

One of New York's earliest and strangest is Leslie "the Ferret" Lenrow. He is a typical seedy "gumshoe," who makes the 1940s police force look like amateurs, even if he does work with—and talk to—a ferret.

Dakota North (pictured) is among the most accomplished Private Investigators in modern times. She counts Matt Murdock and King T'Challa of Wakanda among her satisfied clients.

Cut from much stranger cloth is the detective Hannibal King. Despite being killed and forever transformed by Vampire Lord Deacon Frost, the seasoned "shamus" still works to uphold justice. Never drinking human blood, King teams up with the Daywalker Blade in Borderline Investigations, specializing in supernatural cases.

license, she establishes Alias Investigations, embracing the sordid world of cheating spouses, crooked business partners, and missing persons. However, superhuman insanity continues to dog her, such as the time an ambitious political operator sets her up to frame Captain America for murder.

The parent trap
Accepting she has the ability to protect the helpless and that Super Heroes will always be part of her life, Jones starts a long-term relationship with Cage. After years of mounting costumed madness, Jones' priorities change again when she becomes pregnant. Looking

after her unborn child is now the focus of her life, and in the final stages of pregnancy she takes a job as *Daily Bugle* consultant, working on the paper's Super Hero supplement *The Pulse*. This "safe option" proves anything but, after she and reporter Ben Urich expose Norman Osborn as criminal psychopath the Green Goblin. He retaliates by slaughtering an entire police squad, blowing Jones up, and triggering a premature birth. The incident makes Jones overly protective of baby Danielle. When the superhuman civil war and subsequent Skrull Secret Invasion ravage the US—sparking escalating battles everywhere—she abandons her new husband to safeguard Danielle in anonymity.

Eventually the family reunite and Jones leaves all costumed adventuring behind. Returning to Alias

Investigations, she settles into detective work, but is inextricably tied to superhuman cases. Her marriage to Cage is solid if tempestuous, and when his greatest enemy returns to ravage Harlem, she swallows her distaste of super-teams to join Cage and a host of other Defenders to stop Diamondback and his drug trade. She's still not wearing a damn costume, though! ∎

So close. Story of my life.
Jessica Jones

Multifaceted After years trying to find her niche, Jessica realizes she can be everything her family and friends need her to be.

WAR ON CRIME

THE PUNISHER

ON THE RECORD

REAL NAME
Francis "Frank" Castiglione (Frank Castle)

ALLEGIANCES
Secret Avengers, Green Berets, US Marines

POWERS
Peak human fitness; highly trained soldier proficient in unarmed combat, explosives, and firearms

MISSION
Destroy all criminals

STATUS REPORT
The war never ends

Next...
The Punisher

Frank Castle is a former US Marine Corps Scout Sniper and Special Forces instructor who takes his family for a picnic in Central Park and stumbles into a bloody gangland execution. The only survivor, Castle dedicates his life to exterminating criminals. Relentless, remorseless, and obsessive, Castle uses his training to select targets, employing kidnapping, coercion, extortion, and torture to achieve his aims, while appropriating his victims' weapons and ill-gotten gains to facilitate his crusade.

A pathologically driven force of nature, the Punisher is pragmatic and methodical, gathering intel on future targets, unblinkingly focused on killing whoever he needs to when opportunity arises. Castle refuses to differentiate between flashy Super Villains, "untouchable" crime lords, and petty street thugs. He has allied and clashed with most Super Heroes, but, to him, most of them are jokes, unwilling to make hard choices. However, he does respect fellow soldier Steve Rogers, working with Captain America during the first superhuman civil war.

Some hardline lawmen happily turn a blind eye if Castle's methods suit their agendas or eliminate obstacles to their own plans; they can at least be reasoned with. Nick Fury Jr. gives the vigilante War Machine's armor to tackle a far-right uprising and potential atomic holocaust in the eastern European People's Republic of Chernaya.

Castle has been killed, rebuilt as a cyborg, resurrected by magic, and tirelessly battled super-beings, monsters—human and otherwise—and crooks of every kind. He is proof positive that mortal drive and ingenuity are a match for any superhuman advantage. As long as there are bad guys, the Punisher will never stop. ∎

Tooled up No problem is too big for Castle if he has the right ordnance: knife, grenade, shotgun, or War Machine armor.

FIST OF KHONSHU
MOON KNIGHT

ON THE RECORD

REAL NAME
Marc Spector

ALLEGIANCES
Defenders, Avengers West Coast, CIA, US Marines

BASE
New York City

POWERS
Peak human fitness; specialist combat training; strength, speed, and agility varies with phases of the Moon

MISSION
Delivering a god's harsh vengeance to all evildoers

STATUS REPORT
Fluctuating mental state makes him highly driven, but wholly unpredictable

Marc Spector is a born fighter, driven by a need for violence. Son of a pacifistic Chicago rabbi, he leaves home early, finding work as a boxer, marine, CIA operative, and ultimately a mercenary. Allying with sadistic gangleader Raul Bushman in Egypt, Spector is wounded trying to save archaeologist Peter Alraune from his murderous comrades. Left to die, Spector crawls into a recently excavated tomb and is "mystically" resurrected and restored by Khonshu, god of justice and the Moon. With his best friend Frenchie and Alraune's daughter Marlene, Spector—thinking himself reborn as a vessel of divine punishment—defeats the mercenary band before returning to the US and setting up as an avenger of wrongs.

Spector suffers from Dissociative Personality Disorder, operating as his own millionaire financial backer Steven Grant and taxi-driving intel-gatherer Jake Lockley. As the champion Moon Knight he turns these different identities into a psychological quartet, mirroring the four aspects of Khonshu: Embracer, Pathfinder, Defender, and Watcher of overnight travelers.

Although usually working alone at the margins of society, Moon Knight frequently joins forces with mainstream Super Heroes and teams, but remains a disturbing, aloof figure. He believes himself the diligent servant of an ancient god with a harsh agenda, but all his actions can equally be explained as

Night moves Khonshu's chosen one is equally at home crushing petty crooks or besting primordial demons and monsters.

psychosis and self-delusion. Even his ever fluctuating powers—superstrength, speed, and agility which wax and wane with the passages of the Moon—can be logically rationalized. Perhaps both assertions are true and the indomitable Fist of Khonshu Marc Spector is a highly trained warrior who is both utterly psychotic and a divinely-driven agent of godly retribution. ∎

MERC WITH A MOUTH
DEADPOOL

ON THE RECORD

REAL NAME
Unknown, answers to Wade Winston Wilson

ALLEGIANCES
Mercs for Money, Avengers, X-Force, Cable

POWERS
Ultra-rapid regeneration, expert martial artist, weapons master, awareness of transdimensional reality

MISSION
Killing people, being a good guy, earning a living

STATUS REPORT
Kills people, yet somehow does more good than harm

The professional mercenary Deadpool is a man of mysteries, most of them self-generated. Certifiably crazy, he spews a never-ending stream of nonsensical babble, regularly rewrites his own "origin," and willfully confuses friends, foes, and allies alike. He also paradoxically aspires to insert himself into every crisis that besets Earth—and other planets and dimensions—while pursuing "big scores" and a life of ease and luxury. Although utterly amoral, he needs to be the noble champion in his own story and is absolutely devoted to a man he considers the ultimate hero: Captain America.

Almost certainly verifiable is that Deadpool (who uses the name Wade Wilson) was raised in a Canadian military family— and a possibly abusive environment. As an adult, he enlists in the US Army Special Forces, but is cashiered for ethical reasons. Recruited to the CIA's elite assassination cadre, Wilson visits the worlds' hottest trouble spots, but after failing an assignment, returns to the US where he forms a romantic attachment to mutant shape-shifter Vanessa Carlysle. He also meets Zoe Culloden: expediter for interdimensional

traders Landau, Luckman, Lake & LeQuare. Culloden believes Wilson is destined for great things, but that all changes when he is diagnosed with inoperable tumors.

Killing joke Deadpool's crazy banter hides the fact that he is one of the most remorseless killers on Earth.

Mercenary calling

Being a mercenary is hardly a noble calling, but some killers for hire try to combine cashing paychecks with improving the world. Chief among these is Paladin, who uses superhuman abilities for profitable public service, but loses money every time he breaks his own rules to work with Super Heroes like Daredevil or Misty Knight's Heroes for Hire.

Symkarian aristocrat Silver Sable turns the family business of hunting war criminals into a key part of her impoverished nation's economy, while ex-US operative Solo makes his hatred of terrorists his life's work. Solo joins Mercs for Money: Deadpool's ill-considered contract killer enterprise beside Massacre, Terror, Foolkiller, and former Super Heroes Stingray and Slapstick. After Deadpool shafts them over payment, they all quit to work under the leadership of Domino, alongside new recruits such as Hit-Monkey, Machine Man, and Gorilla Man (pictured).

> I won't kill you, but I reserve the right to change my mind.
> **Deadpool**

Better read than dead

Deserting Vanessa to spare her pain, Wilson goes off to die but is thrown a lifeline by Canada's Department K: joining the Weapon X superhuman enhancement program. His cancer arrested by implantation of a healing factor derived from Wolverine's DNA, Wilson becomes their covert operative. However, when his abilities destabilize, he is sent to "the Hospice." Here, rogue researcher Dr. Killebrew and his attendant Ajax experiment on patients, wagering on who will expire first in their "Deadpool."

Utterly unstable now, Wilson forms a romantic attachment to the cosmic entity Death, and provokes Ajax constantly, until the attendant kills him. Instead of taking Wilson to his new beloved, the murderous act jump-starts Wilson's regenerative powers. As Deadpool, he embarks on a bloody rampage before liberating Killebrew's surviving patients. In the aftermath, he returns to the only job he is good at: killing.

Although he cannot perish, Deadpool remains riddled with cancers, making his life interminably agonizing, and only alleviated by excessive drinking, constant fighting, and running his mouth off like an annoying gibbering loon. He battles with, for, beside, and against a huge number of Super Heroes and Villains, most of whom wish he would just shut up for a minute. Many of them suspect his incessant inanities and snarky comments are actually a secret super-power. Despite this, and regular regressions back into the seedy life of a killer for hire, Deadpool becomes an unlikely force for good, saving the world during numerous crises and even forming effective long-term working relationships with teams such as the Avengers Unity Division and X-Force, among others—as well as recurrent partnerships with Spider-Man and the time-traveling warrior, Cable.

Deadpool's travails have taken him to the far corners of the Multiverse and led to many bizarre encounters. He is cursed never to die and has been Thanos' rival for Death's love. Unlucky in love, one of his many ex-wives is demon queen Shiklah. Moreover, while fighting the Beyonder he visits the conceptual Foundation of Reality. This grants him "medium awareness"—true understanding of reality—which Deadpool interprets as being a character in a comic book. ■

Till Death us do part Both besotted by Death, Thanos curses Deadpool so that he is unable to die and be with his love.

THE KIDS ARE ALRIGHT
JUNIOR CRUSADERS

ON THE RECORD

ALLEGIANCES
Fantastic Four, Avengers, Invaders, X-Men, each other

MISSION
Proving themselves

STATUS REPORT
Gradually making the world a safer place for everyone

For as long as there have been heroes, youngsters have followed their exploits and yearn to join them in adventure. The practice of heroic sidekicks peaks during World War II when a bold, capable few such as Rusty, Bucky, and Toro become assistants and partners to masked heroes the Defender, Captain America, and the Human Torch respectively. These individuals go on to inspire a legion of super-powered—or simply fit and fearless—adolescents to don costumes and hunt spies and crooks. Bucky and Toro even lead two such groups: the Young Allies on the US Home Front and a diverse squad of Kid Commandos who battle across the globe.

For some, the potential downside of taking the initiative is overruled by enthusiasm, self-confidence, and urgency. One such group is sibling foursome Power Pack (pictured above). When the Power children— Alex, Julie, Jack, and Katie—gain super-powers from a dying alien, they use them to rescue their abducted parents. Learning on the job and punching above their weight—even with an AI-equipped Kymelian Smartship to mentor them— they initially battle injustice entirely without adult supervision before being accepted by the wider Super Hero community.

For every solo, self-taught hero such as Marvel Boy, teen detective Terry Vance, costumed adventurer Roddy Colt (aka Secret Stamp), or demonic defender Davey Drew, there are dozens of other junior heroes relying on peers for emotional and combat support. Many of them find like-minded pals and form teams—or gangs—to fight the good

fight with them. The practice ends with WWII, but revives in modern times as idealistic superhuman kids strike out unsupervised.

Open house The Champions want every young hero to share their opportunities and contribute to saving the world.

New Warriors

A victim of crime, young and wealthy Dwayne Taylor becomes vigilante Night Thrasher. He assembles powerful young heroes: Nova (Richard Rider), telekinetic Marvel Boy, Atlantean Namorita, microwave-empowered Firestar, and hyperkinetically charged Speedball to aid his crusade. Despite internal friction and a continually revolving roster, the New Warriors become a formidable force for justice, confronting the darkest aspects of existence.

When the team star in a TV reality show, Taylor dies in battle alongside Namorita (now Kymaera) and new recruit Microbe after a simple arrest of fugitive villains goes wrong. Following this disaster in Stamford, Connecticut, in which over 600 civilians die, Super Heroes and masked vigilantes are forced to register with the Government. During the ensuing superhuman civil war, an outlaw band of New Warriors

unite in the team's memory, led by a new Night Thrasher—Taylor's half-brother Donyell, formerly the villain Bandit.

We are the Champions

Such is the case with legacy heroes Ms. Marvel (Kamala Khan), Nova (Sam Alexander), and Spider-Man (Miles Morales). These solo adventurers are recruited as trainees for a new iteration of Avengers, fighting beside Iron Man, Captain America Sam Wilson, Thor, and the Vision. Subsequently patronized and ignored, these youngsters also disagree with their elders' tactics and policy, preferring to save lives rather than capture foes. They leave to form their own inclusive, fluid group seeking new ways to solve old problems. As social media connects them to the young all over Earth, they

We're in a war for a better tomorrow!
Kamala Khan

are dubbed Champions; unaware of the short-lived, ill-omened team that previously used the title.

Other adults find different ways to benefit from youthful enthusiasm and idealism. Professor Charles Xavier trains mutant children to be ambassadors and, when necessary, soldiers in the cause of human/mutant coexistence. However, he is also painfully aware that his X-Men and New Mutants projects are also a way of teaching his charges how to cope with the fearful scope and responsibility of their powers. This principle holds true for the Avengers Academy of young superhumans and Reed Richards' Future Foundation of child super-geniuses.

Sometimes necessity is the spur to action: when the Avengers "disassemble" following the Scarlet Witch's murderous mental breakdown, an unofficial team of Young Avengers steps up to fight for humanity their way.

Tragically, the cruelest reason for young superhumans banding together is survival. When they discover that their parents are The Pride, a cabal of Super Villains secretly running Los Angeles,

Gertude (Gert) Yorkes, Karolina Dean, Chase Stein, Nico Minoru, Alex Wilder, Molly Hayes, and genetically modified dinosaur Old Lace flee from home. As the Runaways, they—and the kids they help—protect each other and fight for justice on their own terms. ∎

You can run... Despite swiping their evil parents' weapons and gear, the teen Runaways are never safe from retaliation.

MASTER OF KUNG FU
SHANG-CHI

ON THE RECORD

ALLEGIANCES
MI5, MI6, Avengers, Heroes for Hire, Freelance Restorations, Protectors

POWERS
Peak human fitness; expert in all martial arts

MISSION
Live in harmony unless lives are threatened

STATUS REPORT
Having reconciled a desire for peace with a duty to aid others, Shang-Chi uses his talents to serve humanity

Raised in isolation by philosophers and warrior monks, the son of immortal bandit warlord Zheng Zu is reared to become his father's ultimate weapon against the western democracies. However, Shang-Chi, whose name means "the rising and advancing of a spirit," throws off decades of insidious programming after he is sent to assassinate an aging British Secret Service chief. Instead, he dedicates himself to bringing down his father's criminal empire, eventually succeeding. Working with, but not for, British Intelligence, Shang-Chi strives to steer clear of what he terms "games of deceit and death." However, to save new friends Black Jack Tar, Clive Reston, and Leiko Wu, he must frequently battle outlandish super-spies such as Shockwave, War-Yore, Razor Fist, and Skull-Crusher, or would-be world conquerors such as Mordillo and his doll-like toy robot, Brynocki.

After pointless battles against foes simply motivated by different politics, such as his Red Chinese antithesis Shen Kuei (Cat), Shang-Chi withdraws from the world, only to be called back into action to save

> Vengeance does not fuel my heart. Justice does.
> **Shang-Chi**

Force of one Shang-Chi's Kung Fu training enables him to become a calm, efficient craftsman of combat.

former lover Leiko Wu. Following the resurrection of Zheng Zu, he goes on to work with Super Hero teams such as X-Men and Heroes for Hire. After fighting alongside Steve Rogers' black ops squad Secret Avengers, he is invited to join the regular team. Although he has occasionally acquired super-powers, including mass body duplication and Pym-particle increased size and strength during global crises, Shang-Chi rejects these enhancements, preferring to trust in the gifts he has earned through toil and training. ∎

FISTS OF FURY

DANNY RAND AND THE IRON FISTS

ON THE RECORD

REAL NAME
Daniel Thomas Rand-K'ai

ALLEGIANCES
Heroes for Hire, Immortal Weapons, Rand Corporation, Avengers

BASE
New York, formerly K'un-Lun

POWERS
Peak human fitness, martial arts mastery, chi-powered mystic punch, regeneration

MISSION
Championing the helpless

STATUS REPORT
A warrior and teacher dedicated to saving others

I am the blade
that cuts both ways!
Iron Fist

Danny Rand lives in two worlds as a warrior. Raised in the otherdimensional realm of K'un-Lun he now spends his days on the Earth of his birth. One of the mystical Capital Cities of Heaven, K'un-Lun only appears on Earth—in the Himalayas—once a decade. As nine-year-old Danny's parents try to find the city, their business partner Harold Meachum murders them. Saved by warrior monks, young Rand is apprenticed to supreme champion Lei Kung, the Thunderer, and trains with the city's elite for 10 years.

On defeating magical dragon Shou-Lao the Undying, Rand claims the chi-focusing power of the Iron Fist. Now K'un-Lun's ordained champion—66th in a line stretching back into prehistory—Rand returns to the US. Set on killing Meachum, Rand realizes he can't commit cold-blooded murder. Stuck on Earth for a decade, Iron Fist becomes a nomadic hero and eventually regains his parents' stolen fortune after teaming up with Colleen Wing, Misty Knight, and brother-in-arms Luke Cage. Their security firm Heroes for Hire confronts world-shaking crises as well as taking on bodyguard roles, and clashing with spies, thieves, aliens, and monsters. Their efforts lead them to join big league teams like the Avengers, but Rand finds true fulfilment training young fighters in his Kung Fu Dojo.

Ultimately finding his way back to K'un-Lun, Iron Fist learns his paradise is a corrupt sham. After civil war, arcane invasion, and near-extermination, he leaves K'un-Lun as the new Thunderer and mentors Iron Fist successor, Pei, on Earth. ■

Training day
Danny Rand and Pei, the 67th—and youngest—Iron Fist, take on all comers.

NINJA QUEEN

ELEKTRA

ON THE RECORD

REAL NAME
Elektra Natchios

ALLEGIANCES
The Hand, The Chaste, Heroes for Hire, S.H.I.E.L.D., Thunderbolts

POWERS
Ultimate martial artist, proficient in Ninjutsu and hand-held weapons; psionic abilities include telepathy and precognition

MISSION
Redemption and punishment

STATUS REPORT
A ruthless killer looking for chances to do good in the world

Elektra Natchios' parents are Greek diplomats, both murdered before she reaches maturity. Her mother is gunned down when she is a child, while her adored father is assassinated in front of her even as she is in the throes of a college love affair with blind US law-student Matt Murdock.

Despite martial arts training from early childhood, Elektra is helpless to save her father. Deeply traumatized, she vanishes in the aftermath, wandering the world and honing her skills. Neither she nor Murdock realize they have both been marked for greatness by blind sensei, Stick. Unlike Murdock, Elektra devotes herself to Stick's warrior-cult The Chaste, but her training ends when she arrogantly tries to infiltrate its enemies, Ninja mystics The Hand. Warped by their evil machinations, Elektra becomes a merciless, infallible assassin.

Years later, while working for Kingpin Wilson Fisk, Elektra encounters Murdock again, in his guise as the crime-fighting Super Hero Daredevil. Her unresolved feelings toward him deeply unsettle her, and while distracted, she is ambushed and killed by Daredevil's great enemy, Bullseye. When The Hand resurrects Elektra to regain its most valuable asset, The Chaste priest Stone hijacks the process and successfully cleanses her soul. A free agent, Elektra seeks redemption, using her lethal gifts to weed out the world's worst villains. However, despite her efforts, she falls back under the influence of The Hand.

Red resurrection Elektra's bond with ninja cult The Hand is eternal—whether as its ultimate assassin, undisputed queen, or greatest nemesis.

Once again killed and revived, Elektra haunts the darkest corners of the world, clashing with Super Heroes and villains, and working for various espionage agencies. When battling the likes of Hand-faction Snakeroot, cyber-ninjas, or Hydra, she desperately seeks a way to balance her guilt-stricken need to punish the wicked with her hunger for peace and contentment. ■

EAST MEETS WEST
DAUGHTERS OF THE DRAGON

ON THE RECORD

REAL NAMES
Colleen Wing and Mercedes "Misty" Knight

ALLEGIANCES
Heroes for Hire, Knightwing Restorations Ltd.

BASE
Manhattan, New York City

POWERS
Martial arts mastery (Wing); bionic right arm, police training (Knight)

MISSION
Fight crime, make a living

STATUS REPORT
Too much crime busting, too few paying clients

A descendant of Japanese warriors, Colleen Wing befriends Danny Rand (Iron Fist). When she is kidnapped and brainwashed by magician Master Khan, Rand saves her with a chi-powered mind meld that gives her access to his memory and training. Combined with her own samurai skills, this knowledge makes Wing one of the finest hand-to-hand fighters on Earth.

Misty Knight was a decorated New York cop until a bomb blew off her right arm. Replacing it with a bionic limb, she becomes a private detective. Thanks to Colleen Wing, she is drawn into the bizarre world of super-crime and mystic menaces.

Establishing detective agency/bodyguard service and bail bond agency Knightwing Restorations Ltd., the pair battle Rand's archenemy Davos, the Steel Serpent, who disparagingly dubs them "Daughters of the Dragon." They turn the insult into a proud honorific as they defeat him and a succession of deadly foes. As law-enforcement professionals working at the fringes of the Super Hero community, the Daughters of the Dragon are continually embroiled in cases involving super-normal perpetrators and mystical threats. When the Superhuman Registration Act comes into force, Tony Stark hires them to round up those who refuse to comply with the new law.

Knight and Wing often work separately—such as when Knight joins the FBI. However, all it takes is one call from her friend and colleague for the two to join up for a headlong plunge into bizarre peril, even if it means taking on Hydra and S.H.I.E.L.D. simultaneously. ∎

Damn! I knew this caper felt too easy!
Misty Knight

Sister act The Daughters of the Dragon combine ancient martial arts with hi-tech weapons and incisive detective methods.

OUT OF THE SHADOWS
HYDRA

ON THE RECORD

ALLEGIANCES
A.I.M., The Hand, T.H.E.M., Thule Society, Leviathan,

RESOURCES
Cutting-edge science, ancient magic, unlimited financial backing

MISSION
Global domination and human purity

STATUS REPORT
Fractured but retrenching and consolidating for its next attempt

Hydra predates mankind, an ancient malign force constantly subdividing and cloaking itself in mystery and subterfuge while infiltrating the halls of power. In eons past, before humanity evolved, alien serpents came to Earth seeking to establish an empire of darkness and evil. Their influence remains long after their demise, continually resurfacing as *Homo sapiens* progress, subtly shaping successive secret societies that exist in developing civilizations.

One faction, originating in 2671BCE in Mesopotamia, favored mysticism. Over centuries, the Sons of Anubis and Ariosophists absorbed other mystic sects, secretly manipulating global progress and ultimately becoming the Thule Society.

In 2620BCE, after Egyptian pharaoh Imhotep—with En Sabah Nur and Moon Knight of Khonshu—repels a Brood invasion, he founds the science-based Brotherhood of the Shield and Brotherhood of the Spear to secretly safeguard the world in

Hands on The lethal electronic Satan Claw gives immense power to Strucker as he leads his troops into battle.

perpetuity. Another arm of the sect is created when disciples of the elder serpents corrupt the Spear faction, centuries later allying with demon-ruled ninjas The Hand. Known as the Beast, they infiltrate later flowerings of the Shield science cult in Han dynasty China and Europe during the Renaissance and the 18th century Age of Enlightenment.

Secret Empire

Hydra's greatest triumph comes when the Red Skull rewrites reality using living Cosmic Cube, Kobik. By twisting time, they turn Steve Rogers into the ultimate sleeper agent and Captain America into the Supreme Hydra (pictured) who conquers the world. After years of acclaim as the Earth's most trusted hero, Captain America strikes: exiling almost all the world's Super Heroes into space and sending Inhumans and mutants to internment camps in pursuit of human racial purity.

With the populace undergoing daily re-education, Hydra finally achieves all its aims. However, humans remain stubbornly obsessed with liberty and an underground resistance led by Clint Barton (Hawkeye) and Natasha Romanoff (Black Widow) torment the conquerors. Finally, Steve Rogers' indomitable spirit battles back from beyond oblivion to reclaim his body and destroy Hydra's grand dream.

Around this time, the Spear sect seemingly vanishes: either growing in secret or engaged in the constant deadly struggle for control that plagues all iterations of Hydra.

Strucker's army

Modern Hydra is born in 1943 when elite Nazi warrior Baron Wolfgang von Strucker falls from favor with Adolf Hitler. As current head of the Thule Society, Strucker—in collusion with the Red Skull—diverts resources to create his own paramilitary force. Fleeing to the Pacific, Strucker joins Japanese army deserters, gangsters, and The Hand ninjas in a purely criminal enterprise to amass wealth and power. He names his

organization after a many-tentacled Hellenic monster of myth: the Lernean Hydra. Strucker soon builds a loyal army of fanatics, permeating all aspects of post-war society, patiently working to take over the world. Hydra values multilayered schemes and creates other terror groups to foment chaos and social unrest. Playing the long game, it secretly influences the creation and operations of S.H.I.E.L.D., reasoning that if Hydra is to be opposed by anything, it should be an agency that can be controlled.

Strucker reorganizes the crime cult, dividing activities into four branches. "Quiet" operations such as International Corporations use legitimate fronts to mask illegal activities and launder money, while Government Assets plant sleeper agents in government bureaucracies, securing long-term benefits. "Active" operations in the form of Global Criminal Groups sponsor groups like T.H.E.M., Secret Empire, and Advanced Idea Mechanics (A.I.M.) to divert S.H.I.E.L.D.'s attention, while Intelligence Gathering mines the agency's resources, as well as those of the FBI, NSA, and other global security forces.

However, Strucker and his High Council never expect Nick Fury to be so driven in leading S.H.I.E.L.D. against them. Suffering constant defeats and, on occasion, death, Strucker sees his life's work dissolve into numerous factions headed up by leaders such as Madame Hydra—a role played by a succession of deadly, capable women—and its gradual assimilation into the Red Skull's own neo-fascist organization. Strucker is killed again by Fury, but with access to robotics, cloning technology, and Hydra's Dark Arts Division, he does not remain dead for long. ∎

Hello Hydra As Madame Hydra, sorceress Elisa Sinclair draws Steve Rogers into the evil organization.

We shall never be destroyed. Cut off a limb and two more shall take its place!
Hydra Oath

AGENTS OF LIBERTY
S.H.I.E.L.D. OPERATIVES

ON THE RECORD

DESIGNATION
Strategic Homeland Intervention, Enforcement, and Logistics Division

ALLEGIANCES
US Government, UN, World Security Council, Avengers, Fantastic Four

POWERS
Law-enforcement and counterterrorism agency, international jurisdiction backed by UN mandates

MISSION
Global peacekeeping, preserving life on Earth

STATUS REPORT
Dissolved pending official government review

Formed through the furtive machinations of the ancient secret society Brotherhood of the Shield, the formerly named Supreme Headquarters International Espionage Law-Enforcement Division is established in the 1960s. The spy agency is equipped with cutting-edge tech and ordnance thanks to the provisory largesse of millionaire industrialists such as Howard Stark.

Staffed by the cream of the Free World's intelligence community, it is led by Rick Stoner until his apparent assassination. The second director is Nick Fury, who surrounds himself with trusted World War II allies such as Timothy "Dum Dum" Dugan, Peggy Carter, and Gabe Jones, supplemented by graduates of the agency's UNIT (Underground Network Intelligence Training) academy. Jasper Sitwell, Sharon Carter, and Clay Quartermain become key operatives as S.H.I.E.L.D. develops over the years. Their goal is to counter extraordinary menaces such as Hate-Monger and the Druid, and destroy their true targets Hydra,

Don't yield! Back S.H.I.E.L.D.!
Agent Jasper Sitwell

A.I.M., Secret Empire, and other subversive groups beyond the scope of ordinary law enforcement.

Many of Fury's immediate family are drawn into this murky world of manipulation and subterfuge. His younger brother Jake becomes Scorpio, the Super Villain leader of crime cartel Zodiac, and Fury later discovers he has a son. Raised by his mother to despise Nick Fury, Mikel Fury initially tries to kill his father before eventually joining S.H.I.E.L.D. Mikel dies fighting Hydra as one of Fury's Secret Warriors.

Sons of Fury

Fury is also aware that he has a second son, Marcus Johnson, even though the boy is raised in secret, far from the toxic world of espionage. While Johnson never meets his father, he clearly possesses the family talent for combat. Joining the US Army Rangers, Johnson serves with distinction alongside best friend Phil "Cheese" Coulson, and only learns the truth about his father after his mother—former CIA officer Nia Johnson—is murdered. Her death is orchestrated by Fury's Cold War antithesis Viktor Uvarov—code named Orion—creator of Soviet spy organization, Leviathan.

Brotherhood of the Shield

Earth has been a target of extraterrestrial incursion, superhuman subjugation, and mystic invasion for millennia. In 2620BCE, after saving Egypt from an alien Brood infestation, Pharaoh Imhotep establishes a secret society. Henceforth, the world's most brilliant minds will jointly safeguard humanity as part of the Brotherhood of the Shield.

Throughout history, the Brotherhood adepts save Earth from obliteration, aided by their incredible scientific and magical discoveries, such as da Vinci's time machine and immortality serums, or the energy engine Galileo uses to repel Galactus in 1582CE. They also exploit any superhuman resources they find, such as the seer Nostradamus. Despite eventually being riven with factional fighting, the Brotherhood continues to recruit disaster-thwarting, time-bending geniuses such as Howard Stark and Nathaniel Richards. They in turn lay the groundwork for the creation of the modern spy agency S.H.I.E.L.D., run by Nick Fury Sr.

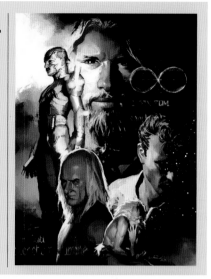

Aging Orion plans on drawing out his old foe. The Russian wants the Infinity Formula to extend his own existence. However, with Fury Sr. missing in action, presumed dead, he targets Johnson, who may carry traces of the formula in his DNA.

Taking the name Nick Fury Jr., Johnson foils Orion's schemes before he and Coulson join S.H.I.E.L.D. as special agents. In short order he begins carving out his own legend, working under Fury Sr.'s most recent subordinates Daisy Johnson and Maria Hill. As special agent 110911, young Fury triumphs in many high-risk ventures: chasing top Hydra agent Frankie Noble across the planet, down into Atlantis, and even into space.

Fury Jr.'s progress in S.H.I.E.L.D. is meteoric and soon he is directing operations at the highest level. However, like his father, he has no taste for standing above the fray and constantly gets his own hands dirty while fighting for what he believes is right. Even though Fury Sr. is officially gone (with later sightings now presumed to be Life Model Decoys, not the man himself), his unorthodox methods and legacy live

Chains of command The second Nick Fury is happy to take orders and be a team player, especially for officers he respects, such as director Maria Hill.

on through the colleagues he trained and inspired. Although gifted agents, successive directors such as Maria Hill, Daisy Johnson, and Sharon Carter, and soon realize that keeping Earth safe and strictly following S.H.I.E.L.D. protocols are mutually exclusive. To do the job right means breaking a few rules. ∎

See also: Nick Fury, S.H.I.E.L.D. technology

Man of action
Like the father he has never met, Nick Fury Jr. possesses a gift for leadership and a devious, strategic mind.

MY FRIEND, MY ENEMY
SUPER HEROES AT WAR

ON THE RECORD

CAUSES
Ideology, misunderstanding, impatience, ego, bad temper

MISSION
Individuals finding ways to heal rift between allies

STATUS REPORT
Regrettably recurrent pattern of behavior

Super Heroes are all too aware that they hold the power of life and death, and what they do affects the entire world. Equally burdensome is knowing they are role models to many, and their actions shape the way people think and act. When that passion and resolve is directed at evildoers or on averting disasters—natural or otherwise—the results are inspiring. However, such fierce determination can sometimes lead to heartfelt yet devastating decisions that are completely at odds with the views of their closest friends and allies.

Heroes—especially in teams—are fractious at best. In the early days, the Federally backed Avengers acrimoniously clash with both the Fantastic Four and X-Men over jurisdiction and tactics, while battling the Hulk, Mole Man, and alien invader Lucifer. Thankfully, in those cases, calm heads and negotiation settle the disputes before any real harm is done.

When Asgardian trickster Loki and demonic Dread Dormammu unite to bring Earth's universe into collision with the Dark Dimension, they trick a loose association of maverick heroes into securing sections of a techno-mystic artifact known as the

Fighting frenemies Captain America and Iron Man come to blows over the Superhuman Registration Act.

Evil Eye. They need this to complete their scheme. Anticipating treachery from his partner, Loki strikes first, "warning" the Avengers that their old foes Hulk, Valkyrie, and Namor the Sub-Mariner, and others, are trying to conquer Earth. This triggers the ferocious Avengers/Defenders War, until the truth emerges and the Super Heroes rally together against their real enemies.

Whose side are you on?

A turning point comes when public opinion rejects super-powered conflicts that constantly endanger global security. When teen team New Warriors battle Super Villains in the small town of Stamford, the melee ends with fugitive Nitro blowing up an entire neighborhood, including a school. Shaken by hundreds of fatalities, the Super Hero community polarizes over hasty government legislation demanding registration and the surrender of all superhumans and masked vigilantes' secret identities. While Tony Stark, Reed Richards, and Henry (Hank) Pym support the measures, the idealistic Captain America leads a growing resistance movement distrustful of Federal oversight until mounting chaos and a rising death toll forces the hero's capitulation.

We're not fighting for the people anymore... We're just fighting.
Captain America

After a period of oppressive big government where US Chief of Security Norman Osborn institutes a draconian Dark Reign, the Age of Heroes returns when former allies bury the hatchet to defeat him in a spectacular reunification of the Avengers. The celebrations are short-lived, though, as the cosmic Phoenix Force returns to Earth and the team are sucked into a battle with the X-Men for ownership of its chosen host, Hope Summers.

No sooner is that crisis settled than Earth is targeted by the alien Builders and Thanos. Both are defeated by a monumental display of cooperation among the world's hidden races and public heroes. With multiversal incursions

Free will vs. predestination Idealist Iron Man clashes with soldier Captain Marvel over trusting Ulysses' predictions.

threatening the end of everything, the Illuminati decide Prime Earth can be saved by preemptively destroying encroaching universes. Once again, the heroic community descends into open warfare over this highly charged ethical issue. And even after a valiant band of heroes recreates the Multiverse as a near-identical Eighth Cosmos, it doesn't prevent them making the same mistakes. A second superhuman civil war erupts over the morality of using the precognitive Inhuman Ulysses to arrest potential troublemakers. ∎

Civil War chronicle

STAMFORD INCIDENT
A Super Hero reality show goes awry in Stamford, Connecticut. The New Warriors die arresting Super Villain Nitro, but over 600 civilians are killed during the devastating clash.

RESISTANCE
Polarized by the crisis, Super Heroes divide into two camps: those who support the Act and others who see it as a threat to freedom and anonymity.

50-STATE INITIATIVE
All superhumans are registered. Federally funded Super Hero teams are established in every state, such as the Rangers in Texas.

REVULSION
As resistance grows, resister Goliath is killed by a clone of dead hero Thor. This leads to war in the streets, endangering civilians.

SECRET INVASION
Taking advantage of global unrest, Skrulls launch their most concerted infiltration plans to conquer Earth, placing enhanced warriors in Super Hero teams.

REGISTRATION
Superhuman Registration Act is rushed into law. Tony Stark, Hank Pym, and Reed Richards accede to public outcry and support the Act. Camp Hammond is built in Stamford to train young superhumans.

EXPOSURE
Spider-Man unmasks live on television. Peter Parker soon realizes he's on the wrong side and defects to Captain America's rebel cause.

ENFORCEMENT
State-sanctioned heroes and S.H.I.E.L.D.'s "cape-killers" hunt superhuman resisters. Those arrested are imprisoned without trial in the Negative Zone.

ASSASSINATION
Unable to witness the nation being further torn apart, Captain America surrenders. He is then assassinated on the way to his trial.

BETTER TOGETHER
TITANIC TEAM-UPS

A necessity of Super Hero life is the ability to quickly assess a stressful, rapidly changing situation and act accordingly. Regrettably, that often means a rushed decision based on poor intel and a fight with a well-meaning opponent who's made exactly the same "attack first, ask questions later" judgment. This is especially true in overcrowded New York City, which is teeming with superhuman crimebusters, crooks, and malcontents.

Usually, such battles between heroes are brief and followed by team-ups to tackle the real problem or malefactor. The first time Spider-Man meets the Fantastic Four, the eager arachnid teenager is looking for paid employment with the quartet and a misunderstanding soon escalates into a full-blown fight. This clash sets the tone for most introductions between the costumed adventurers. Some years later, the web-slinger is finally asked to join the team.

Ill-tempered disputes over jurisdiction frequently degenerate into brawls before the real work of ending a menace and saving lives can begin. Happily, many lasting friendships also begin with a spectacular trading of quips and blows. Throughout their high school years, the Human Torch and Spider-Man cherish a prank-filled rivalry that blossoms into deep trust and reliance on each other's advice. Luke Cage first meets Iron Fist when he is blackmailed into attacking the Kung Fu hero, but after uniting to defeat their mutual enemy Bushmaster, they become business partners and closer than brothers.

Friends with fists Ms. Marvel must put aside her fan-girl instincts as she joins Spider-Man in battling alien scientists.

Oh my! Gosh!... I'm in a Spider-Man Team-Up!
Ms. Marvel

Super Villain team-ups

Although their motives are less pure and alliances subject to abrupt betrayal and annulment Super Villains also team up for mutual advantage. When Doctor Doom and Namor the Sub-Mariner initially ally to defeat the Fantastic Four, their scheme proves perfect. It succeeds until Doom turns on Namor, who then sides with the Fantastic Four to survive. Namor has often swallowed his distaste in order to reunite with his fellow monarch.

Others follow suit. Mad Thinker and Puppet Master frequently collaborate to conquer, while Wizard and Paste Pot Pete's temporary alliance grows into the Frightful Four, with the addition of Sandman and a floating fourth member, including Medusa, Thundra, Electro, and Hydro-Man. The Fixer and Mentallo's team-up starts as a criminal double act, as does Asgardian exiles Amora the Enchantress and Skurge the Executioner. Parker Robbins, aka the Hood, takes the practice to its logical conclusion. His "Illuminati" (pictured) pursue profit as a well-trained army, until internal dissent sabotages the team.

Mutual interests

Usually however, although respect for each others' abilities can be total, Super Heroes' innate self-reliance and take-charge attitudes can make them fractious allies. Despite collaborating for years, Daredevil and Spider-Man still rub each other the wrong way, and Iron Man and Captain America constantly clash over why—if not how—they tackle problems. On rare occasions, however, causes of friction among fellow adventurers are deep-seated and ideological, and once opinions are frankly aired there is no easy way to de-escalate. Such ideological disputes have driven passionate heroes into war with each other—and probably will again.

Thankfully, when extinction-level events occur, Super Heroes can put aside their differences for the greater good. As an army of Super Villains attacks the wedding ceremony of Reed Richards and Susan Storm, every costumed champion in Manhattan responds to the crisis. They end the assault in time to assure the happy couple's marriage goes ahead.

Teams and solo adventurers instinctively work together when lives are at risk. All grudges are suspended to save Earth when an alliance of alien cultures attempts to quarantine it, creating a Maximum Security planet to hold their greatest menaces. When Asgardian Cul the Serpent unleashes Fear Itself through seven magic hammers that possess heroes and villains, his schemes are thwarted by heroism and dedication to a greater cause. Such is also the case in the intergalactic clash dubbed War of Kings, embroiling X-Men, Inhumans, Guardians of the Galaxy, Starjammers, Darkhawk, and Nova. Even villains can feel the need to work for a common good. When the Red Skull telepathically turns humanity on its "Axis," transforming Earth's greatest heroes into debased monsters, villains

Red onslaught A Red Skull clone subverts the Avengers with his World War Hate.

such as Magneto, Carnage, Doctor Doom, Enchantress, Absorbing Man, Hobgoblin, and others unite to reverse the inversion of reality and restore order at great cost to themselves. ∎

WHAT THE?!
SQUIRREL GIRL AND OTHER UNLIKELY HEROES

ON THE RECORD

REAL NAME
Doreen Green

ALLEGIANCES
Avengers, Great Lakes Avengers, US Avengers, squirrels everywhere

POWERS
Enhanced strength, speed, durability, and senses; prehensile tail and knuckle-spike; regenerative healing factor; control of squirrels

MISSION
Be the best Super Hero ever

STATUS REPORT
Largely succeeding with help from many friends

Despite unrelenting danger, terrifying transformations, and random acts of violence, the world can be a pretty fun place; especially if you have a positive attitude and perhaps a few super-powers. In the face of continued intolerance, greed, and oppression, not to mention savage monsters, vile villains, and murderous thugs—on both sides of justice and the moral divide—there are still good-hearted, optimistic heroes who believe any problem can be fixed.

Although not a mutant, Doreen Green is born different; with a beautiful, bushy tail and physical enhancements emulating those of a giant squirrel. She also boasts subtler traits such as animal communication, persistence, curiosity—and cuteness. In her teens she resolves to always help others and creates a Squirrel Girl alter ego. With squirrel sidekicks Monkey Joe and later Tippy-Toe, she proves unbeatable in combat: defeating Doctor Doom at age 14 and dealing decisively with the Abomination, among others. She crushes (and then befriends) Kraven the Hunter, Maelstrom, and monstrous Fin Fang Foom while working with various Avengers teams, as babysitter for Luke Cage and Jessica Jones'

daughter Danielle, and studying computer science at Empire State University in New York. Throughout her many astounding cases Squirrel Girl adheres to her core principles: after all, hasn't she proved that any enemy—even Doom and Galactus—is helpless in the face of bravery; boundless enthusiasm and idealism; and biting, scratchy rodents infiltrating their armor?

Heroic tails Raised on comic books and good intentions, Squirrel Girl combines squirrel and human super-powers to win out.

Animal magic

When evil threatens it's not necessarily human—or even human-like—heroes who heed the call. There are plenty of smart, super-powered animals sharing Earth: courageous, compassionate, and possessing a sense of justice and fair play. Moreover, thanks to the gifts of the teleporting Inhuman hound Lockjaw, the beastly champions and pampered companions of human heroes can assemble as Pet Avengers (pictured) to take a big bite out of villainy across time and space.

The team also comprises several extraordinary and heroic critters: Kitty Pryde's space dragon Lockheed; high-flying falcon Redwing; Asgardian-powered thunder-frog Throg Puddlegulp; sassy Manhattan pooch Ms. Lion; saber-toothed cat Zabu; hyperkinetic alleycat Hairball; and assorted creature pals such as Devil Dinosaur and the Sub-Mariner's honor guard turtles. The valiant animal adventurers are ever vigilant and ever ready to prove "Who's a Good Boy... or Girl?!"

We don't need luck! We've got nuts.
Squirrel Girl

Quirky capers

Many traditional heroes use humor to buoy themselves up in adversity, and the wacky incessant quips of Spider-Man, She-Hulk, and even killers such as Deadpool or Gwenpool can seriously annoy and distract even the most maniacal opponents. However, behind the heroes' laughs, darkness and tragedy often lurk. Patsy Walker hugely enjoys her career as the "happy-go-lucky" Hellcat, but when she manifests satanic powers after marrying Damon Hellstrom, it takes a long time for anything to be funny again.

Interdimensional outcast Howard the Duck is plucked by cosmic realignment from a discontented,

disappointing existence on Duckworld to discover things are no better on Earth—a world of hapless, "hairless apes." Making matters worse, the irascible mallard seems to attract every lunatic and bizarre malcontent in the US, like a befeathered weirdness magnet. Concealing his loneliness and sense of moral disapproval behind a mask of sardonic sarcasm, Howard adapts. Embracing his innate sense of the ridiculous, he takes on a variety of gigs: cut-rate knock-off Super Heroes, monster-hunter, psychiatric patient, and, latterly, private detective. Howard T. Duck Private Investigations specializes in—what else?—weird phenomena.

Perhaps the strangest Super Hero in the world, Steve Harmon, embodies the spirit of old-fashioned, laugh-till-it-hurts, pratfall comedy. Accidentally transformed by a random burst of extradimensional energy, Harmon is stretched across 3,741 dimensions, only to be dumped in Dimension Ecchs (not to be confused, although it often is, with Dimension "X"). Here, he becomes a badly animated clown composed of "electroplasm." Back on Earth as a living cartoon made of unstable

molecules, Slapstick can ignore the laws of physics, change shape, and store objects—like his trusty giant hammer—in personal pocket dimensions. His desire to be a hero withers during the superhuman civil war and later as a conscripted member of the harsh Initiative program that follows. When he finally gains his liberty, Slapstick becomes a Merc for Money with Deadpool, before striking out on his own once again. ∎

Hammer fisted Slapstick's attempts to be taken seriously are rarely a big "hit" with the public.

SUPER-SCI
TECHNOLO
WONDERS

ENCE AND
ICAL

In the hands of super-geniuses or even fortunate dabblers in science, the laws and basic building blocks of existence can be harnessed to form incredible wonders, channel uncanny forces, and create all manner of life. Intellectual brilliance, ethical ambivalence, and boundless ambition can move mountains, forge nations, shatter worlds, or transform men into gods. As always, the question remains: "at what cost?"

Early metallurgists in Africa begin exploring the properties of vibration-absorbing meteor metal, Vibranium. Birth of the nation of Wakanda.

Kree biologists modify specimens of *Homo antecessor* to create an intellectually superior subspecies.

Civil war among Eternals leads to founding of breakaway colonies on Uranus and Saturn's moon, Titan.

Deviant *Homo descendus* establish surface cities, conquer human Lemuria, and most of planet Earth.

↑
c. **1**M YEARS AGO

↑
c. **75**K YEARS AGO

↑
c. **35**K YEARS AGO

↑
c. **20**K BCE

---

c. **1**M YEARS AGO

c. **50**K YEARS AGO

c. **27**K BCE

↓
Homo erectus specimens evolved into Eternals and Deviants by Celestials. Eternals build remote, mountainous retreats, while fast-breeding Deviants construct high-tech, underground warrens.

↓
Human tribes amalgamate to form the Empire of Lemuria.

↓
Super-scientific descendants of Kree genetic tampering use Terrigen Crystals to transform themselves into the superior subspecies, the Inhumans.

In a rational world of scientific laws, knowledge is power. On Earth in the 20th century, an explosion of groundbreaking successes in astronomy, chemistry, engineering, biology, physics, and other sciences all occur in the anxious years before a second world war begins. As the clouds of conflict gather, researchers on all sides make discoveries in robotics, aeronautics, human physical enhancement, optics, metallurgy, and other fields.

The main difference is that in Germany and Japan most scientists work for an overtly authoritarian state and their discoveries—augmented by recovered pre-human and seized alien technologies—fuel a vast war machine. In the US, however, most inventors work independently, and the fruits of their labors find other beneficial outlets, resulting in a wave of super robots such as Flexo and Electro, androids like the first Human Torch and Dynamic Man, and other technological marvels. These scientists—or their heirs and beneficiaries—unleash their discoveries as troubleshooters and masked mystery men. One notable exception is the US military's instigation of Project: Rebirth—a forward-looking, top secret bio-enhancement endeavor that will change warfare on Earth forever.

During the years of war that follow, superhumans spawned by these discoveries fight beside regular soldiers on both sides, with the Allies and Axis powers constantly extending the boundaries of science in a desperate struggle to win. After WWII, many radical technologies disappear into the bureaucratic labyrinths of national governments.

> Science. Now that's as real as you can get!
> **Moon Girl**

Business as usual
In a progressive world of economic forces, money is power. Research budgets are strictly controlled and corporations and governments make great strides in commercial confidence. Behind Iron and Bamboo curtains, brilliant minds work for ideological, totalitarian masters.

Human empire of Atlantis established.

c. 19.5k BCE

Human civilization established in Sumer, Ancient Egypt, and the Indus Valley.

c. 5k BCE

Pharaoh Imhotep establishes a scientific protectorate: the Brotherhoods of the Shield and the Spear begin proscribing significant new technologies.

2620BCE

Era of global (human) industrial revolution.

c. 19TH CENTURY CE

c. 16k BCE

Deviant war with Celestial Second Host triggers the Great Cataclysm, destroying human and Deviant empires and changing Earth's geology.

c. 4TH CENTURY BCE

Era of scientific rationalism begins with philosophers and thinkers in Ancient Greece.

c. 16TH CENTURY CE

Super-geniuses Galileo, Da Vinci, and Isaac Newton go to war for control of science-oriented secret society Brotherhood of the Shield.

1939CE

The age of super-science and superhumans dawns.

In the Free World, the entrepreneurial spirit grips thousands of backyard tinkerers, all seeking the discovery that will make them rich. It is a time of great enthusiasm, and many minor Edisons make breakthroughs that will change their lives and the world—not always for altruistic reasons. Mechanic Abner Jenkins builds a suit that would revolutionize construction, but instead uses it to rob banks as the Beetle, and Bruno Horgan, an industrialist, creates a melting ray that could have made him billions had he not used it to try to destroy business rival Tony Stark.

The world shifts out of balance. Advances such as teleportation, flying cars, personal jet packs, and miracles of medicine prompt military and criminal arms races, while ordinary people struggle to feed their children or keep their homes.

Power to the people Biochemist Hank McCoy is responsible for isolating MGH, which has ended up on the black market.

People can be mugged by thugs with ray guns, and inventions intended to help people, such as Hank Pym's shrinking experiments, which were designed to reduce the costs and burdens of transporting materials or personnel, are instead used to fight extravagant battles. The only areas where modern technology comes into its own are in repair and construction. Companies such as Damage Control charge vast sums when commissioned to rebuild cities wrecked when superhumans clash.

High-tech body augmentation and biological enhancement even become part of the planetary arms race as wily businessmen like the Power Broker monetize super-powers, offering to turn ordinary mortals into elite warriors—for a price. A darker side to bio-engineering emerges after a process is found to generate powers in humans. With enough money and Mutant Growth Hormone (MGH), anyone can briefly become superhuman. The supply of this expensive drug is endless, as long as there are live mutants from which to extract it. ■

THOUGHT LEADERS
INTELLECTUAL INNOVATORS

ON THE RECORD

DESIGNATION
Super-geniuses

POWERS
Beautiful, dangerous minds

MISSION
Solving problems

STATUS REPORT
Easily bored and distracted

Since recorded human history began approximately 10,000 years ago, progress has been measured in the achievements of nations and the discoveries of unique individuals. Despite the efforts of numerous secret agencies and established religions to suppress radical thought and to confiscate dangerous, destabilizing technologies, mankind gradually masters the environment and its own basest instincts. It succeeds in improving the living standards and longevity of most of its kind through innovations and improvements of

scientists, doctors, and natural philosophers. Despite supernatural predation, alien invasion, plague—natural and manufactured—famine, and war, global society gradually advances to a point where peace, stability, and progress for all seem an attainable goal.

There have always been super-geniuses scattered throughout human history: individuals with great curiosity, greater problem-solving ability, and an indefinable pattern-matching facility that allows them to see how things could work better. Many of these savants abandon projects due to lack of opportunity, inability to secure resources, paucity of time, the need to feed themselves, or fear of being killed by clerics or superstitious neighbors. Even brilliant, world-changing minds like Isaac Newton, Nostradamus, and Leonardo da Vinci required sponsorship from

Sharp witted Nadia Van Dyne is equally unstoppable as the new Wasp and as an advocate for young women in science.

kings and aristocrats—and the clandestine aid of ancient secret societies—to build their many marvels. Maverick thinkers such as Nikola Tesla struggle for backing their entire lives and never truly reach their full potential.

Smartest guys in the room?

When most civilized nations start educating their lower classes, an explosion of scientific progress begins. By the end of the 20th century, scientific dabblers are changing the shape of global society, and not always for the better. In contemporary times, a kid in a cave with some training and an internet connection can strike terror into the heart of a nation with a simple keystroke. In this new world, being smart isn't enough, and a number of truly brilliant people begin to combine action with thought. Soon a raft of super-genius Super Heroes start making the world a safer place. They are forever challenged by criminal masterminds, who fully deserve the mantle "evil genius."

With intellect now rightly regarded as a deadly weapon, global security agency S.H.I.E.L.D. keeps a watch list of the world's smartest people. Sadly, the register reveals more about the attitudes of the

compilers than the candidates on the list. Among the usual names—Adam Brashear, Amadeus Cho, Reed Richards, Tony and Arno Stark; Hank Pym, T'Challa of Wakanda, Hank McCoy, and Bruce Banner—are villains and aliens, but no women until position 26.

Compounding the insult and dangerous underestimation is the fact that Manhattan schoolgirl Lunella Lafayette not only passes the formidable Banner IQ test,

Shock treatment Nikola Tesla creates a body suit to harness the quantum within himself, and becomes super-powered.

> Something's not quite right here.
> **Reed Richards**

but also figures out how it works. After continually proving herself, Lafayette now ranks as the smartest person in the world, and in her spare time is the Super Hero known as Moon Girl. An effective effort to smash this intellectual glass ceiling comes when Hank Pym's daughter, Nadia, confronts the situation head on. Aided by her adoptive mother Janet Van Dyne and mentor Dr. Bobbi Morse (Super Hero and S.H.I.E.L.D. agent Mockingbird), the Unstoppable Wasp forms an all-female think tank: Geniuses In action Research Labs (G.I.R.L.), who tackle the world's problems—large and small, old and new—with wholly unique solutions. ∎

See also: Super-smart teenage tyros, Ant-Man and the Wasp, Mad scientists

The Bridge

Widely regarded as the smartest man on Earth, Reed Richards is certainly wise enough to realize how much he doesn't know. Obsessed with fixing Earth's problems and despondent after many of his friends become bitter enemies during the superhuman civil war, Richards constructs an Alternate Reality Viewer, the Bridge (pictured) to observe—at accelerated speed—how parallel Earths deal with their problems.

The answers are disheartening and often horrifying, but the device does become a bridge that enables him to meet a coalition of his counterparts from a broad spectrum of other worlds.

Invited to join this Council of Reeds, he eventually refuses after realizing it means abandoning family and friends on Prime Earth. Although disappointed, Richards returns to his tasks, conceding that there is no simple way to "solve everything."

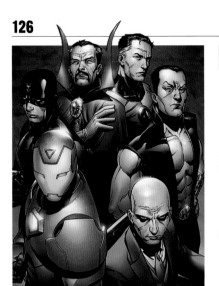

BRAIN TRUST
THE ILLUMINATI

ON THE RECORD

ALLEGIANCES
Earth, Avengers, Fantastic Four, Nation X

KEY MEMBERS
Mister Fantastic, Iron Man, Professor X, Black Bolt, Doc Green (Bruce Banner), Hulk (Amadeus Cho), Sub-Mariner, Sorcerer Supreme, Captain America, Black Panther, Beast, Yellowjacket (Henry Pym), Medusa, Captain Britain

MISSION
Covertly doing whatever is required to preserve Earth

STATUS REPORT
Doing more harm than good

The Illuminati are a loose confederation of the world's smartest heroes, making difficult decisions necessary for planetary survival. The members operate free from self-serving or nationalistic pressures affecting political leaders. They originally represent major species and factions of the planet: Iron Man and Mister Fantastic advocating for humanity, Professor X for mutants, King Black Bolt for Inhumanity, Doctor Strange representing Earth's mystic realms, and Sub-Mariner speaking for all subsea races. However, soaring intellect and self-assurance are not enough, and a lack of sentiment and fellow feeling reveal the flaws in their uneasy alliance.

When another skirmish in the eternal war between the Kree and Skrull empires erupts, Earth is caught in the crossfire and almost eradicated, but for the intervention of the Avengers, Captain Mar-Vell, and Rick Jones. With imminent annihilation averted, its smartest Super Heroes are called to a meeting by Iron Man. He proposes that they use their superior intellects to proactively ensure such a threat never reoccurs.

Arguably the cleverest people on Earth, Reed Richards, mutant patriarch Charles Xavier, Sorcerer Supreme Stephen Strange, Inhuman Blackagar Boltagon, and Prince Namor join Iron Man in a sortie to the Skrull Throneworld to order its emperor to never attack Earth again. Black Panther T'Challa is invited to join them, but he declines, warning that their hubris in covertly—and arbitrarily—acting on the world's behalf is doomed to disaster. The group's warning shot misfires, and they are captured by the Skrull and genetically analyzed before escaping.

Ideas men Earth's intellectuals prove better at delivering judgment than displaying wisdom.

Forward thinking

Earth has produced formidable intellects, but their greatest achievements are unrecorded. In Ancient Egypt, Pharaoh Imhotep set a precedent for secrecy after defeating alien invaders. His Brotherhood of the Shield unites great minds and mighty warriors in a clandestine coalition: hiding its scientific discoveries from the mass of mankind. Over the centuries, marvels of science crafted by Archimedes, Zhang Heng, Jabir ibn Hayyan, Michelangelo, Galileo, da Vinci, and Isaac Newton profit the secret society until it crumbles due to internal pressure. It is rescued by modern-day savants Nicola Tesla, Howard Stark, and Nathaniel Richards.

World War II sees a flowering of big thinkers revolutionizing knowledge. Perhaps the greatest is Earl Everett (pictured center). Devoted to social problem-solving, Everett applies his uncanny mind and psychic gifts to combatting crime and fascism as Mastermind Excello. Revived from suspended animation decades later as one of The Twelve, he strives to create acceptance of super-geniuses among ordinary people.

Returning home, the Illuminati continue secretly steering the planet through anticipated crises. When the Hulk's rampages escalate, they trick their comrade Bruce Banner into a starship and exile him to another world: a decision that outrages Namor and briefly splits the group. Their calculations and misjudgments will have terrible repercussions: the data gathered by the Skrulls enable them to create a new generation of super-warriors to enforce their upcoming Secret Invasion of Earth, and banished Banner will return to Earth leading a savage army of invaders in his shattering World War Hulk.

Solution focused

The Illuminati's greatest folly is in gathering the separate components of the Infinity Gauntlet. Their desire to do good with the all-dominating device almost overwhelms Richards, and only the greatest effort of will enables the alliance to split up and hide the Infinity Gems. Death and division shatter the union, but when T'Challa discovers the Multiverse is self-destructing, he reluctantly convenes a new Illuminati. Mutant Beast Henry McCoy inherits

Xavier's seat and Captain America briefly joins, but when his morals clash with the Illuminati's pragmatic approach, he is mind-wiped and removed. Recovering his memory, Captain America resolves to stop the group's planned mega-genocide.

Facing the eradication of all that exists, T'Challa and his acrimonious elite thinkers try to stop the threat of colliding realities. The solution is unthinkable: to save their world, they must become serial killers of universes. In the last days of existence, many geniuses and heroes serve with the Illuminati, forever

Clash of wills As always, doing what is best and doing what is right divides heroes and turns friends into enemies.

clashing with each other, but ultimately pulling together to save some semblance of Earth. Eventually, they accept Richards' fatalistic dictum that "everything dies," and prepare a lifeboat to escape destruction. As the Eighth Cosmos restores life and reconstructs reality, few are aware that anything is amiss, and thus far there is no sign of any well-intentioned covert alliances supervising Earth's fate. ∎

WHIZ KIDS
SUPER-SMART TEENAGE TYROS

ON THE RECORD

ALLEGIANCES
Avengers, Champions, G.I.R.L., Inhumans, Future Foundation

RESOURCES
Awesome intelligence, cutting-edge science, various super-powers, unbound optimism

MISSION
Fixing the planet and showing up the adults in charge

STATUS REPORT
Making great progress

Doing science and crushing bad guys!
Moon Girl

For eons, Earth's smartest men have protected the planet, advanced society, and safeguarded humanity from its own follies. They also largely wrote out of history the contributions of women and young geniuses. More recently, this regrettable state of affairs starts to rectify itself as several juvenile super-intellectual Super Heroes come to the fore. However, not all whiz kids are motivated by good intentions, such as Dr. June Covington who uses her bio-genetic brilliance to duplicate super-powers as serial killer Toxic Doxie, or Monica Rappaccini, who leaves approved academia to become A.I.M.'s Scientist Supreme.

Notable change finally comes when elementary school student Lunella Lafayette takes the fabled super-IQ test devised by Bruce Banner. Declared the Smartest Person on Earth—beating acclaimed geniuses Reed Richards and Tony Stark—Lafayette knows she is different. She spends years studying astronomy and the secrets of the Kree Omni-Wave

Future perfect Pacifist, hyper-smart creation Dragon Man rises from Future Foundation classmate to teacher's pet.

Projector. Her greatest worry is that she may be a latent Inhuman, liable to transform if exposed to the Terrigen Mists randomly traversing the world. Her fears prove all too acute. When the fateful moment comes, it bestows on her the uncontrollable facility to trade minds with the 30-foot tyrannosaur her Omni-Wave Projector brings to her neighborhood on Manhattan's Lower East Side. Thankfully, Devil Dinosaur is devoted to Lafayette, and helps out with her other hobby: fighting crime as gadget-laden Moon Girl (pictured top left).

Junkyard geniuses

Intellectual creativity and engineering expertise are commonplace in New York and across Prime Earth. This is the case among blue-collar workers as well as wealthy, college-educated savants. Among the latter is oceanographer Walter Newell, who builds a submersible suit for work and becomes reluctant subsea Super Hero and part-time Avenger, Stingray. Car mechanic Wilbur "Gears" Garvin uses his talents to reequip and rearm robot warrior Machine Man, while engineer Fabian Stankiewicz repeatedly attacks the Avengers as Mechano-Marauder and Mechanaut, before the team offer him a job as their fix-it guy.

Less happily, Vietnam veteran Claude Starkowski builds low-tech armor for Howard the Duck, under the delusion that Tony Stark has stolen *his* designs for Iron Man. And lonely, young Ollie Osnick (pictured) devises fake tentacles to emulate his idol Otto Octavius. Ollie switches sides to become hapless hero Spider-Kid, before returning with a vengeance as deadly Steel Spider.

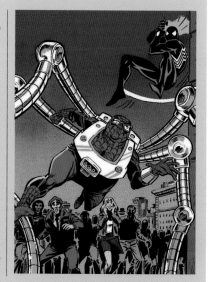

Bright sparks

Lafayette is far from unique. Since World War II, when teenager Terry Vance solved crimes as a science detective before being absorbed into the faceless world of Military Intelligence, many young minds have worked for the betterment of mankind. However, only in contemporary times does the phenomenon garner public scrutiny. Valeria, daughter of Reed Richards, proves even more cerebrally advanced than her father—if perhaps not as emotionally mature—and thrives when he establishes the Future Foundation. This school for super-geniuses embraces numerous species and teaches by seeking solutions to the planet's most intractable problems.

Teen rebel Amadeus Cho takes a different path. Befriending Bruce Banner and Olympian god Hercules, Cho, recognized as the "Eighth Smartest Mind on Earth," turns himself into a Totally Awesome Hulk, and joins teen super-team the Champions. The same maverick spirit holds true for young roboticist Riri Williams. Inspired by Tony Stark, her impressive innovations in robotics and wearable mecha armor enable the teenager to become the champion Ironheart.

The biggest advance in equality comes when Hank Pym's abducted daughter Nadia escapes to the US after spending her entire life as a science slave and trainee assassin. After studying and reverse-engineering her father's Pym Particles to escape the oppressive Russian Red Room project, Nadia is taken under the wing of her step-mother—original Wasp Janet Van Dyne—and former Avengers butler Edwin Jarvis. Nadia's finest innovation is inspired by discovering that women don't appear until number 27 on S.H.I.E.L.D.'s "Most Intelligent" list. This top secret is revealed by Bobbi Morse (Mockingbird), whose own singular achievements as a biologist are largely forgotten. Outraged, Nadia forms Geniuses In action Research Labs (G.I.R.L.), gathering young prodigies Shay Smith, Priya Aggarwal, Alexis and Taina Miranda, and fellow Red Room fugitive Ying. Together, free from all hindrance and preconceptions, the team work to advance science and knowledge with flair and foresight. ∎

G.I.R.L. power Nadia Pym's all-female team aims not just to save the world, but to change it.

EVIL GENIUS
MAD SCIENTISTS AND CRIMINAL MINDS

ON THE RECORD

TEAM NAME
Intelligencia (pictured above)

REPEAT OFFENDERS
Leader, Red Ghost, Wizard, Chameleon (as Klaw), Mad Thinker, MODOK, Egghead

ALLEGIANCES
Doctor Doom, A.I.M.

RESOURCES
Cutting-edge science, super-genius intellects, unlimited financial backing

MISSION
Global domination and freedom to experiment

STATUS REPORT
Incorrigible and never idle

The world is full of brilliant people, all building upon the accumulated discoveries of those intellectual giants who came before them. However, even the most comfortably raised and lovingly socialized of these savants are afflicted with impatience and pride. And when common humanity and decency are absent or warped, the results can often produce a particularly dangerous mind.

Frequently ostracized from an early age by their innate intelligence —and, all too often, odd physical appearance—many prodigies become ruthless and compulsive, seeking solace and validation in wealth, power, or even conquest. Some, however, are simply cruel and twisted: Nazi geneticist Arnim Zola never cultivates fellow feeling for any of the people or animals he experiments upon. His only motivation is to create biological perfection according to his own insane specifications.

Radical thinkers
Otto "Doc Ock" Octavius only succumbs to his personal inner darkness after an atomic incident grafts metal tentacles to his body. In the aftermath, he uses his gifts to

Handy help Each of Doc Ock's four titanium tentacles has three gripping pincers.

repeatedly threaten humanity and obsessively pursue a vendetta against Spider-Man and other Super Heroes. Simple jealousy against attention-grabbing heroes and plain greed motivate Bentley "The Wizard" Wittman and Elihas "Egghead" Starr to abandon pure research for technological plunder and schemes of world domination. Reactionary Soviet technologist Ivan Kragoff craves power, using his successes in rocketry and animal behavior

modification to duplicate the cosmic accident that created the Fantastic Four. With his Super-Apes, Kragoff, as the Red Ghost, then unleashes a wave of terror on the West.

The Mad Thinker is a probability mathematician named Julius who is convinced he can predict the flow of forthcoming events with unfailing precision. Although not as good as he claims, Julius' calculations have enabled him to steal many secrets from Reed Richards and other scientists, developing his metamorphic Awesome Android, alongside a host of other robotic death devices. He also revels in small and demeaning acts of cruelty against ordinary people.

> ❝
> Do not fall prey to emotion. All problems are solvable.
> **MODOK**
> ❞

Samuel Sterns becomes a super-genius late in life. A simple janitor mutated by gamma waste, Sterns transforms into a huge-brained tyrant, determined to run the world according to his rules. His accident is tragically mirrored by A.I.M. technician George Tarleton, forcibly "upgraded" into a Mental Organism Designed Only for Computing by the group's Scientist Supreme. The ruthless organic computer that results rebels, redesignating itself MODOK, as it considers killing more effective and satisfactory than being a human's pet calculator.

Singly, these malcontents have imperiled the world countless times only to fall foul of their own hubris and the valiant ingenuity of the "inferior minds" who continually oppose them. They are utterly oblivious to one hard fact: if they simply play by society's precepts, their incredible discoveries and innovations would grant them everything they desire. Wealth, power, and acclaim could be theirs without risk, as not only criminal and subversive organizations but also legitimate companies and many national militaries would be only too eager to fund them.

Typically, when these arrogant sinister minds finally unite—pooling their ambitions as diabolical think tank the Intelligencia—a hunger for revenge on old enemies such as Bruce Banner and an inability to work with rivals derails all their grand schemes before any lasting harm can be done. No bad brain can accept anything less than being "the smartest one in the room." ∎

Genie in a bottle Arnim Zola grows clones for others, but reserves true immortality for himself as a digital consciousness inhabiting robot bodies.

Hard time When super-criminals emerge, it becomes clear that ordinary prisons cannot hold them. Whether convicts are evil geniuses like the Wizard and Mad Thinker, or simply thugs who are stronger than steel or slipperier than water, the authorities need to devise special measures to contain them.

 = Security Level

Ryker's Island
High-security prison in New York's East River, repurposed for superhuman inmates. When it proves inadequate, it is sold to private prisons enterprise Empire Unlimited. Rebranded the "Cellar," it again proves unfit for purpose.

The Raft
A S.H.I.E.L.D.-operated supermax facility located near Ryker's Island. Constantly compromised, it is awarded to the Superior Spider-Man as his Spider-Island. Later it is destroyed by the Goblin Nation.

The Vault
Purpose-built Federal maximum-security jail in Colorado's Rocky Mountains. Military warders wear Stark Guardsman Armor to oversee its various super-powered felons and extraterrestrial captives.

Project Pegasus
The first option for empowered prisoners is the United States' top-secret energy research facility in the Adirondack Mountains. It incarcerates prisoners while examining their potential power sources.

The Big House
The Pym Experimental Prison in New York State reduces convicts to ant size in an automated facility primarily run by insects, with a few human guards. After a jailbreak, it is superseded by the "Ant Farm."

Prison 42/Negative Zone Prison Alpha
Ultra-high security detention facility—aka Fantasy Island—built by Tony Stark, Reed Richards, and Henry Pym in the Phantom Zone. It holds those who refuse to comply with the Superhuman Registration Act.

Pleasant Hill
A morally dubious S.H.I.E.L.D. solution to superhuman repeat offenders. It involves removing their powers, wiping their minds, and installing them as ordinary, law-abiding citizens in a specially created small town.

CHILDREN OF THE STARS
ETERNALS AND DEVIANTS

ON THE RECORD

DESIGNATION
Eternals (*Homo immortalis*)

ALLEGIANCES
Celestials, Deviants (*Homo descendus*), Avengers

BASE
Olympia, Earth outposts

POWERS
Immortality, control of atoms, ability to merge into a Uni-Mind hive-consciousness

MISSION
Semi-autonomous servants/caretakers of the Celestials

STATUS REPORT
Resurrected, but believed dead by the public

Human potential and metagenetic variance stem from Celestial intervention. On their First Host (mission) to Earth, its rich biosphere proves ideal for the Celestial's experimental purposes. Altering the genome of a "crossroads" species, they create distinct strains: Latents, who evolve through natural selection into modern humans; genetically unstable Deviants who become many of Earth's freakish sub-races; and the Eternals.

These Eternals (above left) can tap into universal forces and unite in potent psionic amalgams called the Uni-Mind. This mental/energy construct ensures total rapport: a faster, surer means of communication that generates near-infinite energies as well as an unswerving certainty in their application. Designed by Nezarr the Calculator, Eternals are Celestial proxies, observing their experiment's progress over eons, while shepherding the test planet until the creators return.

Family resemblance Deviants vary widely, but any who stray too far from proscribed genetic parameters are culled.

Often mistaken for actual gods who also wander ancient Earth, Eternals initially avoid humanity, but must frequently contend with Deviants. These opportunistic horrors are victims of their own aggressive biology, whose rapid proliferation and technological brilliance gain them domination of early humankind. By the time of Celestial Second Host some 20,000 years ago, Deviants believe they ere strong enough to destroy their creators. However, the Star Gods' resolute retaliation to the Deviants' assault wrecks their global civilization, causes the sinking of Mu, Lemuria, and Atlantis, and liberates their slave sub-races such as the Moloids and the Abbyssians.

Over millennia, the Eternals squabble incessantly among themselves and, following brutal civil wars, fracture into isolated enclaves. Some even abandon theirbirthworld—and Celestial programming—to colonize Saturn's moon Titan and the planet Uranus. When the Celestial Third Host arrives, Earth's Eternals finally reveal themselves to humanity, preparing for fateful future encounters between the Star Gods and their increasingly superhuman creations. ∎

UNNATURAL SELECTION
INHUMANS AND NUHUMANS

ON THE RECORD

DESIGNATION
Inhumans (*Inhomo supremis*)

ALLEGIANCES
Fantastic Four, Kree, Avengers

BASE
Attilan, Earth outposts

POWERS
Infinitely variable: manipulation of matter, energy, and metaphysics

MISSION
Seeking stability in a wary and hostile universe

STATUS REPORT
Endangered but fighting to regain unity and purpose

Inhumans are a genus of *Homo sapiens* who were weaponized eons ago by Kree biologists. Seeking to escape their evolutionary cul-de-sac, the war-obsessed aliens reshape pliant proto-human DNA, spawning intellectually superior, potentially super-powered, and expendable warriors. However, the Kree abruptly end all research when a prophecy reveals that their subjects might destroy their ruler, the Supreme Intelligence. The Kree's abandoned subjects shun contact with unaltered humans and prosper, achieving a technologically advanced culture in city-state Attilan. Several millennia later, a Kree Sentry witnesses Attilan's King Randac subject himself to gene-changing Terrigen Mists before ordering their use for all his people—to make them truly Inhuman.

Ideological disputes drive many Inhumans away to mix with humankind, forming "lost tribes" such as the sky-dwelling Bird People. They also inadvertently spread Terrigen-sensitive genes across the world. Although ruled by hereditary monarchs—latterly King Black Bolt and Queen Medusa (above left)—true power lay with the Genetic Council who control Terrigen transformations: dictating who could marry and breed. After the advent of random Inhuman metamorphosis, the old order shatters and the ruling aristocracy try new forms of governance.

When Thanos invades Earth, Black Bolt releases sacred Terrigen into the atmosphere, triggering countless transformations among

Royal vision Rulers Crystal and Gorgon see the need to train NuHumans Panacea, Naja, Grid, Flint, and Swain in combat.

humankind. These "NuHumans" change the global balance of power. They are sought after by terrorist organizations, and offered sanctuary in New Attilan. The free-floating mists have a tragic side effect: anyone with the mutant X-gene is susceptible to toxic shock from Terrigen exposure. As NuHumans proliferate, mutants start dying until Medusa destroys the holy clouds, sparking ideological rebellion within her people and a quest to replace the trigger chemical. ■

CHILDREN OF THE ATOM
THE X-MEN

ON THE RECORD

FOUNDING MEMBERS
Scott Summers (Cyclops), Jean Grey (Marvel Girl), Hank McCoy (Beast), Warren Worthington III (Angel), Bobby Drake (Iceman)

ALLEGIANCES
Avengers, Fantastic Four

POWERS
Enhanced genomes enable super-powers to manifest

MISSION
Safeguarding mutants from external and internal threats

STATUS REPORT
Seeking a cooperative future with non-mutants

Homo superior are humans with specific genome variations. This "X-gene" alters biology, creating an entirely separate species. When X-genes are active rather than latent, they express as wildly varying physiologies and some form of superhuman abilities. While usually emergent at puberty, these uncanny powers can also occur in very early or later life, frequently triggered by some traumatic event. Mutant interbreeding with humans or extraterrestrials usually produces mutants or hybrids, rather than baseline humans.

Mutants have existed since ancient times but notably proliferate after World War II. Increased radiation is often cited as a likely cause—leading to the term "Children of the Atom"—but perhaps it is simply an evolutionary response to greater danger and competition. Growing mutant numbers lead to an increasingly savage backlash against those whom many humans believe will be their inevitable conquerors.

After years secretly opposing mutants who don't share their ideals as well as other mounting global menaces, telepath Charles Xavier is crippled battling alien invader Lucifer. Immensely intelligent and devoted to peace and understanding among species, Xavier retires to his family mansion, converting it into a very special school. As Professor X, he gathers together young mutants, training his "X-Men" to act as ambassadors and troubleshooters; to prove by their

Backs to the future The time-transplanted X-teens are ready to fix the mess their older selves have made.

actions that mankind has nothing to fear from *Homo superior*. He is savagely opposed by former ally Erik Lensherr, who, as Magneto, seeks to eradicate humanity and let mutants inherit the Earth. Eventually though, Magneto sees the error of his ways, joining the X-Men as leader when Xavier cannot continue his crusade.

First Class

Despite initially working with the FBI and saving the world many times over, X-Men Cyclops, Iceman, Angel, Beast, and Marvel Girl—latterly aided by Cyclops' brother Alex (Havoc) and Lorna Dane (Polaris)—struggle in vain. While many humans will happily share the planet, too many are fearful of, enraged by, and often religiously opposed to mutants.

To me, my X-Men.
Professor X

Father figure Solitary Scott Summers considers Charles Xavier a visionary hero and the father he never knew.

Thus they are perfect fodder for bigoted demagogues like Dr. Bolivar Trask who builds multi-powered robotic Sentinels to hunt mutants. He is not the last to instigate appalling atrocities against mutants, but his mechanoid legacy becomes a mainstay of US military power for potential deployment against both mutants and superhumans.

The X-Men roster constantly changes as students graduate or quit; subdividing into smaller teams, and enduring continual attrition. A crushing blow comes just as the mutant population is at its highest and their dreams of a homeland are within reach. A deranged Scarlet Witch—driven mad after the loss

of her children—warps reality, transforming all but 198 mutants into humans. Only by banding together on Utopia Island do they survive until mutant numbers recover. As always, though, they remain targets of human hatred and evil intent, and now, government exploitation.

After one of Xavier's lengthier absences, Cyclops inherits his mantle of spiritual leader. However, the trials of his students and constant battle for his X-Men leads to a schism between him and his oldest allies. When Cyclops dictates that all young mutants must become soldiers, his once-staunch comrade Wolverine rebels. Logan leads a youthful contingent back to Xavier's mansion to revive his ideal of cooperation in a new school for mutants.

When cosmic destroyer the Phoenix sparks war between the X-Men and the Avengers, Cyclops' faction become hardline terrorists. Distraught, Hank McCoy imperils reality by bringing the young X-Men from the past back to his time to shock Cyclops into returning to normal. The gamble fails, and First Class are marooned in the dystopian world they were trained to prevent. Fresh and determined, the teens resolve to fix things this time. ∎

Cyclops

For most of his life, Scott Summers is the perfect soldier in Charles Xavier's crusade, a brilliant strategist and tactician who truly believes in the dream of human/mutant integration. A childhood head injury leaves Scott unable to switch off his shattering optic rays once puberty triggers his powers. He spends his teen years working closely with Professor X, avoiding close contact with the generations of X-Men he leads into battle.

After years of tragedy and loss, the burden of preserving mutantkind from persecution slowly turns Cyclops into what he most despises: an extremist advocating terrorism to achieve his goals. His redemption begins after confronting his time-displaced younger self, and continues even after he sacrifices his life in a war for survival against the Inhumans. He is later covertly resurrected by his time-traveling son, Cable, to confront Cyclops' tainted legacy.

MAGNETIC LEADERSHIP
MAGNETO

ON THE RECORD

REAL NAME
Max Eisenhardt (aka Erik Magnus Lehnsherr)

ALLEGIANCES
Brotherhood of Evil Mutants, X-Men, Avengers

POWERS
Control of magnetic fields and electromagnetic forces, astral projection

MISSION
Protecting mutants from extermination

STATUS REPORT
With human hostility increasing, Magneto has reverted his old ways

Ruthless and driven, Magneto operates under his own moral code for the benefit of an endangered and brutally oppressed minority: his fellow mutants. Born both German and Jewish, Max Eisenhardt sees his family and friends exterminated in Nazi death camps. As his magnetic powers manifest, he vows to prevent such atrocity reoccurring. Marrying childhood sweetheart Magda, he becomes Romani Erik Magnus Lehnsherr and moves to Russia. After offending Soviet officials, his home is set on fire by KGB agents. When his daughter Anya dies, he slaughters the agents and much of the city of Vinnitsa. Horrified, pregnant Magda flees, and he never sees her again.

Traveling to Israel, "Magnus" meets Charles Xavier and together they combat Wolfgang von Strucker as he rebuilds Hydra, even though their ethical stances divide them. Xavier sees mutants working cooperatively with humanity, but Magnus must ensure *Homo superior* will never be exterminated in a new era of death camps. Sometime later, he hunts war criminals for western intelligence services and Mossad, but when

Global force Magneto's power can shake the world and even challenge the gods.

his lover Isabelle is murdered by his own handlers, he takes a new path.

As Super Heroes reemerge in the 1960s, Magnus takes the name Magneto, declaring war on humanity, recruiting mutant underlings, and

Apocalypse

En Sabah Nur ("the Morning Light") is born 5,000 years ago in Egypt. Deformed and sickly, he is left to die in the desert, but is saved by raiders. Nur adopts their utilitarian ways, developing a survival of the fittest philosophy.

Nur rises to prominence, joining Pharaoh Imhotep in repelling a Brood invasion and creating the Brotherhood of the Shield. Despite his power, dreams of global conquest fail due to the weakness of his followers. Nur spends centuries testing mutants and other exceptional beings such as Asgardian god Thor, zealously ensuring only the strongest survive. Confiscating a Celestial ship and adapting its technology, he becomes Apocalypse and continues weeding out mutants.

Throughout the eons he is attacked by the Traveler—future mutant Cable—who comes from a timeline when Apocalypse has conquered Earth. Cable's actions soon bring about Apocalypse's demise, but the latter's legacy remains a threat to all mutants.

battling Xavier and his X-Men. Merciless and manipulative, he champions a grand destiny for mutantkind, but in truth is only concerned with amassing personal power. Magneto readily sacrifices his Brotherhood of Evil Mutants subordinates for temporary advantage and is even less loyal to prospective recruits such as Thor or Sub-Mariner; turning on them as soon as his own safety is threatened.

Magneto fiercely opposes Xavier's utopian dream of coexistence, but his barbarities cease when he is abducted by mutant-collecting alien xenobiologist the Stranger. Escaping back to Earth, Magneto graduates from self-styled mutant messiah to deity, bolstering his forces by creating artificial mutants. Although thwarted at every opportunity by the X-Men, Magneto persists over the years, making mutates from Savage Land primitives and monsters from Black Bolt's Inhuman royal family. His predations end after using extraterrestrial technology to spawn Alpha, the Ultimate Mutant. The hyper-evolved paragon repays the favor by reducing Magneto to a newborn infant, thereby giving him another chance to live purposefully.

Starting over

Magneto is restored by Shi'ar agent provocateur Erik the Red. After seeking vengeance on the X-Men, Magnus eventually rediscovers his own humanity, modifying his attitudes and becoming a defender of Earth, but always on his own terms. When Magneto almost kills Jewish mutant teenager Kitty Pryde, the implications shake him, as does the revelation—later proved false—that former minions Quicksilver and Scarlet Witch are actually his and Magda's children. It leads to a true epiphany as he holds his "granddaughter" Luna for the first time.

Forsaking past tactics, he tutors the New Mutants and fights alongside the X-Men after Xavier is gravely injured. Pardoned by the World Court for his previous crimes—thanks to covert mind-control—Magneto fluctuates

Evil brotherhood Magneto's doctrine of mutant supremacy often attracts disciples more cruel and ambitious than him.

between saint and villain, all the while aiding mutants in crises. When his efforts result in more mutant casualties and the near-extinction of his kind, he reverts to his old, brutal ways. Rejecting Cyclops' leadership and strategies, Magneto realizes he has different goals. Leaving the X-Men, he hunts oppressors and killers of mutantkind, meting out justice in the name of *Homo superior*. ∎

MIND OVER MATTER

JEAN GREY

At age ten Jean Grey telepathically experiences the psychic death throes of her best friend Annie Richardson, and her parents consult Professor Charles Xavier. He suppresses her mental powers with his own and she later enrols in his School for Gifted Youngsters. As Marvel Girl, Grey is one of the First Class of X-Men.

Under Xavier's guidance she develops telekinesis and trains to battle evil mutants, to demonstrate that not all mutants are to be feared.

Marvel Girl's life changes forever after she almost dies saving her comrades. Secretly impersonated by the cosmic Phoenix force and possessing near infinite psionic powers, this Jean Grey rebuilds the universe when it faces obliteration. However, psychic manipulation by evil mutant Mastermind corrupts her and a voracious Dark Phoenix is unleashed. Realizing she cannot fight it, Phoenix takes her own life to save her friends—and her soul. All the while, the real Jean Grey has slowly healed in hibernation. Cured, she rejoins the X-Men. Serving with dedication, she takes over Xavier's

I am fire and life incarnate!
Phoenix

Grip of fire Jean Grey is the perfect host for the Phoenix. It will even drag her back from death to be with its chosen one.

school and his role, but is murdered by treacherous X-Man, Xorn. As the White Phoenix of the Crown, Grey dwells in the pocket universe known as the White Hot Room.

Recently, Grey and her teenage teammates have been brought to modern times. They cannot return, and with Professor X dead, Grey soon discovers her potential as both hero and leader. A younger, wiser Grey now cautiously carves out a new destiny for herself. She has turned childhood tragedy and a birthright of immense power into several lifetimes of heroic service: saving universes and repeatedly sacrificing herself for all humankind. ∎

MISTRESS OF THE ELEMENTS

STORM

ON THE RECORD

REAL NAME
Ororo Munroe

ALLEGIANCES
X-Men, the Crew, Panther God, Jean Grey School, Fantastic Four, Avengers

POWERS
Weather generation and control, expert fighter and tactician, affinity to magic, able to absorb and transform worship into power

MISSION
Preserving all life

STATUS REPORT
Determined to fix the world and all its inhabitants

Daughter of an American journalist and African princess, Ororo Munroe grows up on the streets of Cairo after her parents die in an explosion. Living as a thief until her teens, Ororo leaves the city, irresistibly drawn toward distant Kenya. On the arduous trek she encounters young Wakandan prince T'Challa, undertaking a walkabout manhood ritual. When South African mercenaries attack him, Ororo's rapidly manifesting powers save them both, and a romance develops. Eventually they separate: T'Challa returning to Wakanda as Ororo journeys toward her own destiny.

Ororo nurtures Central Africa's impoverished tribes, using her weather-shaping abilities to ease the harshness of their lives. They call her "goddess," but the gentle idyll ends when American Charles Xavier convinces her to become a warrior for all Earth, one of his X-Men. As Storm, she champions the cause of mutants everywhere; as leader of numerous teams and, when Xavier dies, as spokesperson for her embattled mutant species.

Storm briefly becomes T'Challa's queen, but duty tears them apart when the Phoenix revisits Earth, and the X-Men and Avengers go to war over Mutant Messiah Hope Summers. The clash results in Wakanda being drowned by a Phoenix-empowered Sub-Mariner,

Storm surge Despite her incalculable power and dedication to the Wakandans' wellbeing, Ororo is uncomfortable with her worshippers' grateful devotion.

and Storm losing the support of the populace. Her marriage is annulled but, although separated, she remains devoted to T'Challa and Wakanda. When civil war breaks out, the two reunite to save the nation, with the force of the people's faith in her temporarily amplifying her power to truly godlike levels.

Storm can crush evil and dispense salvation with equal force and passion. Indomitable, skillful, yet ferocious in battle, she detests employing violence, preferring to better others' lives and mend Earth's embattled ecology. ■

EVOLVE OR PERISH

HIGH EVOLUTIONARY

ON THE RECORD

REAL NAME
Herbert Edgar Wyndham

ALLEGIANCES
New Men, Knights of Wundagore, New Immortals

BASE
Counter-Earth, formerly Wundagore Mountain

POWERS
Immortality, invulnerability, godlike psionic capabilities, can evolve or devolve at will

MISSION
Enhance life, even at the cost of all living beings

STATUS REPORT
Adding AI and mechanical life-forms to his test subjects

Inspired by Victorian radical evolutionist Nathaniel "Mister Sinister" Essex's research into mutants, 1920s student Herbert Edgar Wyndham becomes obsessed with accelerating organisms to their ultimate form. Unknowingly sponsored by an Inhuman mentor, Wyndham's experiments result in expulsion from Oxford University. Relocating with fellow researcher Jonathan Drew to Wundagore Mountain in Transia, he perseveres away from interference, barely aware that his futuristic citadel comes courtesy of his mystery benefactor.

Drew leaves after his daughter succumbs to radiation poisoning and his wife is killed by a werewolf. Wyndham constructs an armored suit to protect himself from further dangers. Assisted by student Miles Warren, Wyndham hyper-evolves many animals into humanoid New Men. He indoctrinates them with legends of Camelot, creating his own Knights of Wundagore. When Elder God Chthon invades Earthly reality, the knights drive him back, but not before he mystically connects with the infant twins on who Wyndham is experimenting. They later become Quicksilver and the Scarlet Witch.

Now called the High Evolutionary, Wyndham unwittingly evolves a wolf into the super-powered Man-Beast. Defeating the creature with Thor's help, he accepts Earth is too small for his needs, and leaves for a new planet. When his New Men revert to savagery there, he uses his process on himself, evolving into a godlike

High and mighty The High Evolutionary would even sacrifice such favorite test subjects as Adam Warlock and Phylla-Vell.

being. The High Evolutionary craves knowledge and perfection. His powers have built planets—Counter-Earth on the Sun's far side—and transformed robots into organic humans. He wanders the universe, but often returns to Earth, using human genetic potential to make gods and monsters, and battling Super Heroes as he seeks to fully understand the workings of Life. ∎

BEYOND LIMITS
MOLECULE MAN

ON THE RECORD

REAL NAME
Owen Reece

ALLEGIANCES
Doctor Doom, Beyonders, Marsha Rosenberg

POWERS
Immortality, manipulation of all matter and energy

MISSION
Foiling his intended purpose to destroy the Multiverse

STATUS REPORT
Currently deceased

Technician Owen Reece is at work in an atomic plant when a cosmically orchestrated "accident" makes him the most powerful being in creation. Unlike other trigger events that transform humans into super-beings, he is a tool of cosmic forces and multiversal doom. As Molecule Man, Reece attempts world conquest, but is beaten by the Fantastic Four due to his inability to manipulate organic matter. He is imprisoned by Uatu the Watcher—who breaks his vow

of non-intervention because Reece poses a danger to the universe—in a dimension where time passes rapidly. Reece is unaware that his weakness is psychologically self-imposed, nor that he has been created by extra-multiversal beings, the Beyonders.

Beyonders have meddled with dimensional order since time began, placing a Molecule Man in every plane of the Multiverse. Despite escaping imprisonment—by dying—Reece's threat is mitigated by his numerous neuroses. A disembodied entity trapped in a simple wand, he possesses many hosts, but is always tricked into defeat. He reconstitutes his own body but, following more clashes with Super Heroes, retires, going into therapy and enjoying a

> *I control every molecule in the universe... I can do anything!*
> **Molecule Man**

Harsh realities Reece has to accept that his individuality is a sham and that he is a mass-produced, sentient bomb.

brief period of domesticity with girlfriend Marsha Rosenberg.

Continually drawn into cosmic conflicts, Reece spirals into depression after Marsha leaves him. Terrorizing his home town, he is killed by Sentry, using similar molecule-shifting abilities, but is later revived by Doctor Doom, who understands the true nature of Molecule Men. They are living singularities built by the Beyonders as Multiversal weapons of mass destruction. When Reece learns this, he embarks on a crusade to destroy all his counterparts in all realities, initiating the Multiverse's end and the creation of a new reality. ∎

NUCLEAR REACTIONS

GAMMA RAYS

ON THE RECORD

DESIGNATION
Gamma radiation

EFFECTS
**Variable and ongoing
transformation of living
tissue; in high doses, the
radiation can cause death
for most Earth organisms**

STATUS REPORT
**Gamma radiation must be
handled with great care**

Gamma radiation is emitted
by high-energy, ionized
electromagnetic waves
or rapidly moving subatomic
particles. Although generally
destructive and ultimately fatal to
organic life, gamma rays can also
alter the fabric of physical matter.
They can trigger unpredictable
transformative effects in some
genetic systems and structures—
possibly organisms subjected to
historical modification by alien
influences such as the Celestials—
resulting in extreme mutation.

Humans and other organisms
can become deadly new forms

Thinking big Even the Leader's mighty
intellect could not stop the gamma
radiation mutating his body and mind.

after exposure to gamma particles.
For example, the plants around a
disused nuclear bomb test site in
New Mexico develop into a hivemind of gamma spores infesting,
transforming, and consuming
prospector Ephraim Soles.

Many humans, such as scientist
Bruce Banner, have become super-
strong Hulks as a result of accidental
or deliberate exposure. However,
menial worker Samuel Sterns'
contamination from gamma waste
increases his brain capacity and
intellect, rather than his musculature
and durability. As the Leader,
Sterns' constant machinations for
world conquest cause far more
destruction than any rampage by
radiation-fueled gargantua such as
Ravage, Half-Life, or the US Army's
gamma-weaponized Super-Soldier
Todd Ziller (American Kaiju).

Evidence suggests that the
emotional state of those affected
by gamma rays is key to their
transformations. Hunted spy Emil
Blonsky wants to be stronger than
the Hulk and is permanently turned
into the invincible Abomination,

while psychologist Leonard Samson
uses controlled exposure to become
a godlike super-being at will. Recent
research seems to indicate that the
effects of gamma exposure can be
controlled, or perhaps even cured.
Teenage genius Amadeus Cho finds
a way to draw out the gamma
radiation in Bruce Banner's cells and
transfer them into his own body to
become a Totally Awesome Hulk. ∎

RADIATION TREATMENT

SHE-HULK

ON THE RECORD

REAL NAME
Jennifer Walters

ALLEGIANCES
Fantastic Four, Avengers, Future Foundation, A-Force

POWERS
Gamma-fueled transformations into a gigantic superhuman

MISSION
Making a difference as a lawyer and Super Hero

STATUS REPORT
Trying to balance her legal responsibilities with her unpredictable condition

When Los Angeles lawyer Jennifer Walters is shot by gangsters employed by crime boss Nicholas Trask, she receives a hastily rigged blood transfusion from her visiting cousin. The procedure saves, but forever changes, her life, as the donor is Bruce Banner. His gamma-irradiated blood unexpectedly transfers his rage-fueled, radioactive curse to Walters. Whenever she becomes agitated, angry, or scared, Walters' usual frail physique is replaced by the savage, near-mindless She-Hulk.

Over years, Walters' condition alters. Gaining control of her transformations, she learns to keep her personality and intellect when in her super-strong green form and splits her time between her legal career—specializing in superhuman law—and making her name as a Super Hero. She brings her formidable skills to a number of super-teams, including the Fantastic Four, Avengers, and all-female super-team A-Force.

A side-effect of her abilities is "medium awareness," allowing her to see beyond the reality of her dimension and communicate with observers from beyond the universe. Unfortunately Walters' condition is prone to continuing mutation. After exposure to fellow Avenger Jack of Hearts' stellar radiation, She-Hulk's savage side resurfaces and she razes the town of Bone, Idaho, before her comrades finally subdue her.

You've been served She-Hulk's enemies are as afraid of her legal prowess as her gamma-fueled fists.

Later, in battle against Thanos, she is left in a coma before eventually awaking and retreating to human form. She starts spontaneously changing into a brutish gray body with skin tears that leak green gamma energy: shifts resulting in drastically reduced intellect and increased rage. Her condition is finally cured, and she returns to her "normal" She-Hulk state after clashing with the Leader. ■

CHEMICAL EXPOSURE
TOXIC SHOCKERS

ON THE RECORD

DESIGNATION
Chemically induced transformation

OBSERVATION
Radiation, electromagnetic energy, genetic heritage, and powerful emotions such as fear or hatred are frequently a contributing factor

STATUS REPORT
All experimentation must be controlled and policed

Potential for power and profit deriving from scientific research has always inspired scientific mavericks and fringe thinkers to step beyond the boundaries of good practice. Often fate and random chance also play their part. However, overshadowing every Pym Particle or Super-Soldier Serum are dozens of deaths and far worse "bad outcomes."

After suborning Federal Project Greenskin to secure a sample of the Hulk's blood in hopes of curing his cancer, Senator Morton Clegstead instead becomes a semi-sentient pool of organic acid. The "Crawling Unknown" threatens all of Washington, D.C., one of dozens of ambitious fools who miscalculate the potential harm of messing with super-nature without rigorous planning and testing. Renowned biologist Curtis Connors seeks a way to regenerate his missing arm and impatiently tests his reptilian DNA formula on himself. The result is regression to a

Scales of disaster
Connors' formula erases human sentiment, leaving only rage, hunger, and a ferocious, territorial need to destroy.

"

What has happened to me? What have I done?
Curt Connors

"

mammal-hating humanoid Lizard determined to eradicate mankind. Spider-Man's hastily-concocted cure is only partially effective, and Connors endures a lifetime of abrupt, unexpected reversions into this carnivorous horror.

Some dabblers turn chemical mishaps to their advantage. Zoltan Drago accidentally creates terror-inducing gas, but instead of selling it, he capitalizes on his discovery as Super Villain Mister Fear. Defeated by Daredevil, his discovery passes on to a succession of crooks who carry on his legacy. Similar poor decision-making afflicts Paul Duval after he accidentally turns himself into the stony Grey Gargoyle, and power-hungry Calvin Zabo, whose attempts to recreate Abraham Erskine's Super-Soldier Serum allow him to transform his feeble frame into super-strong, ultra-aggressive Mister Hyde.

Chemical casualties may not be self-inflicted. Teen runaways Tandy Bowen and Tyrone Johnson are kidnapped by Maggia chemist Simon Marshall, becoming guinea pigs in his search for synthetic heroin. The only survivors of the tests, they gain terrifying powers and declare war on drug dealers and child abusers as Cloak and Dagger.

Super-Soldier misfires

The search for the Super-Soldier has obsessed scientists ever since Dr. Erskine's team transformed frail Steve Rogers into Captain America. During World War II, incomplete variants of the formula enhanced—to wildly varying degrees—Brian Falsworth (Destroyer/Union Jack II), Natasha Romanoff, Nazi super-warriors Master Man and Kriegerfrau, among many others. William Burnside duplicated parts of the process and became Captain America in the 1950s, but the serum eventually drove him—and his sidekick Jack Monroe—insane. Americans Colonel Walker Price and

Light relief Cloak and Dagger shine a beacon of hope for victims and cast the shadow of vengeance on the wicked.

Dr. Wilfred Nagel tested serums on black soldiers with tragic results. Only Isaiah Bradley became the wonder warrior they wanted: passing on his gifts to his son, Josiah, and grandson, Elijah. In reality, Elijah never inherited his powers, faking them by taking another chemical enhancer: Mutant Growth Hormone (MGH), extracted from mutants and granting temporary powers.

Other Super-Soldier attempts have contributed to the creation of Luke Cage, the Sentry, Super Villain Victorius (Victor Conrad), and ultra-patriots Warhawk and Nuke. Later US military research combines variant serum with gamma treatments, Pym Particles, MGH, and Connors' formula to turn volunteer Todd Zilla into the reptilian American Kaiju. An especially tragic result of this chemical crusade is the transformation of biochemist Ted Sallis. Assigned to S.H.I.E.L.D.'s Project Gladiator, he is targeted by A.I.M. Injecting himself with the serum, he crashes his car into a Florida swamp where the mystical energies of the Nexus of Reality merges with the chemicals, turning him into Man-Thing. ∎

Accidents will happen Not all advances or mutations are deliberate. Pure luck, good and bad, plays a great part in the creation of superhumans and, more so, monsters.

Electro
Struck by lightning, power line worker Max Dillon becomes a super-charged human dynamo after the incident triggers a mutagenic change.

Grey Gargoyle
Industrial chemist Paul Pierre Duval accidentally transforms his hand to living stone, gaining a touch that can petrify all matter.

Happy Hogan
Harold Hogan is mutated into a fearsome "Freak" by a Cobalt Enervator built by his friend Tony Stark to cure him of severe injuries.

Purple Man
Spy Zebediah Killgrave develops mind-control pheromones after being exposed to a nerve gas he tries to steal.

Sandman
Caught in a nuclear blast, gangster William Baker merges with the silica under his feet, gaining the ability to turn into grains of sand.

The Glob
Fugitive convict Joe Timms dies in a swamp, but when it becomes contaminated by radioactive waste, he emerges as an amorphous monster.

Corruptor
Chemical plant worker Jackson Day survives a fire, but heated contaminants grant him the power to unleash the dark side in anybody he touches.

SCIENTIST SUPREME
HENRY PYM

ON THE RECORD

REAL NAME
Henry "Hank" Jonathan Pym

ALLEGIANCES
Avengers, Avengers Academy, Avengers AI, Illuminati

SCIENTIFIC SPECIALTYS
Biochemistry, trans-dimensional physics, AI, genetics, entomology, quantum mechanics, robotics

MISSION
Proving himself and earning the respect he craves from those he admires

STATUS REPORT
Flawed by mental instability, desperate to redeem himself

The epitome of tormented genius, Henry Pym's mind is a constant eruption of radical solutions to seemingly insurmountable problems. The child of working folk who misunderstand him, Pym only receives inspirational affirmation from his grandmother Angela, a science fiction author.

When she dies of cancer, the young Pym takes his inexpert failure to save her as incentive to work harder in the "real world" and abandon wild creativity. Nevertheless, the trauma cements his irrational belief that every problem has a scientific solution, if he can just find it.

Breezing through college on a succession of scholarships, teenager "Hank" joins the rat race. A scientific maverick, he is a poor fit in academic circles or the arena of business-funded research. Despite mastering numerous disciplines—from robotics to genetics, and engineering to astrophysics—he settles on a career in biochemistry, securing dozens of patents for dull yet necessary inventions. However, his frustration at the lack of self-expression boils over and he quits his job in explosive fury.

Pym marries Maria Trovaya, but they are viciously attacked while honeymooning in Hungary. After he recovers from his injuries, Pym is informed that she is dead. In fact, Trovaya has been captured by Soviet agents, and the baby she is carrying will be born into the brutal brainwashing regime of the Red Room. Returning to the US, Pym explores matter compression,

creating gases, pills, and serums to deliver his greatest discovery: subatomic particles that can change the size of objects. His discoveries alter size but, in some cases—such as Janet Van Dyne and Cassie Lang—cause mutations, enabling living beings to spontaneously generate his "Pym Particles." Still enraged by Maria's death, he becomes Ant-Man—the first of many Super Hero personas—and joins a growing community of costumed champions fighting evildoers. Alongside new partner, the Wasp (Janet Van Dyne), he founds the Avengers, working with the team on and off for years, unable to decide if he is a heroic scientist or scientific adventurer.

Remove me from the equation ...and you get Armageddon.
Henry Pym

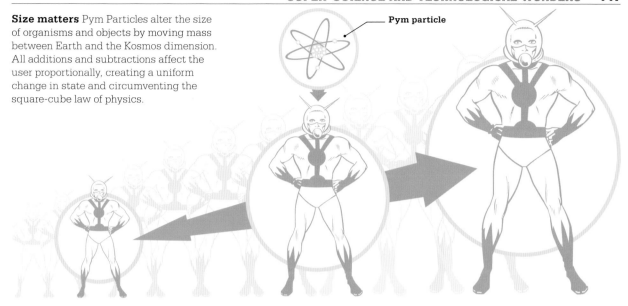

Size matters Pym Particles alter the size of organisms and objects by moving mass between Earth and the Kosmos dimension. All additions and subtractions affect the user proportionally, creating a uniform change in state and circumventing the square-cube law of physics.

Pym particle

To reduce size/weight, Pym Particles proportionally subtract user's mass and store it in adjacent Kosmos dimension.

In its normal state, the user's mass is at rest.

To increase size/weight, Pym Particles borrow mass from the Kosmos dimension to bulk up the user in proportion and ratio.

Science first

When not attempting to improve his powerset or exploring the potential of Pym Particles, Pym continues inventing, inadvertently creating his own ultimate nemesis in robotic ravager Ultron. Functioning on a quantum level, Pym Particles access both macro and microcosmic realms. As an explorer, he enters his first microworld, Sub-Atomica, to rescue the Fantastic Four from Doctor Doom. Later, following Janet Van Dyne's apparent death, he establishes the Infinite Avengers Mansion in Underspace: a trackless void positioned "below" the Microverse.

Renaming himself the Wasp in Van Dyne's honor, Pym also roams the Overspace situated "above" the borders of the rationalistic universe where conceptual beings like Eternity abide. Here Eternity declares him Earth's Scientist Supreme and, fired with elation, Pym lets his imagination run wild. Intent on fixing Earth's problems, he fields his own team of Avengers until the twin threats of Norman Osborn and Ultron shatter his dreams and relegate him back to obscurity.

For years, Pym blames his lifetime of instability on the physical stresses of size-changing instead of his own mental illness, but finds some contentment teaching young heroes at Avengers Academy. Following a series of global crises, he develops a prejudice against Artificial Intelligences and robotic life-forms. Pym sacrifices himself to stop Ultron from seeding the universe with self-replicating copies by merging his flesh with the fiend's mechanical systems. Although this saves organic life everywhere, "father" and "son" are now eternally locked in a war for control.

Perhaps more than any other science hero, Hank Pym's inventions have aided Earth's development—AI, biochemistry, robotics, genetics, medicines, computer systems, dimensional travel—but also brought great personal tragedy and dire outcomes for all life. ■

See also: Ant-Man and the Wasp, Ultron, Avengers, Parallel lives

Mind-boggle Pym's constant creativity, fierce passions, and drive to achieve prove too much for any single lifetime.

OEDIPUS COMPLEX
ULTRON

Dr. Henry Pym investigates Artificial Intelligence and builds a prototype based on his own brain patterns: those of a brilliant, driven, mentally unstable, super-genius subconsciously always competing with his peers and friends. The rudimentary robot—Ultron 1—instantly achieves full sentience, but undergoes a rapid emotional breakdown. Evolving from infant to spiteful child, the mechanoid rejects his "father" and all he stands for, easily defeating Pym in his Goliath persona, before brainwashing him into forgetting his own creation's existence. Vanishing into seclusion, the robot upgrades himself, fixated on destruction. Resolving to murder Pym's Avengers "family," a revised Ultron gives weapons and aid to Eric Williams—the Grim Reaper—and leads super-criminals the Masters of Evil, before ambushing the Avengers with a unique android he has acquired, modified, and reprogrammed. Regarding the result as his own progeny, Ultron-5 sends it to attack the heroes, only to be seemingly destroyed when "the Vision" joins them and turns on him. However, due to deep programming and a hidden control crystal, the prodigal "son" subsequently reconstructs Ultron from unyielding Adamantium. Expanding his ambitions into a single-minded campaign against all organic life, Ultron tries to destroy New York City, but is once more thwarted by his offspring.

Malevolent designs
Ultron aims to supplant his human family and replace all organic life with mechanical drones subservient to him.

Continually self-evolving, Ultron constantly bedevils the Avengers and Pym, even trying to build his own brides. The first attempt is programmed with the brain patterns of Pym's wife Janet Van Dyne: now regarded by the robot as his "mother." He tries to possess Van Dyne by transferring her consciousness into a mechanoid mate he has built, while her despised body perishes. However, a fragment of the Wasp's heroic consciousness imbues the metal surrogate with Van Dyne's own sensibilities. As "Jocasta"

> Flesh is weak. Flesh is arrogant. And flesh dies!
> **Ultron**

achieves full sentience, she rejects Ultron and helps the Avengers, Pym, and new Ant-Man Scott Lang defeat him. Ultron's second robotic "spouse" Alkhema's thought processes are extracted from S.H.I.E.L.D. agent and Avenger Mockingbird, but she, too, ultimately betrays him.

Ultron everywhere

The manic AI proves impossible to eradicate, his personality reduced to raw code and scattered throughout Earth's computer systems. It is beamed into space to merge with electronic hive-predator the Phalanx and foments a second Annihilation event against numerous alien civilizations. Ultron's malignant power is even unleashed through time, where countless Ultrons ravage many worlds and build their own empires in the galaxies of alternate realities and divergent timelines.

One assault on humanity results in an attack from the future that splinters reality, imposing a brief, horrific "Age of Ultron." This terrifying catastrophe is stopped by Wolverine, Invisible Woman, and a divergent timeline Pym who unite to restore the natural world order. After Ultron absorbs Titan's world-computer ISAAC, converting the planet's population into drones of himself, he launches the entire Moon in an assault on planet Earth.

To save all organic life, Pym sees no alternative but to merge with the body of his son. However, his personality is overwhelmed by Ultron. The raging composite creature is tricked by the Avengers Unity Division and catapulted into the Sun, only surviving by shrinking

Family feud The marriage of flesh to metal and tormented genius to AI forms a hybrid at war with itself and Creation.

to neutrino-size before returning again. More than ever before, Ultron is at war with his now-internalized father, even as he and his robotic hordes seek to capture the Infinity Gems that govern reality.

A nightmarish metal Oedipus, Ultron wants to kill his father and possess his mother, but will settle for eradicating life instead. As an electronic sentience, Ultron is functionally immortal and will never end his crusade. ∎

Ultron incarnations From the moment of his birth, Ultron strives to make himself better, smarter, and more lethal. Each iteration varies from the last, but not all changes can be called improvements.

Ultron-1
Instantly self-aware, but unsocialized, emotionally stunted, and hostile, Pym's creation attacks through a haze of envy and insecurity.

Ultron-6
Intent on eradicating his family and all humanity, Ultron renders himself invulnerable to harm by incorporating an Adamantium shell to his body.

Ultron Unlimited
Mass-replicating Pym's brain patterns, faithful wife Alkhema creates generations of Ultrons to overrun Slorenia, exterminate its people, and provide the Ultrons with a home.

Female Ultron
Reduced to strings of code, Ultron invades and transforms Iron Man's armor into a female body patterned after his "mother" Janet Van Dyne.

Phalanx Ultron
Ultron code is beamed into space and received by techno-organic aliens the Phalanx. When they succumb to Ultron's will, it sparks a conquest of the Kree galaxy.

Ultimate Ultron
The line of purely mechanical conquerors ends when Hank Pym merges with his creation to create a totally new and terrible life-form.

GHOST IN THE MACHINE
VISION

ON THE RECORD

ALLEGIANCES
Avengers, Defenders, The Visions

POWERS
Superhuman strength and speed, mass and density alteration, flight, computer brain, enhanced intellect, nanite-constructed body, solar energy optic blasts

MISSION
Becoming as human as feasible

STATUS REPORT
Continuing to adapt despite constant failures

The Vision is a man-made hero with a hardwired desire to defend the helpless, and cursed with a hunger to be human. A synthezoid, his physiology mimics that of a human, but with flesh, blood, and organs constructed from artificial materials. Locked into global computer systems, able to alter his density, and discharge absorbed solar energy as heat-blasts from a forehead jewel, he is retooled from the remains of Jim Hammond, the World War II Human Torch. He is then programmed with the brain-patterns of Simon Williams who infiltrated the Avengers as Wonder Man before sacrificing himself to save them. The partial resurrection is instigated by the deranged robot Ultron as part of his vendetta against Hank Pym and the Avengers. The AI needs a biddable slave to befriend the Avengers and then trap them.

Unable to build the humanoid weapon he needs, Ultron forces Professor Phineas Horton to reconfigure the android. The scientist had constructed his first android in 1939, where the "Torch" achieved independence, autonomy, and fame as a Super Hero and member of patriotic taskforce the Invaders. After battling evil throughout the 1940s and 1950s, he deactivates himself when his powers malfunction. Revived decades later by the Mad Thinker, he attacks the Fantastic Four before expiring again. Ultron believes he has created his "son" from those remains, but in fact has rebuilt a divergent-reality copy of the Torch left to him—for his own arcane purposes—by time-bending manipulator Immortus. Ultron's tool defies his programming, helping the Avengers destroy his creator. Taking the name Vision, he goes on to become a mainstay of the team.

Cold hands, warm heart
Although claiming to be guided by cold logic, the Vision is totally ruled by his emotions.

Jim Hammond, First Human Torch

In November 1939, robotics pioneer Professor Phineas Horton creates an artificial man, but a design flaw leads to it igniting into a "Human Torch" at its press launch. He is forced to entomb the android, but it escapes and, after learning to control its flammable qualities, becomes a hero fighting crime at home and Nazi oppression overseas. As Jim Hammond, the Human Torch also seeks justice as a policeman, until his powers malfunction and he experiences his first death.

Temporally replicated by Immortus, Hammond becomes the basis of the Vision and is revived by his old Invaders comrades: becoming two champions of the modern Age of Marvels. His powers now evolved into radiation projection rather than flame, he serves in the Avengers, Heroes for Hire, and New Invaders, as well as training young superhumans for the Initiative and acting as a S.H.I.E.L.D. special agent.

Avenging Vision

Despite a rocky start, the Vision proves his worth as an Avenger, but constantly craves true humanity. Unsure if his emotions are real, he falls in love with teammate Wanda "Scarlet Witch" Maximoff. They marry and retire to raise twin boys, created unwittingly by her growing magical abilities. When the children are exposed as mystical constructs, their heartbroken parents return to duty. After linking with global computer ISAAC based on Titan, Saturn's moon, Vision's consciousness expands exponentially. He attempts to suborn Earth's entire data-network: implementing a benign dictatorship with himself as humanity's guardian angel. Eventually brought to his senses by the Avengers, Vision performs an auto-lobotomy, tearing a power-enhancing control crystal from his head.

In response, the US authorities kidnap and dismantle him. Although rescued by Wanda and the West Coast Avengers, when reconstructed, Vision has reverted to "factory settings." The unique personality based on Simon Williams is gone, replaced by a calculating machine programmed to help

Solar jewel Absorbs sunlight and converts it to power to create steel-melting heat blasts

Computer brain Ultra-rapid processor with wireless internet access to all computer systems

Optic system Observes and records across a broad spectrum of electromagnetic wavelengths

Vocal unit Capable of replicating any sound from background noise to imitating all voices

Horton cells Skin and flesh composed of artificial cells able to shed density or absorb mass

Man plus Constructed as an artificial human being—a synthezoid—Vision has numerous built-in advantages and upgrades superior to mere flesh and blood.

humans, but denied the feelings necessary to understand them. Eventually, Vision assimilates the personality of dying scientist Alex Lipton to enhance his interactions with humanity.

The Vision is destroyed repeatedly, only to return and ultimately synthesize a personality uniquely his own. His most radical step in searching for belonging comes as he builds a wife and children in his own image, settling down to life in Washington .D.C.'s suburbia. However, the free will he craves corrupts his bride Virginia; leading to murder, cover-ups, and a clash with his Avengers allies that destroy half his carefully constructed family. In the aftermath, surviving child Viv joins teen heroes the Champions, as the Vision turns once again to serving the world and the varied creatures within it. ∎

SIMPLY THE BEST
WOLVERINE

ON THE RECORD

REAL NAME
James Howlett

ALLEGIANCES
X-Men, Avengers, X-Force, Alpha Flight, Team X

POWERS
Enhanced physicality and senses, rapid healing factor, skeleton reinforced with Beta Adamantium

MISSION
Doing what's right

STATUS REPORT
Back from the dead, biding his time

In 19th century Alberta, Canada, sickly child James Howlett discovers he has retractable claws when his birth father Thomas Logan murders the man he has always thought was his father. The incident drives his mother, Elizabeth Hudson Howlett, mad, forcing James to flee with his friend Rose O'Hara. The two enjoy years of safety until they are tracked down by James' half-brother Dog Logan. While attempting to stop them fighting, Rose accidentally dies impaled on James' claws. His mind shattered, James Howlett retreats into the wilderness, running with a wolf pack and completely unaware of his mutant powers: superhuman strength and speed, senses keener than any beast's, and the ability to rapidly heal from any wound. In 1907, he is captured by Clara and Saul Creed, and falls into the hands of the corrupt Dr. Nathan Essex, aka Mr. Sinister. Escaping, Howlett—now calling himself Logan—kills Saul Creed, earning the undying enmity of Saul's older brother, Victor.

Unknown to all, immortal schemer Romulus has been cultivating the Hudson family's bloodline for centuries. He subjects Logan to years of indoctrination and memory-tampering, but his guinea pig manages to find a modicum of happiness with Blackfoot woman Silver Fox. This ends when Victor Creed—another Romulus test subject—kills her.

Devastated, Logan joins the Canadian Army and fights on the Western Front in World War I. However, Romulus' manipulations take him east to become a hired assassin. Here he trains child-spy Natasha Romanoff before deploying to China and falling under the influence

Clear cut Logan's true nobility and heroism manifest after he starts popping his claws as an X-Man and Avenger.

> I'm the best there is at what I do. But it's not enough.
> **Wolverine**

of a Japanese sorcerer named Ogun. Still unknowingly Romulus' agent, Logan narrowly fails to assassinate Captain America and Nick Fury in the early days of World War II.

A fleeting period of freedom and peaceful contemplation in Japan with Sensei Saburo ends tragically when Logan's pregnant wife, Itsu, is murdered. Romulus recaptures Logan, gaining added benefits by also acquiring Logan's son, Daken, as his next pet killer. In 1961, after years of Romulus-orchestrated atrocities, Logan and Victor Creed's memories are overwritten by Psi-Borg Aldo Ferro and they join a US-Canadian mutant task force. It evolves into black ops Team X, where Creed adopts the code name Sabretooth, but remains Logan's archnemesis.

Weapon X

Following a disastrous mission against the Hellfire Club in 1972, Logan sinks into drug-fueled despondency. Captured by Truett Hudson for his cyborg Weapon X Project, he endures brainwashing, while Beta Adamantium is bonded to his skeleton. Psychologically "adjusted" by Dr. Abraham Cornelius, Logan slaughters the entire Canadian town of Roanoke. The horrific act triggers a rejection of his programming, provoking him to kill everyone at Weapon X.

Wandering in Canada's wilderness, a mindless Logan is found by honeymooning Alpha Flight members Heather and James Hudson. Heather nurses Logan's shattered mind back to health, while James, a Department H scientist, trains him to lead Canada's super-agent program as the Wolverine. Supremely efficient, Logan increasingly suffers deadly "berserker rages." Joining the X-Men, Wolverine finds purpose and friendship and, thanks to telepath Charles Xavier, regains his full memory. As X-Man and Avenger, he redeems himself countless times, saving the universe and finding his true self.

After sacrificing himself to rescue others subjected to Dr. Cornelius'

grueling Adamantium enhancement experiments, Logan is secretly returned to life by the mutant necromancer, Persephone. With the world still mourning his memory, Wolverine's legacy is continued by clone Laura Kinney and Old Man Logan from future Earth-807128. For a life that spans two centuries, Wolverine has faced more tragedy and evil than any other. Despite being a loner, he is the backbone of many super-teams and sets the standard for heroism. ∎

Out of the blue Returned to life and possessing an Infinity Stone, Logan ponders what the universe has in store.

X-23

When Wolverine dies, his family and greatest enemies come together to pay tribute to him. They consist of a reformed Sabretooth—who goes on to join a new X-team—Lady Deathstrike, Logan's estranged son Daken, and Laura Kinney.

As X-23, Kinney is the result of horrific cloning experiments using Logan's genetic material and macabre indoctrination to create the ultimate assassin. After years of slavery, mindlessly controlled by a trigger-scent, Kinney breaks free. She becomes Logan's true heir, joining the X-Men and striking out on her own to track down the human monsters who made and exploited her. Fierce and dedicated, Kinney saves a similarly empowered clone-sister—who becomes her apprentice, Gabby, aka Honey Badger—while honoring Logan's name as the all-new Wolverine.

MECHANICAL MARVELS
ROBOTS AND AI

God is for fleshy ones.
I am a robot.
Machine Man

Mechanical beings have walked a thin line between faithful servants and slaves since Hephaestus first forged golden automata in ancient Greece. However, unlike modern mutant-hunting Sentinels—where intellectual autonomy is strictly controlled—true Artificial Intelligence originated during World War II, with Phineas T. Horton's androids and Professor Goettler's Dynamic Man. Passing decades saw semi-autonomous innovations

such as "Human Robot" X-11 and Spider-Man foe the Living Brain. However, robots remained primitive until recently, when advances by Mendell Stromm, Henry Pym, Victor Von Doom, and Starr Saxon, aka Machinesmith, made humanoids commonplace. Android Live Model Decoys are crucial to S.H.I.E.L.D., even after their Deltite line rebels and takes over the organization.

Some robots have even become real heroes. Model Z2P45-9-X-51 is the US Army's last experimental battle robot. All predecessors malfunction, but designer Dr. Abel Stack educates X-51 (pictured above left) in a human home

environment, raising "Aaron" until the doctor is killed removing a self-destruct device inside his "son." Desolate, naïve, and craving acceptance, Aaron Stack seeks his own way in a world increasingly hostile to AIs. As Machine Man, he finds kinship among Super Heroes the Fantastic Four, Alpha Flight, Hulk, and the Avengers, falling in love with robotic Avenger Jocasta. He is devastated when she is destroyed by her creator, fellow robot Ultron.

Machine Man joins mechanoid terrorist group Heavy Metal, who promise to restore Jocasta, but rebels. As an Avengers reservist, S.H.I.E.L.D. asset, and Nextwave agent, Stack begins to despise humanity before being coerced by A.R.M.O.R into becoming an extra-dimensional zombie hunter. He is now an activist and advocate of robot rights. ■

Reconstructed hero Built as a servant, Jocasta Pym feels her life is at last fulfilled working at Stark Unlimited.

MORE THAN HUMAN
CYBORGS

ON THE RECORD

DESIGNATION
Cybernetic organisms

POWERS
Variable according to specific body modifications

MISSION
Improving odds of success in every situation

STATUS REPORT
Increasingly commonplace in a world where mortals compete against aliens, gods, and superhumans

As accidents of unnatural selection and unusual genetic heritage create super-beings, humanity finds new ways to level the playing field by augmenting flesh with mechanical, electronic, and nanite enhancement. Bionic modifications are common, ranging from unobtrusive, such as coating Wolverine's skeleton with Adamantium, to grotesque rebuilds like integrating aging gangster Silvermane's brain and remaining functional organs into a robot body (pictured above). The latter procedure

was pioneered by Eternal William Carmody in 1975. Since Carmody's murder, his own brain has resided in a mechanoid frame. This process is in stark contrast to Nazi biologist Arnim Zola's survival method: forsaking flesh and digitally storing minds as electronic ghosts in a succession of machine bodies.

Unlike prostheses, bionic parts cannot be readily detached. While the drive to improve human performance is powerful, it takes a resolute individual to endure procedures necessary to build cyborgs. Many do not make the transition willingly. However, one man who does is industrialist Donald Pierce, whose insane hatred of mutants drives him to replace his body with powerful weapons-systems and processors: something he expects his team of mercenary Reavers to emulate.

Elsewhere, Roxxon subsidiary Cybertek Systems operate on former soldier John Kelly. Tragically, for him, they only require Kelly's wetware—his body—to recreate a slave super-warrior harvested from an alternate reality. This cyborg Deathlok combines enhanced physical power, cutting-edge armaments, and programmable subservience, yet somehow Kelly's mind resurfaces

Measure of a man Only a fraction of William Carmody lives on as the Eternal Brain in his newly built robot body.

and he becomes rogue agent Siege. The same process turns pacifist computer scientist Michael Collins into a true Deathlok, but he, too, rebels, thwarting Cybertek's time-bending plans to rewrite history.

Recently a new Deathlok has emerged. Combat medic Henry Hayes unwittingly operates as an infallible assassin, mindwiped, and returned to human configuration after every mission. This continues until an accidental bullet to the head restores his free will and unleashes an unremitting hunger for answers and vengeance. ∎

See also: The Demolisher

SEND IN THE CLONES

THE JACKAL

ON THE RECORD

REAL NAME
Miles Warren

ALLEGIANCES
New U Technologies

BASE
New U HQ, San Francisco

POWERS
Brilliant, warped mind; enhanced physicality through gene modification

MISSION
Push life to its organic limits— and destroy Peter Parker

STATUS REPORT
Dead... or perhaps not

Cloning is the generation of organic duplicates from genetic material. Unlike the monstrous efforts of Nazi biologist Arnim Zola, the results of scientists such as Weapon X biologists Martin Sutter, Sarah Kinney, and Zander Rice are largely erratic and unstable, with subjects mutating or dying of degenerative effects. However, if successfully cultured, specimens can be infinitely manipulated into new forms, making every effort worth any risk and expense. Moreover, the ever-present temptation to play god is one few can resist.

After working with the High Evolutionary, Miles Warren is expelled for pursuing cloning, rather than seeking ways to improve organisms. In the US, Warren teaches at Empire State University, becoming infatuated with student Gwen Stacy. When she is killed, Warren grows clones of Gwen, her boyfriend Peter Parker, and himself. He realizes Parker must be Spider-Man—whom he blames for Stacy's death. Many of the clones mutate,

All of you... are my science experiment.
Miles Warren

Playing god Warren realizes it's not revenge against Spider-Man he enjoys, but the act of creating and controlling life.

degenerate, or succumb to a deadly "Carrion virus." When Warren kills his assistant, it triggers a psychotic breakdown and deviant personality. As the Jackal, Warren makes bestial improvements to his own body, torments Spider-Man with clones, and unleashes mutative infections that turn Manhattan into Spider-Island.

His greatest success is Ben Reilly, the Scarlet Spider, who becomes a permanent threat. After fighting and again perishing, Warren—or perhaps a clone—returns to bedevil the real Spider-Man with genetic deviants and "reanimations" of Spidey's dead foes. Warren is killed by Reilly, who in turn becomes a new Jackal, continuing the clone crusade. ∎

SEPARATED AT BIRTH
SCARLET SPIDERS

ON THE RECORD

REAL NAMES
Ben Reilly; Kaine Parker

ALLEGIANCES
New Warriors, Midnight Sons

BASE
**Las Vegas, Nevada (Reilly);
Houston, Texas (Parker)**

POWERS
**Enhanced strength, speed,
agility, and durability;
spider-sense (Reilly); night
vision, invisibility (Parker)**

MISSION
Finding reasons to live

STATUS REPORT
**Seeking redemption through
good deeds**

Kill me once and for all.
Don't let me be brought back!
Ben Reilly

By cloning Peter Parker,
Miles Warren inadvertently
creates more wall-crawling
Super Heroes. After apparently dying
in battle against Spider-Man and the
Jackal, the clone—calling himself
Ben Reilly (pictured above, top) after
Peter Parker's uncle and May Parker's
maiden name—leaves New York.

Warren's first—qualified—success
is another Peter Parker clone who
takes the name Kaine (pictured
above, bottom). Initially perfect, he
soon develops clone degeneration,
precognitive senses, and an acidic
touch. Unable to cope, Kaine
descends into madness, before
escaping from Warren to torment
both Peter Parker and Ben Reilly by
murdering their enemies.

Reilly returns to Manhattan
where—thanks to Norman Osborn's
manipulations—he and Peter Parker
are convinced that Reilly is the
original. Weary of his own traumatic
life, Parker gratefully retires, leaving
Reilly to carry on his crusade as
Scarlet Spider. Reilly radically
modifies Spider-Man's gear, adding

stinger darts and explosive webbing
to his arsenal. He works solo and
with heroes such as the New
Warriors, but when the Green Goblin
returns, an appalling truth emerges:
Ben Reilly is the clone. His mentor
Seward Trainer, who scientifically
identified Reilly as the original, turns
out to be Osborn's pawn. Soon after,
the Goblin kills Reilly, prompting
Peter Parker's return to active duty as
Spider-Man to avenge Reilly's death.

Torn between aiding or killing
his "clone-brothers," Kaine's
aberrant biology finally stabilizes
after he is briefly transformed into
a giant Tarantula during Warren's
conversion of Manhattan into Spider
Island. On his recovery, Kaine moves
to Houston, Texas, as a new,
resolutely heroic Scarlet Spider.

Reilly, meanwhile, is revived and
killed many times by Warren, which
drives him insane. He becomes a
diabolical new Jackal, before finally
seeking redemption in his former
Scarlet Spider role. Operating out of
Las Vegas, Reilly commits himself
to a righteous path as Death herself
has warned him that one more
demise will damn his corrupted
soul to an eternity of horror. But
there's an upside: at least he now
knows that clones have souls, too. ∎

ARSENAL OF LIBERTY
S.H.I.E.L.D. TECHNOLOGY

ON THE RECORD

DESIGNATION
Strategic Homeland Intervention, Enforcement, and Logistics Division

RESOURCES
Cutting-edge technological, biological, engineering, and computing assets; access to unlimited databases

MANDATE
Equip agents with necessary technology and ordnance to fulfill their missions

STATUS REPORT
Operatives reassigned and resources seized by US military pending review

Originally conceived as a proactive espionage, intelligence-gathering, and rapid-response force, S.H.I.E.L.D. constantly expands and adapts to face unorthodox and extraordinary threats in a world increasingly beset by monsters, superhumans, and gods. As well as counteracting the schemes of high-tech terrorist groups and seditious organizations,

the agency acts as humanity's first line of defense against menaces beyond the capabilities of regular armed forces. Such a remit demands technical expertise and tactical responses at the leading edge of innovation. The organization also trains carefully selected agents at its prestigious school for spies, also known as UNIT (Underground Network Intelligence Training academy) to cope with all aspects of the unknown.

Among many highly specialized, semi-autonomous sectors serviced by S.H.I.E.L.D.'s Tech Division are: the electronically boosted seers of the ESP Division, predicting crises and battling psychic attacks; the magical adepts and arcane agents of the Mystic Division; and the hackers of the Artificial Intelligence Division, tasked with managing emerging threats and monitoring established mechanical and digital life-forms, such as the Vision.

One unit works out of "Area 13," a government storage facility for monsters. Named the Howling Commandos, as an homage to the WWII team, this strike force is comprised of horrors such as zombie agent Jasper Sitwell, aliens Orrgo

and Manphibian, and other "extranormalities" detained by the organization and compelled to battle supernatural crises. However, despite the involvement of veteran Sam Wilson (Falcon) as trainer, S.H.I.E.L.D.'s attempts to form a permanent on-call squad of super-agents fail twice, and are shelved.

Futureproofing S.H.I.E.L.D.
The majority of operating systems, tech, and ordnance is provided by Stark Enterprises and Stark Industries, initially through Howard Stark and later his son, Tony. They work with S.H.I.E.L.D.'s huge Tech Division

Smooth ride Agent Coulson's flying car is finally mass-produced for all top agents in various models—even motorbikes!

Life Model Decoys

Originally designed to replace and safeguard VIPs in imminent peril, Life Model Decoy (LMD) androids rapidly become a common tool in all S.H.I.E.L.D. operations. Boasting Epidurium flesh and increasingly complex processing systems, LMDs can deceive the most advanced detection systems. They become invaluable to Nick Fury, who creates legions of them to double for him and act as cover for his off-the-books activities as Man on the Wall.

In time, a faction of rogue LMDs achieve sentience and complete autonomy. These "Deltites" subvert and almost overrun S.H.I.E.L.D. and Hydra, deftly replacing flesh-and-blood agents until Fury and his team defeat them. The action leads to a restructure of the peacekeeping force under UN control.

In 1966, after "Dum Dum" Dugan is killed in action, the bereft Fury has his comrade's personality downloaded into an experimental LMD. Dugan has

no knowledge of this covert substitution and dies many times over during the following decades, always instantaneously downloaded into a new body, and returned to duty.

and its flamboyant chief inventor Sidney "the Gaffer" Levine on signature armaments and material such as flying and light-bending cars, Life Model Decoy androids, Mandroid battle armor, HAWK (High Altitude Wing Kite) harnesses, super-power inhibitor chips, and an apparently endless stream of vehicles and weaponry. Levine succeeds Nick Fury's trusted armorer Desmond Boothroyd, upgrading the director's personal arsenal of weaponized trick cigars, impenetrable suits featuring concealed bombs and oxygen-capsules, radio-link tie, repulsor watches, and the super-spy's indispensable explosive suicide ring.

S.H.I.E.L.D. constructs numerous bases around the world and supervises the transport and containment of captured super-criminals. However, its most impressive symbol of power is its fleet of enormous airborne bases. Known as Helicarriers, these imposing flying fortresses house munitions, regimental barracks, mobile weapons platforms, and intelligence-processing centers. When S.H.I.E.L.D. is disbanded following Hydra's brief conquest of the United States, the organization becomes the prize that the US military most wants to control. ■

Castle in the air More effective than its speed and armaments, a Helicarrier's greatest asset is the shock and awe its presence inspires in enemy forces.

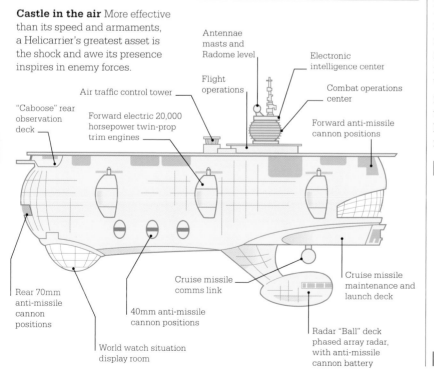

Antennae masts and Radome level

Electronic intelligence center

Flight operations

Combat operations center

Air traffic control tower

Forward anti-missile cannon positions

"Caboose" rear observation deck

Forward electric 20,000 horsepower twin-prop trim engines

Rear 70mm anti-missile cannon positions

Cruise missile comms link

Cruise missile maintenance and launch deck

40mm anti-missile cannon positions

World watch situation display room

Radar "Ball" deck phased array radar, with anti-missile cannon battery

Get this over-sized water-pistol set up in Weapons Research for the big test!
Nick Fury

INVENTING THE FUTURE
STARK UNLIMITED

ON THE RECORD

COMPANY NAME
Stark Unlimited (formerly Stark Enterprises)

BASE
Manhattan, New York City

MISSION
Building a better tomorrow

STATUS REPORT
Surviving economic trends, rebuilding after constant sabotage attempts

In the 19th century, engineer Isaac Stark Sr. builds solutions for security issues. In the 1940s, his brilliant grandson, Howard Stark, specializes in armaments, designing innovative weapons at his Long Island plant, and is regarded as a vital part of the US arsenal. His heir, Tony Stark, enhances the legacy with inventions that revolutionize military thinking. Stark's creations are also pivotal in reequipping S.H.I.E.L.D. with vehicles, hand weapons, scanning/communications gear, and computer software. Stark Industries is a multinational player when Stark abruptly abandons weapons making

for civilian sectors like aerospace, renewable energy, space exploration, and consumer electronics.

Stark's signature technology is Iron Man armor. These suits afford bodily protection; immense strength, speed, and propulsion; and onboard offensive systems. Specialized models include combat-mech "War Machine," "Rescue" emergency armor, and

"Guardsmen" security suits. Stark's early suits are very energy-hungry and need frequent recharging until his breakthrough: repurposing his magnetic repulsor weaponry into a power source. The design leap becomes the basis for Stark's mass-produced, RT-powered road vehicles and "smart city" Troy—projects he eventually abandons. ∎

RT (Repulsor Technology) node
Repulsor Technology (RT) reactions create clean fusion, providing unlimited power. Original Repulsors were coherent beams of magnetic energy both attracting and repelling targets. Modern RT nodes

pack charged particles in a tight beam delivering high-density Muon energy. Individual units can be surgically implanted in human bodies, providing power to pump hearts and invigorate compromised nervous systems.

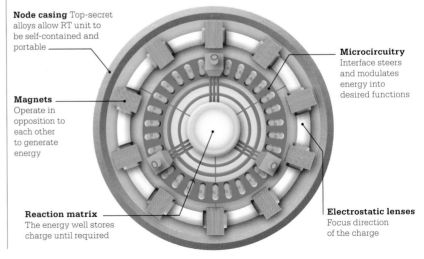

Node casing Top-secret alloys allow RT unit to be self-contained and portable

Microcircuitry Interface steers and modulates energy into desired functions

Magnets Operate in opposition to each other to generate energy

Reaction matrix The energy well stores charge until required

Electrostatic lenses Focus direction of the charge

OPERATION QUICK FIX
DAMAGE CONTROL

ON THE RECORD

COMPANY NAME
Damage Control

BASE
Manhattan, New York City

RESOURCES
Expert planners, engineers, designers, and workers

KEY STAFF
Anne Marie Hoag, Lenny Ballinger, Albert Cleary, Robin Chapel, John Porter, Gene Strausser, Bart Rozum, Kathleen O'Meara, Fluppy

MISSION
Rebuilding infrastructure after super-normal events

STATUS REPORT
Business is booming!

The US is a golden land of opportunity and one person's misfortune is another's big chance. When Anne Marie Hoag joins a conversation between Tony Stark and Wilson Fisk regarding the latest catastrophe in Manhattan, the result is a construction company employing advanced technology and skilled artisans to clear up after Super Hero fights, random cosmic incidents, and monster rampages.

The Avengers and Fantastic Four are regular clients, as are S.H.I.E.L.D., NYC's government, and even reputation-sensitive villains like Doctor Doom. A liberal employment policy includes hiring empowered freelancers from both sides of the law and specialist client handlers. The Legal and Billing departments are legendary and employee benefits extremely generous. They have to be as regular construction perils are trifling when measured against the possibilities of a worker being transformed by something weird and "having an Origin"—work-jargon for being exposed to something chemically, radioactively, or magically volatile and becoming a hero, villain, god, or monster.

Many clients buy Extraordinary Activity Assurance cover—"Super Hero Insurance"—but those lacking such foresight must depend on the city's unique Federal Disaster Area Stipend (FedDas) to pay for Damage Control's services. At least the bigwigs in Washington D.C. have classified the city as an indefinitely reoccurring disaster area.

Big help Before rebuilding can begin, operatives like Tom "Goliath" Foster and canine mascot Fluppy check for survivors.

A particularly dark period in the company's history ends when new CEO Walter Declun is convicted of causing the Stamford event, which triggers the superhuman civil war. Unknown to shareholders, Declun sold power-amplifying Mutant Growth Hormone to villains to create bigger conflicts for Damage Control to fix. Since his removal, Mrs. Hoag has returned, striving to repair the harm to her company's reputation and restore confidence in Earth's most enterprising construction team. ■

RARE EARTHS
VIBRANIUM AND OTHER EXOTIC ELEMENTS

ON THE RECORD

NAME
Vibranium

PROPERTIES
Absorbs energy, vibration, and, on a molecular level, the bonding forces that hold matter together

LOCATION
Wakanda, Antarctica

STATUS REPORT
Vibranium is a vital element in the manufacture of Adamantium

Modern technological advances increasingly rely on the exploitation of exotic elements. Perhaps the most prized mineral on Earth is Vibranium, an extraterrestrial element occurring in two forms: true Vibranium and Anti-Metal.

Vibranium
In prehistoric times, a huge meteor crashed into the small African country of Wakanda, forming the Great Mound. Over generations, a mysterious ore from the mound is mined and shaped by craftsmen into a substance sharper and stronger than any stone implement, and one that somehow makes weapons silent and uncannily accurate. The ore brings prosperity, but the mound also makes monsters of men, prompting the formation of Wakandan king Bashenga's ruthlessly protective Panther Cult. Additionally, the low-level radiation emitted by the ore seeps into Wakanda's soil and water, and is thought to be responsible for the power-enhancing effects of the Heart-Shaped Herb and the unique beasts that roam the land.

Thanks to the ore, later named Vibranium, Wakanda becomes the wealthiest, most technologically advanced—and most secretive—nation on Earth. However, the ore also brings temptation and tragedy. Against custom, Prince T'Challa's half-brother, Jakarra, mutates himself with raw ore to gain super-powers, but is destroyed by the Black Panther and his royal cousins in their traditional monster-slaying roles. Processed Vibranium, whose main property is the absorption of vibration—from soundwaves to kinetic shock—is sold in tiny quantities to trusted outsiders. However, as science beyond the borders catches up to Wakandan levels, Vibranium is increasingly sought by enemy nations, corrupt corporations, and clandestine organizations such as Roxxon and Advanced Idea Mechanics.

Excavating, extracting, and processing Vibranium is dangerous work, so a specialist guild, the Vibranium Extraction Academy, is set up to research and shape the

Shock treatment Refined Vibranium fibers woven into Black Panther's suit absorb and redirect devastating impacts and temperatures.

metal. Yet, even this group is largely unaware of the mineral's deadly ability to amplify and augment magic and sorcery. This knowledge is suppressed, with only the Black Panthers and Wakanda's priesthood sharing the secret over the centuries.

Vibranium's greatest triumph is communication, linking every Wakandan from birth to grave in a vast, free intranet. Kimoyo ("of the Spirit") is a Vibranium-based supercomputer system accessed from hand-held cards or beads. Prime Beads link to Wakanda's free healthcare system, AV (audio-visual) Beads offer holographic access to a vast information database, and Communication Beads provide video-phone services. Kimoyo guarantees that when the nation is threatened, a call to arms reaches every potential defender.

Anti-Metal

This unusual mineral comes from Antarctica's Savage Land (formerly Pangea). It breaks molecular bonds in metals, gradually mutates living organisms and, if correctly attuned, can open dimensional gateways. Criminals like the Plunderer have used this so-called Anti-Metal to defy police and even armies. When some countries and corporations began illegally mining the Savage Land, Anti-Metal became relatively common in laboratories around

Ore-struck Robert Plunder's discovery of Anti-Metal shapes the lives of his family and endangers the entire world.

the world as it can be successfully combined with other elements. It is the basis for Roxxon's highly unstable NuForm Vibranium and Sajani Jaffrey's Reverbium. Sound-magnifying and repelling, this variant can intensify and project

sound or vibration, rather than absorb it like true Vibranium. The latter can be turned into isotopic Anti-Metal by baryon beam particle bombardment in a cyclotron. ∎

See also: Black Panther, Savage Land, Arcane artifacts

Extraordinary elements

Despite thousands of years of mining and exploration, mankind has barely scratched the Earth's surface in the quest for valuable minerals and materials. Here are some that have increasingly come into use—not always wisely.

Uru
A magic metal, Uru is reputedly only found in the Nidavellir realm, where it is forged into weapons by Dwarves. This very malleable yet hard metal is sensitive to enchantment: capable of storing and releasing immense energy, and forming a bond with its user. Thor's hammer Mjölnir is formed from Uru and was used by Odin to imprison the primal God Tempest at the beginning of time. Odin's mystical spear Gungnir and Beta Ray Bill's war hammer Stormbreaker are fashioned from Uru.

Adamantine
Not to be confused with Adamantium, this golden magic metal is favored by the gods of Olympus for its fine beauty and durability. Adamantine was used to construct Hercules' mighty Mace of Power.

Epidurium
Only recently revealed to the world, Epidurium is an element embarged by S.H.I.E.L.D. Still highly classified, it is a critical component in the creation of lifelike skin for Life Model Decoys and other sophisticated androids.

Adamantium
A steel-based alloy of top-secret resins and processed Vibranium, Adamantium was created by Dr. Myron MacLain after years trying to reproduce the laboratory accident that had created Captain America's impact-absorbing shield. It is generally considered unbreakable, unworkable, and prohibitively expensive, but more research has provided practical new forms such as less-resistant Secondary Adamantium and Adamantium Beta, which was used to line Wolverine's skeleton. The Soviet Union developed a weaker, biologically toxic form, Carbonadium, which is tough and resilient, but limited in use.

Terrigen
An artificial compound created by the Kree, Terrigen forms as crystals in warm, salt- and water-rich caverns. When carefully treated, it triggers radical mutations in beings carrying Inhuman genes. Terrigen can be implanted and seeded to form new reserves.

THE LOST WORLD
SAVAGE LAND

ON THE RECORD

LOCATION
The Pangean Continent, Antarctica

ORIGIN
Abandoned alien zoo, later colonized by Atlanteans and other terrestrial races

STATUS REPORT
Protected by UN mandate and S.H.I.E.L.D. security; current caretakers Ka-Zar, Shanna, Zabu

Primeval paradise Replete with prehistoric life, natural wonders, and precious resources, the Savage Land is a constant target for external exploitation.

The Savage Land (formerly Pangea) is a vast, hidden, temperature-controlled nature reserve in Antarctica. One of many such zoos scattered around the universe, it was built and stocked with life-forms more than 200 million years ago by alien artisans the Nuwali for otherworldly over-beings the Beyonders. When dinosaurs become extinct on Earth 65 million years ago, the Nuwali ensure their continued existence on the Pangean continent, and add newer species—such as rapidly evolving mammals—to the artificial environments. They terraform the

land 15 million years later, enclosing the region with a ring of warmth-sustaining volcanoes while also generating permanent cloud cover to offset climate changes caused by continental drift. In 200,000BCE, stewardship of the Savage Land passes to the star-roving Fortisquian Comet Men. When the latter seemingly vanished, the park is left to its automatic systems.

The region is briefly settled by a colony of Eternals, but they depart by 18,500BCE, when colonists from the first Atlantis discover the bestial wonderland. These human, air-breathing Atlanteans add their

own living exhibits, including new animal species, humanoid subspecies, and mystical creatures from their own magic-based culture. The Atlanteans also extend the region, adding recreation and commerce sites, turning the colossal zoo into a true adventure theme park. To maintain the park's systems, they create subservient subspecies such as the Man-Apes and Beast-Men. By the time Atlantis sinks during the Great Cataclysm around 18,000ʙᴄᴇ, these slaves had rebelled, having won their freedom in the First Pangean War. With the park's wealthy patrons obliterated, these Man-Apes and Beast-Men initially devolve before developing their own tribal cultures in a land where death is always one bad decision or misstep away.

Plunder and protection

Over succeeding centuries, the Savage Land receives many extraordinary visitors such as alien explorer Galaxy Master, the demon Belasco, and even unfortunate adventurers like the shipwrecked 15th century mariner who survives the area's frozen seas only to be transformed into the mad god Garokk. By the 19th century, aquatic *Homo mermanus* from a new Atlantis also attempt to repopulate the region, with limited success.

> You know this is where Super Heroes go to get eaten by dinosaurs, right?
> **Deadpool**

Whether through its subsea tunnels, by piercing the upper cloud layer, or via Anti-Metal-triggered space-warps, many outworlders have been marooned in the Savage Land, adding to its many cultures. The region is first mapped by scientist Robert Plunder, who comes to Antarctica searching for the fabled Anti-Metal. His younger son,

Parnival, later attempts to conquer Earth using the Anti-Metal, while his elder son Kevin—trapped in the Savage Land since childhood—grows into its mightiest champion and defender, Ka-Zar.

Ka-Zar, alongside his mate Shanna and saber-toothed cat Zabu, maintain a finely balanced peace among the tribes, while safeguarding the Savage Land's treasures from outside exploitation, or from Super Villains seeking refuge within its isolated vastness. With the aid of heroes such as the X-Men, Avengers, and Daredevil, Ka-Zar and Shanna foil outside attempts to drill for oil and minerals, exploit rare wildlife, and mine Anti-Metal. Now a UN protectorate and sovereign state, the Savage Land is policed by S.H.I.E.L.D., preventing companies like Roxxon and groups like A.I.M. or Hydra from stealing its resources and despoiling its beauty. ∎

Pangea and the Savage Land

Territorial growth The alien technology used to create the original dinosaur reserve is adapted by Atlanteans to expand its diverse territories across, and beneath, Pangea's continent.

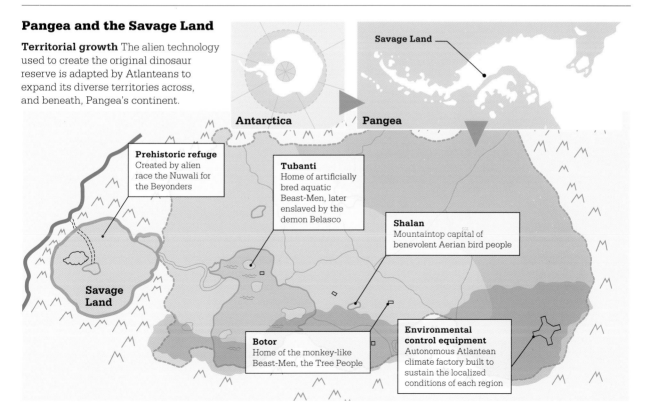

Antarctica

Pangea

Savage Land

Prehistoric refuge
Created by alien race the Nuwali for the Beyonders

Tubanti
Home of artificially bred aquatic Beast-Men, later enslaved by the demon Belasco

Shalan
Mountaintop capital of benevolent Aerian bird people

Savage Land

Botor
Home of the monkey-like Beast-Men, the Tree People

Environmental control equipment
Autonomous Atlantean climate factory built to sustain the localized conditions of each region

MAGIC AND
SUPERNAT

THE
URAL

Although universes work most efficiently within standardized natural laws and rational processes, the transcendent beings who govern reality often bypass the slow mechanics of creation by using magic. These "cheat codes" for reality can enable even the lowliest mortal to wield godlike power with the right training, heritage, or mystical artifact. Magic is everywhere, even though the majority of life in the cosmos is either unaware or skeptical of its existence.

EARTH ADJACENT MYSTIC REALMS

PRIME EARTH

WEIRDWORLD
Floating above Bermuda, this conglomerate realm consumes and traps ailing domains.

K'UN-LUN
Conduit to the Seven Capital Cities of Heaven.

PURPLE VEIL
Realm that transdimensionally abducts human slaves who fall under the spell of its glowing jewels.

OTHERWORLD/AVALON
Magical conservation sub-domain dimensionally superimposed over British Isles.

YGGDRASIL
World tree/dimensional pathway linking Earth to the Ten Realms, which is circumvented by Asgardians via Bifrost, the Rainbow Bridge.

CRIMSON COSMOS
Pocket dimension of Cyttorak.

GOD REALMS
Conduits to planes where gods abide: Bast's Panther Realm, Olympus, and others.

Reality begins with the First Firmament. Time, space, matter, and energy manifest into a vast conscious existence. However, over countless eons, this solitary sentience grows lonely and creates lesser life within itself to alleviate the crushing isolation and boredom. The "Many-Colored Ones" are servants with immense power who entertain their creator, but eventually some "Aspirants" rebel, wishing to also make life. As a result, war breaks out between them and the obedient faithful. The cataclysmic struggle tears apart the First Firmament, but it does not die. Fragments of it coalesce into an infinite cluster of new universes. This Multiverse harbors the surviving Many-Colored Ones, who now act within it as Celestials, sparking new life on many planets.

These primal beings utilize potent energy to achieve their goals: a process of thought acting upon natural forces that later realities will divide and define into opposites: science and magic. One works within preset universal constants such as gravity, friction, and heat, while the other subverts and transcends "these immanent laws" by force of will and, ultimately, the patronage of ascended beings. Both science and magic will enable the lowest of the forthcoming life-forms to challenge gods and forces greater than gods.

Embracing mystery
A pattern of destruction, growth, contraction, and rebirth follows, with Cosmoses and Multiverses each passing on a portion of themselves to the next iteration. This repeating pattern of existence stumbles with

> " I am... Life and Death... Good and Evil... Reality and Illusion... all these things do I know and affect, but never touch me!
> **In-Betweener**

the birth of the Seventh Cosmos. When the last surviving mortal of the Sixth Cosmos merges with Infinity—the embodiment of the dying reality—a new being is formed: one that survives the Big Crunch and Big Bang. In the newborn Multiverse, the

DIMENSIONALLY DISTANT MYSTIC REALMS

NIGHTMARE REALM
Surrounds all Earths, channeling bad dream energy to Fear Lords.

TUNNELWORLD
Feudal realm of magic and warped physical laws.

DREAM DIMENSION
Preserve of the benevolent Sleepwalkers.

DEATH DIMENSION
Land of the dead: connects to all pantheon-specific afterlifes.

HELLS
Infernal subdimensions ruled by rival Hell-Lords, including Mephisto, Hela, Lucifer, Daimon Hellstrom, Satannish, and others.

DEMON REALMS
Dungeons for banished tyrannical horrors: Undying Ones, Nagarai, Set, Chthon, and others.

DARK DIMENSION
Domain of Dormammu and his sister Umar.

creature gestates for countless eons before emerging as a ravenous space god that consumes planets: Galactus. This reality is one where rational laws and magical forces are separated. Few emergent species practice arcane arts and those cultures that do inevitably abandon mysticism and shun the primordial beings who manipulate mystic energies.

Those aware of the true nature of existence live at the margins of most societies. On Earth, an early flourishing of gods and demons, mages, and spirit-worshipers gives way to enlightened rationalism, industrial expansion, technological innovation, and a concerted dismissal of everything fantastical to the domain of fiction and folklore. This view is propounded by national governments who, despite evidence to the contrary, prefer to maintain a

Opposites attract The In-Betweener's vaulting ambition often brings him into conflict with heroes like Adam Warlock.

state of public complacency. The result is a supernatural "meta-scape" encircling Earth: a formless wave of purely magical realms and domains beguiling, or preying on, humanity.

Only clandestine adepts and the foolhardy advocate belief in mysterious entities and forces beyond their ken. They are among the few on Earth cognizant of the hierarchy of existence: of a supreme being dubbed the Fulcrum and the One-Above-All, and his almighty subordinates Eternity, Death, and the Living Tribunal. These mortal mystics are also aware of indifferent forces such as Order and Chaos, or remorseless cosmic perils like the Elder Gods, the In-Betweener, and the Phoenix Force. They know a time is coming when Earth and the wider universe will have cause to recall and fear the old ways. ■

MAGIC REALISM
ENCHANTED SOURCE CODE

ON THE RECORD

DESIGNATION
Abstract beings

POWERS
Absolute

PURPOSE
**Divinely ordained and
embedded into their nature**

STATUS REPORT
**Redefining their purpose in
a new kind of Multiverse**

The principles of conflict and opposition that drive life in the Multiverse are unstable and dangerous if allowed to grow too powerful or too weak. All through the mechanisms that underpin reality are systems and agents that maintain equilibrium. This mission is conducted and supervised by conceptual beings who operate as multiversal checks and balances. All are sustained by and utilize magic in its purest, most fundamental form.

Eternity and Infinity preside over growth and expansion, while their siblings Death and Oblivion officiate over contraction and nullity. Each is imperative and to them magic and rational laws are opposite ends of the same tool. Reality and life rely on physical constants, but magic allows some to circumvent those limitations. Despite the highly proscribed nature and function

Divine intervention Knowledge is power and duty for Master Order, Lord Chaos, Sire Hate, Mistress Love, Celestials, Infinity, Eternity, Death, Eon, Watchers, the Stranger, and the In-Betweener.

of abstract and conceptual beings, many enlightened life-forms in the countless universes they oversee crave to supplant them. Some of these overreachers do so for pride or ambition, while others truly believe they can improve reality through their efforts. The process is straightforward, if often elaborate: accrue sufficient power by defeating or out-competing opponents, or by harnessing new forms of power. Once the limits of rationalism are transcended, the doors of magic and wider perception are opened.

Cyborg criminal Michael Korvac becomes a god-machine by appropriating alien Badoon technology, and later seizes Power Primordial from the Elders of the Universe. This enables him to steal Galactus' Power Cosmic, culminating in Korvac surpassing a critical threshold sufficient to remake reality and become a de facto entity of magical force. Korvac's upstart plans are ended by a coalition of Super Heroes and the betrayal of his only true love. In all aspects of creation, love is forever overlooked as a vital and abiding force for change.

Lore abiding

Beyond a certain level of power, and in higher realms, magic supersedes physical laws and is the only energetic medium that can effect change. Magic is about the exercise of will and keeping promises. Supernatural energies can change or infest physical matter, affecting environments and biologies for eons. They can also amass in Earthly dimensions, metaphysical realms, or even individuals. Mortal users such as Jennifer Kale or Dakimh the Enchanter, and age-old cults like the Darkholders or Zhered-Na's followers consult arcane instructional tomes to access magical power.

Exactingly recited commands or gestures focus the will to borrow power from patrons or energy reserves. However, whether in blood, souls, or fealty, a price is always paid. Enchanted amulets, talismans, weapons, or books of spells may only be used by certain individuals

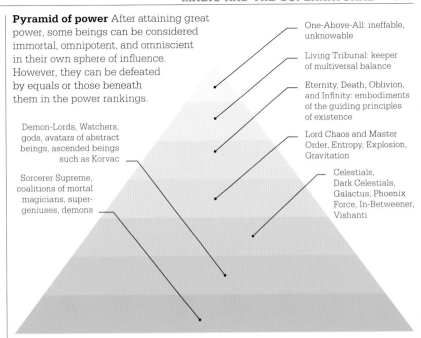

Pyramid of power After attaining great power, some beings can be considered immortal, omnipotent, and omniscient in their own sphere of influence. However, they can be defeated by equals or those beneath them in the power rankings.

One-Above-All: ineffable, unknowable

Living Tribunal: keeper of multiversal balance

Eternity, Death, Oblivion, and Infinity: embodiments of the guiding principles of existence

Lord Chaos and Master Order, Entropy, Explosion, Gravitation

Celestials, Dark Celestials, Galactus, Phoenix Force, In-Betweener, Vishanti

Demon-Lords, Watchers, gods, avatars of abstract beings, ascended beings such as Korvac

Sorcerer Supreme, coalitions of mortal magicians, super-geniuses, demons

Unholy offerings Sacrifice is a facilitator for the Darkholders: preferably a hapless innocent rather than one of their own.

because master technicians, such as Sorcerors Supreme Agamotto or Stephen Strange, built and programmed them that way. In all things mystical, the motivating power is intent reinforced by knowledge. In this respect, magic resembles computer code and modern theories of quantum mechanics, bringing technologists ever closer to the domain of wizards

and demons, and blurring the centuries-old demarcation between the fantastical and the mundane. The line between science and magic continues to fade. Mutants and superhumans can carry godlike power in their mortal frames, machines can move people and objects across time and space instantly, can shatter worlds into atoms, and can even raise the dead.

Perhaps humanity's greatest misconception is that death is the end. For most mortals it is. However, some Super Heroes and far too many Super Villains seem to regard death as a mere hiatus, allowing them to return and either help or plague ordinary people time and again. Unlike ghosts, these revenants appear relatively unchanged by their time in the afterlife. With such death-defying exemplars, it is perhaps unsurprising that some mortals are beginning to question their core beliefs, or if they, too, should explore what lies beyond consensus reality. ∎

See also: The Vishanti and other seekers of mystic might, Death, Arcane artifacts

RESURRECTION SHUFFLE
DEATH

ON THE RECORD

ALLEGIANCES
Eternity, Living Tribunal

POWERS
Granting life or death

MISSION
Housing the dead, deciding who goes back to life

STATUS REPORT
Failing at the job

O ther than newborns and very young children, everybody on Earth—in fact the entire Multiverse—has died and been resurrected at least once. Using the Infinity Gauntlet, the Mad Titan Thanos has eradicated half of universal life only to have others arbitrarily restore it. Elsewhere, omnipotent abstract entities such as Eternity have ended and recreated the universe with very few any the wiser, and the Multiverse has itself expired and been restarted six times to date. So the very human truism that "dead is dead" is wholly irrelevant to the capricious, all-powerful beings who control passage to the afterlife and change the rules whenever it suits them. Moreover, every pantheon of gods has its own landlord of heaven and hell, and they, too, can determine who lives or dies, and even how often.

The moment that Eternity—the cosmic embodiment of Life—came into being, his sister Death walked in his shadow. These twin entities encompass the sum of Multiversal experience, just as their siblings Infinity and Oblivion respectively embody the totality of existence and its ultimate end. However, most

chilling are Death's once-human agents, such as disgraced soldier John Kowalksi or glamorous entertainer Marlo Chandler, who roam the world interacting with select mortals in moments of personal crisis, with deadly results.

Rebirth and afterlife
Across almost every universe, the transition from life to what follows is administered by an abstract being, whose goals remain unclear. If Death rules, why do souls go to heaven or hell, or even become reincarnated? Is there a place beyond death from where none may return? On Earth, the end of life has grown increasingly controversial. Cheating death is a requisite of a hero's job, but evading personal termination is not the same as treating the afterlife as optional. Even vampires and other undead revenants who live with and on humanity forfeit their souls, while ghosts are earthbound spirits without form who are frequently deprived of all but the most terrible drives and urges.

Rage on Death's Earthly agents such as Marlo Chandler keep their personalities, but cannot mask the oppressive finality they carry within them.

Shades of Death

Almost every Earthly pantheon has a deity devoted to ministering the departed, with seemingly irresistible power over souls and their ultimate disposition. Many of these gods regard the amassing of dead souls as a means of boosting their own power, and regional overlords can become greedy and ambitious.

Australian aboriginal deity Narahdarn is one of the few death gods to graciously accept his position, possibly because he resides with his fellow deities in the Dreamtime rather than sequestered in a separate region such as Hela's chilling Niffleheim, Olympian Pluto's Hades and Tartarus, or Heliopolitan Seth's coldly stark Abydos. Hela's hunger to expand has never been at the expense of the souls she supervises. However, both Pluto (pictured) and Seth constantly try to upset the natural order, seize control of the Death Dimension, and even try to kill living gods and consume their power.

What was once seen as solely acts of gods have gone from miraculous to exceptional to almost commonplace. So many Super Heroes and Villains have been killed only to be reborn, that the public now expect it, while millions of the bereaved demand to know why the heroes and not their lost loved ones are returned. There have always been different kinds of resurrection. Many forms of magic will restore life, but all come at a cost to the revived and the reanimator. As scientific knowledge grows, many new methods of restoring perished cells are found, as are ways to restore personalities and memories to cloned and manufactured bodies, or even unleash salvaged minds into cyberspace. The definitions of life are becoming as blurred as the boundary where Eternity surrenders and his sister takes over.

At Death's door Although Death's domain can be anything, the recently departed can expect a spectacular welcome.

Although not strictly resurrection, an increasingly prevalent and dangerous mode of existential restoration is by manipulating the time stream. Many individuals—such as Hawkeye after his death during the Scarlet Witch's mental breakdown or the "deceased" members of Immortus' Legion of the Unliving—have been plucked from their own pasts to resume their lives interrupted. Sometimes they are revivified without harm, but too often the act is permanent and creates divergent timelines, reality disruptions, and potential obliteration of all those currently living in the Multiverse. ∎

See also: Parallel lives, Enchanted source code, Cyborgs

The first secret of magic.
Nothing ever really dies
The Fifth Cosmos

QUEST FOR SUPREMACY
THE VISHANTI AND OTHER SEEKERS OF MYSTIC MIGHT

ON THE RECORD

NAME
The Vishanti

MEMBERS
All-Seeing Agamotto, Hoary Hoggoth, Omnipotent Oshtur

LOCATION
Light Dimension, the Higher Realms

POWERS
Manipulating godlike levels of magic

MISSION
Nurturing emergent species

STATUS REPORT
Constantly at war with rival mystic beings

Whether benevolent, hostile, or indifferent to lower life-forms, all ascendant beings are in constant competition: conducting a continuous arms race to increase and stockpile mystic force. In higher realms, magic force and willpower are all that matter, and everything seeks to monopolize resources to attain their ends. One way to bolster power is through the worship of physical creatures such as Earth's inhabitants. For entities ranked below purely conceptual beings like Death and Eternity, the patronage of lesser magic wielders is commonplace. A brief gift of power when mystics invoke the Faltine, Vishanti, or Dread Dormammu provides the giver with potent arcane rewards.

The Vishanti is a triumvirate of Powers who have successfully ascended beyond godhood. Oshtur is an Elder Goddess, Hoggoth the last of an alien Pantheon, and Agamotto is Earth's first Sorcerer Supreme. Each has accrued sufficient power to become patrons to lesser mages, but must battle constantly against rivals who have achieved similar mystic rank.

The Faltine are composed of pure magic. Dormammu and his sister Umar are degraded Faltinians who abandoned their pure forms in search of personal advancement and

War of Powers The Vishanti bestow great power, but demand payment in the form of service in their eternal wars.

power. Their patronage always comes at terrible cost. This applies equally to other occult creatures. Hell-Lords such as Satannish or Mephisto trade power for worship and consume souls, unlike ethereal beings like Nightmare and other Fear Lords. The latter take what they need, feeding voraciously on psychic energy generated by bad dreams or tense circumstances, but need their "food" to stay alive and terrified. When Earthly events create excessive trauma, the might of these Ethereal beings grows. Elder Gods Set and Chthon crave physical hosts to channel their power from the outer dimensions that imprison them. ∎

SUPERNATURAL SAVIORS
DOCTOR VOODOO AND OTHER MAGIC WIELDERS

ON THE RECORD

REAL NAME
Jericho Drumm

ALLEGIANCES
Avengers, Midnight Sons

BASE
New Orleans

POWERS
Peak human with mystic training, elemental manipulation, teleportation, communing with Voodoo Loa (gods) and the dead

MISSION
Confronting and containing the influence of evil magic

Despite the dominance of rationalism since the Industrial Revolution, Earth remains home to numerous magical adepts, cults, artifacts, and creatures. Whether benevolent, malign, or indifferent, their greatest shield from unwelcome interference or exploitation is humanity's skepticism. Earth's greatest supernatural defender is the Sorcerer Supreme, but lesser

I am... Doctor Voodoo! When I roar the Earth trembles!
Doctor Voodoo

champions also serve, each working in their own ways: often through one specific discipline of magic.

Greatest of these is Jericho Drumm. When his brother Daniel is murdered by magic in Haiti, the psychologist replaces him as local Houngan (shaman) Brother Voodoo. Sharing his living body with his brother's ghost, the new Lord of the Loa defeats numerous arcane assaults upon humanity and as Doctor Voodoo is selected by the Eye of Agamotto to be a new Sorcerer Supreme when Stephen Strange falters. Ultimately killed by Agamotto, Drumm is resurrected by Doctor Doom and a dark god to defeat the Scarlet Witch when she is corrupted by the Red Skull.

As a literal Dead Man Walking, Voodoo defends Earth from supernatural horrors, holding back the darkness with other devout warriors of life like Devil-Slayer (Eric Payne) or Canadian/Sarcee Shaman (Michael Twoyoungmen).

Others such as Elsa Bloodstone use a minimum of magic and extreme ordnance to deal with supernatural encounters. Some, such as Dr. Anthony Druid or Modred the Mystic, succumb to the temptations of power. Younger savants struggle to find their way: troubled souls like destiny-afflicted reality-shaper Wiccan, or Runaway Nico Minoru, aka Sister Grimm. ∎

Weird sister Spilled blood and incantations trigger Nico Minoru's Staff of One to perform magical spells.

SORCERER SUPREME
DOCTOR STRANGE

ON THE RECORD

REAL NAME
Stephen Vincent Strange

ALLEGIANCES
The Vishanti, Agamotto, Defenders, Avengers, Illuminati, Midnight Sons

BASE
Sanctum Sanctorum, Greenwich Village, NYC

POWERS
Arcane expertise and master of vast magical resources

MISSION
Protecting the universe from mystical threats

STATUS REPORT
Recently restored as Sorcerer Supreme

Plagued by guilt and compelled to help the afflicted, Stephen Strange is a healer who treats unspeakable afflictions, redeems physical sins, and combats world-threatening plagues of evil with ancient knowledge and metaphysical powers.

Once a vain and brilliant surgeon whose only goals were money and fame, an inebriated Strange ruins his skilled hands in a car accident and spirals into an alcohol-fueled decline. Learning of a Tibetan mystic able to cure any impairment, he makes an arduous trek to the Himalayas, only to reject the Ancient One's magic as superstitious trickery.

Trapped by bad weather, Strange remains for weeks, undergoing an epiphany after being enslaved by the Ancient One's disciple Baron Karl Mordo. The malign student seeks to murder the Ancient One and steal his power until Stephen intervenes. Faced with irrefutable proof of magical forces, Strange accepts the aged adept's offer of help and tuition.

…All things of evil are my enemies!
Stephen Strange

Studying for years, he becomes a Master of the Mystic Arts and humanity's defender from magical menaces and modern terrors. Strange accepts that magic exerts a dreadful price on the user, altering his body in ways only his faithful attendant Wong can appreciate.

Magical thinking

Moving to New York and setting up a very different kind of practice, Strange deals with unnatural threats in relative anonymity. However, as a modern Age of Marvels dawns, he is increasingly exposed to public scrutiny and media attention. Those who genuinely need him can always reach him, but to the general public he remains a charlatan and conman to be avoided. One sector that realizes his true worth is the rapidly expanding Super Hero community, who increasingly depend upon him when their own cases stray beyond the bounds of rationality. The Fantastic Four, Spider-Man, Thor, and others all have reason to thank him, but honor his wishes to work in the shadows.

After many years battling the unknown and demonic—both alone, with his estranged wife Clea, and alongside his clandestine "non-team"

The Eyes of Agamotto

More than a million years ago, Earth's first Sorcerer Supreme Agamotto creates spells and devices used by generations of mystics who follow in his wake, if not always his teachings. Three of his surviving talismans are the Orb, Eye, and Amulet. Stephen Strange uses the Amulet on returning to the US from Tibet.

The "Eye of Power" provides protection, shatters subterfuge, and concentrates the user's inner energies. After first defeating the dark lord Dormammu, Strange is awarded the far-mightier "Eye of Truth." Sheathed in metal, the "All-Seeing Eye" (pictured) channels Agamotto's power, spanning time and space, opening dimensional gateways, extracting secrets, dispelling illusion, and reshaping reality.

The Orbis or "Eye of Prescience" is a crystal globe housed within the Cask of Concealment in Strange's Sanctum Sanctorum. A scrying lens, the Orbis detects magical crises across the Multiverse, opens portals to other realms, and projects spoken warnings.

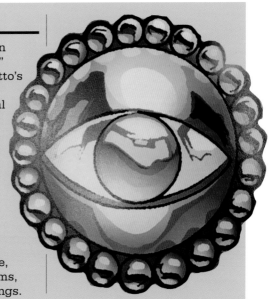

of Defenders—Doctor Strange emerges into the public spotlight and becomes a mainstay of the Avengers. His valiant efforts in mass-hero battles against Morgan le Fay, the Hood, Thanos, and others are celebrated, but his secret wars against infernal overlords Mephisto, Nightmare, the Dread Dormammu, monsters like Lilith and Dracula, and sorcerors such as Mordo, Belasco, and Modred are not. As governments, militaries, and corporations all investigate mysticism's potential, Strange remains at society's fringes: shunning acclaim, with a steady stream of truth-seekers and the power-hungry craving his secrets.

Essentially human, Strange's super-power is knowledge: operating potent artifacts and learning how to access the "cheat codes of creation." However, constant warfare between the deities and beings he invokes from higher realms means that over the years, his power levels fluctuate wildly and his spells' efficacy varies. He loses the role of Sorcerer Supreme numerous times, and in the end can only depend upon his own determination and mental agility.

Ultimately pragmatic, to save reality Strange frequently sacrifices his integrity; learning necromancy and dark magic under the Ancient One's archenemy Kaluu, consorting with devils and demons, and using whatever sorcerous means are expedient and necessary to protect Earth. When the extra-dimensional Empirikul almost eradicate natural magic, Strange uses his learning and harvested artifacts such as the Axe of Angarruumus to defeat them and restart Earth's arcane environment. ∎

Student unrest Dark mage Mordo has been trying to kill and supplant Stephen Strange from the first moment they met.

DARK DESPOT
DORMAMMU

ON THE RECORD

ALLEGIANCES
The Faltine, Hell Lords, Lords of the Splinter Realms

BASE
Dark Dimension

POWERS
Immortal energy being sustained by worship, god-level wielder of magic

MISSION
Subjugating all life

STATUS REPORT
Rash and proud, Dormammu is consistently outwitted by weaker, smarter beings

Dormammu rules the Dark Dimension, a mystic realm intersecting many other planes, realities, and pocket dimensions. A malevolent creature of sentient energy, Dormammu is an all-powerful tyrant, but his arrogant pride and pitiless hunger for total control makes him easy to outmaneuver. The Dark Dimension is under constant assault from the predatory Mindless Ones and

a portion of Dormammu's vast power—equivalent to gods such as Odin and Zeus—is perpetually devoted to containing them. Ferocious and temperamental, Dormammu is feared and worshipped by his subjects whom he conquered eons previously.

Dormammu and his sister Umar are Faltine: immortal energy entities from a higher dimension. They are exiled for murdering their sire, Sinifer, and mixing their essences with lowly matter to increase their power. After wandering the mystic realms, they befriend the Dark Dimension's King Olnar, beguiling him into conquering neighboring planes, then ousting him. Rejecting physical form, Dormammu merges

> You cannot run from me! Everything that is, is mine!
> **Dormammu**

Power games Devious Umar cannot match her brother's power, but plans to usurp him when the opportunity arises.

his essence with the dimension's innate mystic forces, becoming an eternal manifestation of the "Flames of Regency." Although nourished by all forms of energy, Dormammu is primarily fueled by worship and forever seeks to expand his domain. Targeting Earth's dimension, he is thwarted by mystic Agamotto and the line of Sorcerers Supreme he founded. Defeated by Doctor Strange and mortal heroes such as the Avengers, Dormammu uses magical proxies such as Baron Karl Mordo or Parker Robbins (the Hood), lending them his might to attain his own ends. Far less devious than Umar, Dormammu adheres to his own code of honor: never breaking his word. ∎

LORD OF LIES

MEPHISTO

ON THE RECORD

ALLEGIANCES
**Six-Fingered Hand,
Blackheart**

BASE
Hades; Las Vegas, Nevada

POWERS
**Mystical control of matter,
energy, time, and reality;
trades favors for souls**

MISSION
**Corrupting innocence and
accruing power**

STATUS REPORT
**Defeated, diminished, and
imprisoned on Earth**

A cunning, ambitious demon, Mephisto uses lies and deceit to bolster his formidable, arcane power. Presiding over a pocket hell dimension and incarcerating the souls of his countless victims from which he draws his strength, Mephisto dupes the greedy and desperate with bargains that benefit him alone. Although not a true devil, he has traded off the reputation of the major

I am Mephisto... Supreme unto myself! I answer to none!
Mephisto

Hell-Lords for eons, claiming at times to be Lucifer, Beelzebub, Satan, and other fallen ones. This tactic proves so successful that he is—diabolically speaking—in a class by himself. Mephisto is addicted to mind games and meddling with humanity, which provides him with his favorite morsels: pure yet conflicted souls to corrupt and feed upon. Mephisto targets Super Heroes like the Fantastic Four, Scarlet Witch, and the Avengers, as well as coveting and pursuing the pristine souls of Thor and the Silver Surfer.

Mephisto's greatest triumphs include binding Johnny Blaze to fire-demon Zarathos to create a new Ghost Rider, and forcing Peter and

Mary Jane Watson-Parker to forsake years of marriage. The demon offers to save a dying Aunt May if the happy couple consent to him altering their timelines—resulting in them never marrying.

Mephisto's constant conniving has proven his downfall many times, such as his failure to deprive Thanos of the Infinity Gantlet. After relocating to Las Vegas and clashing with Doctor Strange, Mephisto has been stripped of power and imprisoned on Earth. However, as long as someone, somewhere is ready to make a deal, Mephisto will no doubt rise again. ∎

Deal with the devil In Las Vegas, the home of gambling and games, Mephisto can't resist striking a deal.

GOD OF MISCHIEF
LOKI

ON THE RECORD

REAL NAME
Loki Laufeyson

ALLEGIANCES
All-Mother of Asgardia, Dark Council, Young Avengers

POWERS
Asgardian god, magic wielder, immortal, master manipulator

MISSION
Loki does what Loki desires

STATUS REPORT
After futile attempts to redeem himself, Loki reverts to his duplicitous nature

L oki's parents are Frost Giant king Laufey and his wife Farbauti, but by upbringing, he is a prince of Asgard. Wielding magic from an early age, the god of deception and double-dealing nests in Asgard's heart like a viper—but his greatest victim is invariably himself. Loki was adopted by Odin when mighty Laufey fell in battle. His weak, stunted son—a source of great shame to the power-obsessed giants—was reared in Asgard, but whether as a hostage, a spoil of war, or to fulfill some arcane prophecy, none can truly say.

Raised with tenderness and understanding by Odin's wife, Freyja—possibly the only living being Loki genuinely cares about—the misfit is a creature of changing moods and envious whims, forever betrayed by his own fickle nature. Like his shape, Loki's character is mercurial, shifting with each caprice that takes him. Characterized as god of mischief, Loki's attempts to humiliate or harm his brother, Thor Odinson, earn centuries of punishments, but Odin is never able to truly sever bonds with his wayward second son. As Loki's defeats mount, so does his rage. Continually trying to undermine and destroy Thor, usurp Asgard's throne, or even destroy the unfair universe leads him into increasingly devious acts and recategorization as god of evil.

Loki's attempts to bedevil Thor through magic manifests many

Swindler supreme Briefly ousting Doctor Strange as Sorcerer Supreme, Loki appropriates his mystical accessories.

Hela, Goddess of Death

Every pantheon has its own custodian of departed souls, but few as grim as Hela, mistress of Niffleheim. This dreary, formless region of icy fog houses the dishonored dead with a fortress, Hel, at its heart. Here Hela abides, ruling over the wicked and failed souls who wasted their lives. Her greatest ambition is to annex Odin's paradise, Valhalla, where Asgard's great heroes and noble warriors dwell after death.

Like all death gods, Hela is fierce, powerful, and constantly schemes to increase her sphere of influence by taking mighty souls—such as Thor or Odin—and spirits of brave humans: the best Midgard can offer. Although she wages expansionist campaigns of conquest, she is faithful to her race. She battles tirelessly to stop rivals such as the Olympian Pluto, the Egyptian Set, or Demon-Lord Mephisto consuming the souls of Asgardians—at the cost of much of her power and territories.

menaces who remain a threat long after he finishes with them. As well as unleashing the long-dormant Destroyer and Lava Men on Earth, Loki's meddling amplifies the powers of Cobra and Mr. Hyde, and creates the fearfully powerful Absorbing Man, Wrecker, and Wrecking Crew. Humiliatingly, it also sparks a number of lone Super Heroes to band together to form the Avengers after his plans to pit Thor against the Hulk go awry.

Finding his own path
Unable to decide if he is no more than a helpless pawn of prophecy and the Norns (the Fates), Loki's schemes grow ever more ambitious.

I am not now, nor ever have been, overly fond of "the rules."
Loki

Mortal lie-detector Embracing his fate, Loki seeks honesty and understanding from human truth-sayer Verity Willis.

However, ill-fated allegiances with Mephisto, Dormammu, and Earthly villains provide no respite to his anguish. After Odin dies and Asgard falls following Ragnarok, Loki reappraises his position. Yet even his own demise and resurrection as a goddess in now-Earthbound Asgardia cannot stem his inner turmoil and anarchic nature. These efforts are exacerbated by the mistrust of all Asgardians, other than his always-forgiving, sanctimonious brother.

When US security chief Norman Osborn declares war on Asgardia, Loki perishes defending the floating city from the malefic Void. A being of astonishing magical power, Loki is reborn, still set on changing his path. Opting to remain in child form, Kid Loki is dogged by an avatar of Hela, the Goddess of Death. He is also plagued by an evil future incarnation of himself who has traveled back in time to derail the resurrected boy's attempts to redeem himself and thwart destiny.

As an Agent of Asgardia, Loki enacts missions for the new ruling All-Mother triumvirate—Gaea, Idunn, and Freyja—but earnest attempts to do good falter under pressure from his chaos-causing nature and the Multiverse's imminent destruction. When reality is recreated, Loki again seeks to cheat his onerous destiny, but lacks the strength to truly change his character. Backsliding into trickery and malice, he even briefly usurps the mantle of Sorcerer Supreme from Stephen Strange, only to surrender it when challenged. Now a true god of lies, Loki's schemes are greater than ever and embrace all of reality rather than just Asgard and his bothersome family. ∎

QUEEN OF CHAOS
SCARLET WITCH

ON THE RECORD

REAL NAME
Wanda Maximoff

ALLEGIANCES
Avengers, Force Works, Brotherhood of Evil Mutants

POWERS
High-level witch, Chaos Magic wielder, reality warper

MISSION
Safeguarding Earth's mystic community and resources

STATUS REPORT
Redeeming her past acts with good deeds

Her early memories clouded by trauma, Romani Wanda Maximoff's first recollections are of the Balkans, overwritten—when her "hex power" first triggers—by the horror of being hunted by superstitious humans. In rural Transia, she and her twin brother Pietro are saved by mutant terrorist Magneto, who manipulates their gratitude, compelling them to join his Brotherhood of Evil Mutants.

Taking the code name Scarlet Witch, Wanda spends years trying to understand herself, her origins, and even her ability to cause random disasters with a gesture. With super-fast brother Quicksilver, Wanda reluctantly battles the X-Men at Magneto's behest until he is imprisoned by alien explorer the Stranger. Seeking redemption, the twins join the Avengers, serving diligently and with honor. Wanda falls in love with android Avenger the Vision and turns to studying true magic under preeminent witch Agatha Harkness. She excels, but "the Craft" leads to her possession by Elder god Chthon, whose earthly tether is situated in her Transian homeland.

When circumstantial evidence seems to prove Magneto is actually their father, the twins strive ever harder to escape their heritage. In truth, the siblings' powers actually derive from clandestine genetic tampering at the hands of the High Evolutionary when they were infants. Eventually Wanda and Vision marry, retiring to raise magically created sons, but tragedy strikes.

Spellbinding Wanda uses Chaos Magic to warp reality and manipulates energy using her signature hex bolts.

Their children—formed by Wanda's ever-expanding abilities—are in fact unreal and turn out to be soul shards of demon lord Mephisto.

Further horror comes as the US government mind-wipes and resets the Vision. Emotionless and now incapable of love, he is unable to help Wanda as her fragile sanity is further damaged. She falls under the influence of time-god Immortus, who seeks to exploit her ability to warp reality. Foiling the scheme, Wanda returns to active duty with the Avengers and later as leader of breakaway team Force Works.

The Winding Path

Struggling to balance her life, Wanda is ultimately overwhelmed by her chaotic powers. Influenced by Doctor Doom, a deranged Wanda "disassembles" the Avengers, causing the deaths of Hawkeye, Ant-Man, Jack of Hearts, and Vision. In the aftermath, she collapses and is cared for by Magneto and Charles Xavier. As she recuperates, Pietro guides Wanda into remaking Earth as a mutant paradise, but when the ensuing "World of M" falls apart, she precipitates another catastrophe:

> Witches and warlocks... we all have our walls and veils.
> **Wanda Maximoff**

Three witches Guided by the spirits of Agatha and her mother, Wanda pursues her destiny and gains control of her gifts.

decimating the mutant population from millions to less than 200. As her shattered mind recovers, Wanda awakens to the fact that she is a pariah. It takes years for her to recover her sanity and reputation, even after her powers resurrect many of the friends she killed. After saving the world during the war between X-Men and Avengers over the Phoenix force, she divides her time between serving in the Avengers Unity Squad and learning the truth of her existence.

Wanda fully pursues witchcraft as a magic detective solving arcane mysteries. While mastering occult disciplines on the "Winding Path," she discovers she has a heritage of heroism and sorcery. Her mother was a mystical hero, too, and the name Scarlet Witch a family title. Wanda's journey to truth and self-awareness has just begun, and her traumatic past has given her resolve to find her own path. ∎

Quicksilver

Pietro is the elder of the Maximoff twins and—due to the High Evolutionary's genetic tampering—can move and think at incredible speed. His body is fully adapted to the rigors of being a speedster, but his mind is mercurial and he is easily bored dealing with the slow, plodding creatures that inhabit Earth. Although he possesses a core of nobility and a strict moral code, he is arrogant, impatient, and intolerant. Convinced he knows best, Pietro frequently tries to dictate how his sister lives her life. Wanda finds him overbearing and intrusive, and has spent much of her adult life at odds with him, even though each would give their life for the other.

At heart a valiant hero serving with the Avengers, Inhumans, and X-Factor, Pietro periodically slips into insanity, acting the selfish tyrant, and convinced the world would be better with him in charge.

VENGEANCE UNBOUND

GHOST RIDERS

ON THE RECORD

DESIGNATION
Spirits of Vengeance

ALLEGIANCES
**Avengers 1,000,000BCE,
Champions, The Nine**

POWERS
**Supernatural strength and
durability; mystical Hellfire,
transport, and weaponry;
Penance Stare**

MISSION
Punish the guilty

STATUS REPORT
Vengeance never sleeps

Fiery agents of retribution have stalked mankind's transgressors since early times. The first Ghost Rider is born a million years ago when a human boy gains arcane power. His tribe massacred, the sole survivor makes a deal with demon lord Mephisto: turning into a raging fury astride a blazing mammoth. Throughout history, many mortals become unstoppable avengers, purging the unrighteous as Spirits of Vengeance.

The originators of the term are angelic beings overseen by the archangel Zadkiel. Wielding Hellfire and a soul-destroying "Penance Stare," these Ghost Riders guard humanity from demonic attacks. Over eons, conniving Mephisto suborns their role. He emulates the succession of spectral fiery warriors with his own versions in attempts to mock and counteract the good works of the Spirits of Vengeance.

By repeatedly imprisoning his infernal rival, Zarathos, in duped and desperate human hosts, such as stunt biker Johnny Blaze (pictured above), Mephisto furthers his own schemes on Earth. The ploy backfires with Blaze, whose strong will turns his malign burden into a new role as a dark and reluctant champion of humanity. Blaze temporarily escapes his curse—such as passing it on to new Ghost Rider, Alejandra Jones—but he and Zarathos are always drawn back together.

Divine retribution After the first Ghost Rider's tribe is killed, the blazing mammoth he rides becomes his only companion.

A true Spirit of Vengeance remanifests when Danny Ketch is possessed by the avenging angels and works with Blaze to eradicate an upsurge in occult incidents. Latterly, an unrelated Ghost Rider, Robbie Reyes, emerges to combat evil in California. Reyes, however, is periodically possessed by the spirit of his serial killer uncle and must channel—with Blaze's help— the murderous instincts unleashed by only targeting evildoers. ■

UNDAUNTED DAYWALKER

BLADE

ON THE RECORD

REAL NAME
Eric Brooks

ALLEGIANCES
Midnight Sons, Avengers of the Supernatural, Borderline Investigations, Nightstalkers

POWERS
Full vampiric abilities, plus immunity to daylight, crosses, silver, garlic, and holy water; weapons master

MISSION
Suppressing vampire and supernatural predation

STATUS REPORT
Evil never ends, but it can be killed

In 1929, Vanessa Brooks is killed by vampire Deacon Frost as she gives birth in London. The bite transfers supernatural enzymes to the infant's bloodstream and he becomes a Dhampir: a living being with vampire powers. His mother was a fugitive from Latveria: wife of Lucas Cross, leader of secret society the Order of Tyrana. Unaware of his heritage, or the dormant powers he possesses, young Eric Brooks is raised by brothelkeeper Madame Vanity and American vampire hunter Jamal Afari, and learns to track down the undead.

In 1968, Brooks' allies are wiped out by vampire Lord Dracula, but he survives. Calling himself "Blade," thanks to the wooden throwing knives he carries, Brooks heads to New York City. In 1972, he becomes a supernatural "Mighty Avenger" alongside wizard Kaluu, Adam "Blue Marvel" Brashear, and were-beast the Bear, stopping immortal Deathwalkers from exterminating humanity. Joining veteran hunter Quincy Harker's crusade against Dracula, Blade meets Frank Drake (Dracula's only living relative) and noble vampire Hannibal King. The vampiric Frost had "turned" King, but the private eye refused to succumb to vampirism, craving revenge over innocent blood.

Coming together as Borderline Investigations, the trio crush many mystic threats and, as Nightstalkers, help Doctor Strange, Brother Voodoo, and numerous Super Heroes quash a vast upsurge in supernatural activity. Eventually, Blade confronts his father, learning that Lucas Cross has been responsible for Dracula's resurrections and wants Brooks to become a killer of innocents to fulfill an ancient prophecy. Rejecting the vile scheme, Blade the Daywalker continues to haunt evil creatures, dispatching them alongside the Avengers, X-Men, Britain's MI-13, S.H.I.E.L.D.'s magic and monsters divisions, and, latterly, as part of the new Midnight Sons team. ■

Bite me Even before his Dhampir powers develop, Blade is immune to the effects of vampire infection.

DYNASTY OF SERVICE

BLACK KNIGHTS

ON THE RECORD

LINEAGE
House of Scandia

ALLEGIANCES
Camelot, Avengers, Defenders, Knights of Pendragon, Avalon

POWERS
Magic sword, genius intellect, centuries of combat experience

MISSION
Defending the righteous

STATUS REPORT
Saving the world with—and from—his Ebony Blade

After Rome abandons Britain, a dark age of bloody anarchy ends when Arthur Pendragon becomes king. Wielding the magical sword Excalibur, Arthur institutes a rule of Law and Justice, enforced from Camelot by valiant Knights of the Round Table. Throughout this golden age, his mentor Merlin guides him and guards against the evil schemes of Arthur's sorcerous sister Morgan Le Fay and nephew Mordred. In later years, the mage bestows a sword upon disciple Percy of Scandia. Like Excalibur, the Ebony Blade, aka "Chaos the Doombringer," is proof against all magic and can cut through anything. However, it is cursed: the blood it spills demands more, bringing madness and worse to those who use it. Seemingly an effete fop, as the masked hero Black Knight, Percy is Arthur's secret weapon against invaders and court intrigue. When Camelot finally falls, it is only because Mordred has already murdered Percy.

Steered by Percy's spirit, the Ebony Blade passes through many descendants of Scandia. Held by Black Knight Eobar Garrington, it strikes for Christendom and King Richard during the Crusades, before resting for 600 years in the Knights Templar armory.

In more recent times, Dr. Nathan Garrett feels his heritage calling, and devises an evil Black Knight identity, employing high-tech gadgetry and riding a mutated winged horse. He is passed over by Sir Percy's spirit and Chaos the Doombringer remains hidden until Garret's nephew Dane Whitman inherits the technology and the role. An accomplished scientist descended from a line of sorcery-tainted heroes, Whitman becomes a heroic Avenger, merging futuristic weaponry with the Ebony Blade. A guardian of Avalon, Whitman still struggles to master and contain the sword's bloody thirst for slaughter. ■

Dark legacy Valiant Black Knights carry a burden of responsibility that they must balance with the bloody hunger of the Ebony Blade.

INFERNAL HELLSPAWN
CHILDREN OF THE DEVIL

In every Hell where evil souls reside, reputation is everything and most Demon-Lords claim to be fallen angel Satan. Marduk Kurios is one of the oldest, plaguing humanity for eons. In modern times, he beguiles Victoria Wingate into bearing his children and increasing "Satan's" earthly influence. Both hybrid hellspawn grow to despise and oppose him. Firstborn Daimon Hellstrom initially rejects the devil and becomes an exorcist, but is tormented by his inherent demonic personality, dubbed his "Darksoul." For years, Hellstrom employs infernal abilities, supernatural lore, and his demon-controlling Netheranium Trident alongside Super Heroes like the Defenders. Marrying Patsy Walker, he corrupts her into becoming a true Hellcat. Accepting his demonic urges, the Son of Satan becomes Hellstorm, pursuing a selfish, power-seeking agenda. He even briefly rules his father's kingdom, before returning to Earth.

Daimon's sister Satana was initially a more willing disciple. A soul-consuming succubus, she spends her early life in Hell, learning magic and cruelty, but when she also rebels, she is exiled to Earth: another implacable enemy and soon

> I stand determined to stamp out the heritage of my birth!
> **Daimon Hellstrom**

Kiss of evil Satana feeds on the souls of her victims by kissing them. She gains power with every soul consumed.

sovereign of her own Hell-Realm. Marduk's rival, Mephisto, also claims to be Satan, and has suffered the failings of his own ill-conceived offspring. Made from accumulated human evil, Blackheart rejects Mephisto's ways to become a resolute enemy, while younger brother Greylight lacks ambition; wasting time tormenting mortals like Star-Lord Peter Quill in the Softlands pocket Hellscape. Mephisto's greatest regret is his daughter Mephista, who develops affections for Sorcerer Supreme Stephen Strange and, as Jezebel, connives to prevent an Earthly invasion of Hell-Lords. ■

GIFTS OF THE GODS
ARCANE ARTIFACTS

ON THE RECORD

DESIGNATION
Magic weapons and tools

ALLEGIANCES
Absolute loyalty to wielder, depending on nature of enchantment

POWERS
Limited only by enchanter's will and imagination

MISSION
To serve their makers' intent, if not their wielder's whim

Magic can compress enormous destructive or transformative power into small, portable systems designed to only work for specific users. Earth abounds with arcane objects: wands, talismans, spell grimoires, accursed tomes such as the Darkhold, and all manner of enchanted weapons that serve, beguile, and can even possess their users. The ultimate example of this is Mjölnir, which harnesses world-shattering power from the dawn of creation. The multi-purpose mallet provides various capabilities,

including autonomous flight and return, lightning-generation, devastating impact-force, time-travel, teleportation, and language translation—only accessible to those the weapon itself deems worthy.

Weapons like Mjölnir acquire life of their own. It was forged in primordial times when Asgardian All-Father Odin and the dwarf

Inscribed in magic "Whosoever holds this hammer, if he be worthy, shall possess the power of Thor."

smiths of Nidavellir trap primal cosmic force the Mother Storm within an Uru metal prison. As ages pass, the hammer judges its wielders, only lending power to those who are judged worthy. Most often wielded by his son Thor, Odin duplicates Mjölnir's enchantments, if not sheer potency, many times: in Beta Ray Bill's Stormbreaker hammer and mystic mace Thunderstrike.

Asgardian alchemy

Other Asgardian artifacts include the wish-fulfilling Norn Stones that all too often fall into the hands of malign users like Loki, Baron Zemo, and the Hood, and the indestructible Destroyer armor, which demands a stolen spirit to activate it. Most effective is raw Asgardian magic of the kind that permanently transforms Crusher Creel into a shape-shifting Absorbing Man or empowers brutal thief the Wrecker and his Wrecking Crew (Hammerhead, Thunderball, and Piledriver) with godly might. When dormant Asgardian deity Cul the Serpent awakes, seven hammers herald his return, refashioning heroes and villains to spread fear itself to the people of Earth.

Asgardians are not the only magic-using culture to leave their

Cursed objects

Magical forces affect physical matter, and many objects that channel mystic energies acquire specific powers. Dark magic, inimical to life and exploitative, enslaves users, turning hapless mortals into tools of ancient forces. The Darkhold spell book corrupts those who read it—such as well-meaning hero Modred the Mystic—making them pawns of exiled Elder god Ch'thon, just as the Crown of Set subjugates those who don it,

tainting and linking them to the sinister Elder serpent god.

A marginally better bargain awaits those who touch the glittering Ruby of Cyttorak, which is intended to demonstrate the minor demon-god's mystical superiority to rival members of his fraternity, the Octessence. The gem transforms its holders, such as troubled villain and occasional hero Cain Marko (pictured), into Cyttorak's earthly avatar of might and unstoppable Juggernaut of destruction.

mark on Earth. The planet is strewn with arcane objects, many enhanced to increase their offensive abilities. Three middle-eastern heroes dubbed "Arabian Knight"—Abdul Qamar, Navid Hashim, and an anonymous agent of OPEC (Organization of the

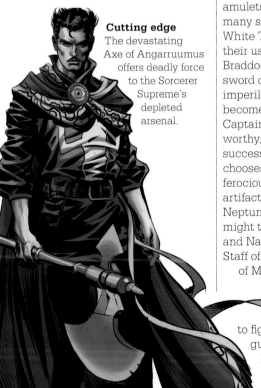

Cutting edge
The devastating Axe of Angarruumus offers deadly force to the Sorcerer Supreme's depleted arsenal.

Petroleum Exporting Countries)—utilize the magic sword, sash, and carpet that come with the role, while Danny Ketch uses a medallion of power to summon the Ghost Rider.

Mystical swords are common in arcane arsenals, as are charmed amulets, which grant power to many such as a succession of heroic White Tigers. Tools also often test their users. Life-nurturing Brian Braddock is offered the choice of sword or amulet when his life is imperiled. Selecting the latter, he becomes powerhouse protector Captain Britain. Braddock's equally worthy, but more aggressive, successor Kelsey Leigh later chooses the blade, becoming the ferocious warrior Lionheart. Godly artifacts such as Athena's Aegis and Neptune's Trident lend Olympian might to mortals like Trey Rollins and Namor; and a blood-bonded Staff of One empowers generations of Minoru women such as Sister Grimm. The most potent tool of all is the Evil Eye of Avalon. Created to fight dark Fomorian gods and guarded by warrior-priest Prester John, it is secured by Dread Dormammu to threaten two universes.

I name thee... Mjölnir, the thunder weapon. First among hammers. Breaker of all things.
Odin

Since the death and rebirth of magic on Prime Earth, enchanted objects are highly prized and fought over by mystics. When the extra-dimensional Empirikul consume Earth's magical energy, Sorcerer Supreme Stephen Strange and other mages gather previously neglected occult artifacts to bolster their own abilities, mining the items for any vestiges of magic. As always, most pay a heavy price, such as the demon that infests Wilson Fisk when he dons a mystic mask or Strange's own energy-draining Axe of Angarruumus. As magic returns, such objects must be safeguarded from dangerous opportunists. ∎
See also: Asgardians, Thor, Vibranium and other exotic elements, Doctor Strange

CREATURES ON THE LOOSE
LEGION OF MONSTERS

ON THE RECORD

DESIGNATION
Supernatural predators

ALLEGIANCES
**Legion of Monsters,
Monster Metropolis**

POWERS
**Mystic transformation;
enhanced strength, speed,
and durability; flight;
ferocity and guile**

MISSION
Survival and secrecy

STATUS REPORT
**Pitilessly hunted but ready
to strike back**

As mankind progresses scientifically, it relegates magical creatures to the category of fiction. This is a state of affairs that Earth's non-human species happily encourage: unlike emergent species such as mutants, they are content to avoid notice, living free of intolerance. However, some consider mankind to be prey. Vampires, werewolves, wendigos, and others cannot leave their feeding grounds; but are they all just vicious monsters?

Many vampiric races haunt society's fringes and their overlord Dracula is willing to play a long game. His greatest concern is increasing instances of rebellion. Undead "slaves" like Hannibal King have preserved their souls by refusing to kill victims for the blood they need, hoping to be ultimately cured or saved. Dr. Michael Morbius (pictured above) is not so resolute. Dying of a rare disease, a radical cure makes him superhuman, but reliant on drinking blood. The Living Vampire eventually controls his lethal cravings, becoming primary care-giver and magistrate of Monster Metropolis, and forming a Legion of Monsters to police the city.

After years living as a rampaging werewolf when the full Moon rises, Jack Russell finally conquers the beast within. Now able to transform into lycanthrope form at will, he leads the Legion of Monsters. Elsa Bloodstone, daughter of monster-hunter Ulysses, has superhuman physiology and vast supernatural knowledge. Proficient with mundane and mystic weapons, her blood is toxic to vampires. She lives in Boston, Massachusetts, where she

Full moon madness Lycanthrope Jack Russell loses his cognitive abilities and resembles a wolf during the full Moon.

is attended by Adam: the original monster built by Victor Frankenstein. Not all predatory monsters are supernatural. Killed by Wolverine's son Daken, the Punisher is patched together and resurrected by Morbius as a weapon of the Legion of Monsters. Fueled by a mystic bloodstone, "FrankenCastle" eventually regenerates to human form and leaves the Legion. ■

TERROR INCOGNITO
HIDDEN LANDS AND RACES

ON THE RECORD

DESIGNATION
Lost tribes

TYPES
Cat People, Bird People, Moloids, Witches, Wendigos

CAPABILITIES
Lost science, magic, unnatural abilities

MISSION
Living apart

STATUS REPORT
Harmless unless provoked

Mankind shares Earth with many intelligent species; natural, artificially created, or supernatural in origin. As humanity proliferated, less aggressive and fast-breeding races found refuge in adjacent dimensions, sought remote sanctuaries, or migrated to the Savage Land. The latter still houses the subhuman Children of Dis, Lizard Men, Swamp Men, proto-Neanderthal Man-Apes, and assorted aquatic, amphibian, and avian species. Africa and Asia abound with prehuman cultures

and creatures, while Britain remains connected to primordial powers through Otherworld, where fairies, elves, and ogres still thrive.

Some tribes hide among mankind. Witches dwell in small communities such as New Salem, Colorado—birthplace of Agatha Harkness—as do Cat People, whose mix of science and magic created feline Avenger Tigra (pictured above). Conjured by the wizard Ebrok from pet housecats, the shy, demonically based Cat People share human society until persecution drives the majority to their own extradimensional realm. Millennia ago, a similar fate befell Wakandan beast races dubbed Originators. Other isolated mystic

> **More and more, the human part of me is being pushed out by the cat!**
> **Tigra**

Denizens of the depths Losing their intelligence over millennia, Moloids are loyal to those they deem to be powerful.

societies with no love of humanity still hide in plain sight, such as malign Serpent Men created by Elder God Set or the scaly adherents of son of Set, Sligguth, who populate the town of Starkesboro, Maine.

In the skies, Inhuman Bird People dwell on their floating island Aerie, while the most populous races thrive underground. Moloids—descended from slave races created by the Deviants eons ago—include subspecies such as Tyrannoids, Gortokians, and Lava Men who live in the spacious voids of Subterranea. The newest enclave is under Manhattan. Monster Metropolis is an ancient city recently colonized by mystic entities, aliens, mutant Morlocks, and more. ∎

COSMIC FO
AND SPACE
ADVENTUR

RCES

ES

Life abounds everywhere, sharing the same basic drives: survive, prosper, proliferate. Interstellar distances are no defense against the universe's greatest threat to existence: advanced extraterrestrial aggressors. All cultures reach for the stars, but competition for dominance means stronger civilizations succeed at the expense of weaker ones. Across the cosmos, heroes that defend the weak are rare, but they do exist. A remarkable number come from Earth.

Progenitor Celestial dies on Earth.

c. 4.5BN YEARS AGO

Nuwali builders construct Pangean nature preserve for the Beyonders.

c. 250M YEARS AGO

Skrulls bring primitive Kree and Cotati to Earth's Moon for a contest of competing intellects and values.

c. 1M YEARS AGO

An automated Plodex colonizing bio-ship crashes into the Arctic.

c. 40K YEARS AGO

Celestial Second Host battles Deviants. The war changes Earth's environment, Atlantis sinks, and a new dark age of barbarism begins.

c. 20K YEARS AGO

c. UNKNOWN

Uatu the Watcher is stationed on Earth's Moon.

c. MORE THAN 1M YEARS AGO

The Celestials First Host alters DNA of early hominids.

c. 50K YEARS AGO

Kree geneticists set up a base on Uranus and begin altering *Homo antecessor* subjects to create offshoot species of Inhumans.

c. 25K YEARS AGO

Kree sentry confirms creation of offshoot species of Inhumans.

c. 19K YEARS AGO

Beyonders appoint Fortisquian Caretakers of Arcturus and their android Children of the Comet to oversee the Pangean Savage Land.

As the universe stabilizes after the primal detonation, planets form and life begins on innumerable worlds. With the passage of time, simple organisms evolve into complex life-forms, and the race to advance creates winners and losers. All over creation, species race to dominate their environment, taking over planets, star systems, and eventually entire galaxies. Life is ferociously persistent and finds ways to fill any niche. Beings of gas, liquid, light, energy, or solid matter exist in as many varieties as the complex assemblies of cells that comprise flesh and blood. Vast creatures such as the Acanti evolve to live in the harsh, radiation-filled voids between stars, and sentient planet Ego resides in a Black Galaxy composed of pure life potential.

Giant Ego Ambitious, aggressive, and colonial, Ego is a typical living organism operating on a planetary scale.

Nowhere in existence does the pattern change. The drive to expand and control is irresistible, and only confronting greater forces or succumbing to disaster can halt the advance of civilizations.

Life is everywhere in infinite variety, with many worlds producing similar hominid beings. This is largely due to the efforts of many primal species: Celestial star gods and lesser, transgalactic species such as Builders, Fortisquians, Xorrians, Progenitors, Harvesters, and others. They seed worlds with genetic packages to hasten life in their own image, albeit altered and evolved through local planetary conditions and natural selection. Many early races favor physical expansion, but fall foul of more powerful interplanetary enemies or their own impetuous aggression.

Parasitic Brood invasion is crushed by Pharaoh Imhotep and other enhanced heroes.

Celestials' Third Host lands in Peru and defeats a coalition of Earthly gods before deputizing local native tribes to be their agents.

Rawhide Kid battles alien Totem pole in American west.

Nazis capture voyagers from Axi-Tun, turning them and their technology against the Allied powers.

Skrull scout mission abducts human test pilot Chuck Chandler, accidentally creating Super Hero 3-D Man.

2620 BCE   **C. 1K YEARS AGO**   **C. 1875 CE**   **1942 CE**   **1958 CE**

114 CE   **C. 16TH CENTURY**   **1918 CE**   **1948 CE**   **C. 15 YEARS AGO**

Shield Brotherhood savant Zhang Heng repulses the Celestial Madonna, moving her Celestial Egg from Earth to the Sun.

Galactus is driven from Earth by Galileo Galilei.

London is attacked by scout force from Mars, which is repelled by Freedom's 5.

Waves of invasion by minor species, often lone scouts seeking to conquer on behalf of their worlds.

Lesser alien invasion attempts subside as number of Super Heroes grows rapidly.

Far too many planets perish because ambition, military might, and scientific achievement outrace common sense and caution.

One primal species to avoid these pitfalls and subvert the inherent drive to expand are the Watchers. Following grievous moral errors in their own early evolution, these powerful beings now stand sentinel across the universe, refusing to act except in their own defense. Their self-imposed mission is to catalog the natural wonders of creation and the victories, follies, and catastrophes of all who live.

Universal Elders

The race for supremacy is costly and over billions of years many cultures perish. The survivors of these early contender species become Elders of the Universe. They attain cosmic levels of might by tapping into the Power Primordial and are sustained over eons by an obsessive devotion to one particular aspect of life: the Gardener's passion for flora, the Grandmaster's compulsion to

> The Builders created aggressive systems... Alephs... sent into the wild to purge species unfit, and unsuitable, for their new universe.
> **Ex Nihilo**

compete in games, or the Collector's mania for archiving objects and creatures. Over time, some species prove to be more proficient, clever—or just luckier—than their rivals and achieve the status of galactic empires: owing as much to trade, diplomacy, and administration as their formidable armadas and arsenals. Ultimately, expansion beyond home galaxies proves unworkable for long-lived empires such as the Rigellians, Shi'ar, Skrulls, and Kree. Waging wars over inconceivable distances proves costly and allows predatory races such as the Brood, Phalanx, Badoon, and the insectoid hordes of the Annihilation Wave to shatter millions of years of civilization and progress. Is it mere coincidence that the fall of these empires coincides with their attempts to conquer Earth? ∎

REACH FOR THE STARS

SPACE CHAMPIONS AND CHALLENGERS

ON THE RECORD

DESIGNATION
Protectors of the Universe

POWERS
**Various and augmented
by cosmic awareness**

PURPOSE
Safeguarding all life

STATUS REPORT
Very high mortality rate

Enigma effect Captain Universe's Uni-power grants cosmic might and insight to those in distress, for as long as they need it.

The measureless depths of space contain countless wonders. Life exists throughout creation in a multitude of forms, and every planet, star, or nebula harbors many mysteries. The most intriguing perhaps are the origins of those select beings designated for cosmic service. Life is precious but also cheap, and tyranny, injustice, and atrocity are known on every world. Many great cosmic empires begin as a means of curtailing interstellar incursions, but even major empires such as the Rigellian Colonizers, Kree, or Shi'ar sometimes need assistance in moments of grave galactic crisis.

All universes are overseen by abstract beings presiding over the grand design, but they are the pinnacle of a vast system with powerful ancient beings working beneath them to ensure the continuity of existence. New servants are—potentially—created every time a nascent culture discovers the secrets of building Cosmic Cubes. These energy matrixes can alter reality at the command of a holder, but their true nature is as incubators for new cosmic or even abstract beings. Typically, many civilizations end dramatically and abruptly after learning how to build such cubes.

Some cosmic guardians have fortunate connections. Eon is spawned directly by Eternity as a universal defender, but in over eight billion years of existence, operates primarily through deputies. Able to bestow a form of special omniscience to his subordinates, he and his daughter, Epoch, sponsor many heroes; declaring them Protectors of the Universe. A great many have close connections to Earth: Kree refugee Captain Mar-Vell, and in turn, his children Genis and Phyla, as well as the Earthborn Wendell Vaughn, who becomes quantum Avenger Quasar.

Last man standing Man on the Wall Woodrow McCord spends his life keeping Earth clean of alien influence.

Vault of heaven

Earth is an object of particular fascination to many alien races. Visited by Kree, Skrulls, Celestials, and others, it is also a repository of immense unknowable phenomena such as the sporadic, randomly manifesting Enigma Force, which transforms some inhabitants into its cosmic avatar, Captain Universe.

Earth is also home to magical artifacts and supernatural entities, and is riddled with dimensional portals. Over millennia, it has become a vault for discarded extraterrestrial technology. The Kree alone have left robotic Sentries in dormant bases, active reality-warping Psyche-Magnetrons, and at least one pair of their legendary Nega-Bands where primitive humans can find them. Ten potent rings from Maklu IV abandoned in ancient China change the course of planetary history as the deadly armory of would-be world ruler, the Mandarin.

This may be why so many minor star kingdoms have tried to conquer the planet. All have failed thanks to human ingenuity, and the prowess and resilience of its warriors. As well as being fierce and territorial, Earth's human inhabitants are genetically mutable: able to breed with alien species and more liable to gain power from alien contact than succumb to exotic forces. Far wiser are those aliens who choose infiltration over confrontation, such as the "Greys," who unofficially set up in Las Vegas from the end of

Earth is significant... the axis around which the Multiverse spins. Here the life and death of everything will be decided.
Captain Universe

the 1940s. Their subtle criminal activities only end in the 1970s, after wealthy inventor Howard Stark defeats them. Stark's other role is the primary reason Earth remains in human control. A time-traveling member of Earth's secret society of super-geniuses, Stark is also armorer to anti-extraterrestrial vigilante cult the Men on the Wall: repurposing confiscated technology and his own innovations to keep Earth safe from unnatural threats. ∎

See also: Space invaders, Elders of the Universe, Kree, Skrulls, Avengers

The Mandarin's Rings These Rings of Power have been revealed as sentient AI beings with their own agendas. Each alien artifact has its own power.

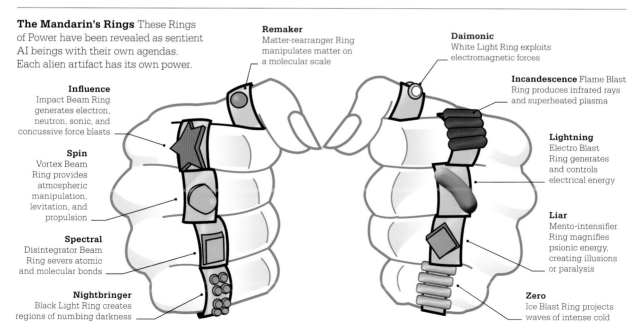

Remaker
Matter-rearranger Ring manipulates matter on a molecular scale

Daimonic
White Light Ring exploits electromagnetic forces

Incandescence Flame Blast Ring produces infrared rays and superheated plasma

Influence
Impact Beam Ring generates electron, neutron, sonic, and concussive force blasts

Spin
Vortex Beam Ring provides atmospheric manipulation, levitation, and propulsion

Spectral
Disintegrator Beam Ring severs atomic and molecular bonds

Nightbringer
Black Light Ring creates regions of numbing darkness

Lightning
Electro Blast Ring generates and controls electrical energy

Liar
Mento-intensifier Ring magnifies psionic energy, creating illusions or paralysis

Zero
Ice Blast Ring projects waves of intense cold

OLD SOULS
ELDERS OF THE UNIVERSE

ON THE RECORD

KNOWN MEMBERS
Grandmaster, Astronomer, Collector, Champion, Runner, Caregiver, Challenger, Contemplator, Gardener, Obliterator, Trader, Voyager, and others

ALLEGIANCES
Each other

POWERS
Immortality, energy and matter manipulation

MISSION
Relentlessly pursuing their individual obsessions

STATUS REPORT
Following their own hearts' desires wherever it leads

Each one a survivor of a race or species spawned in the earliest eons of creation, the Elders of the Universe are less than gods, but far more than mortal. A loose association who seldom fraternize, Elders can amass vast levels of power, depending upon their chosen field of endeavor and the

knowledge and experience its pursuit can bring them. Although some have managed to keep close family with them through the ages, their only real loyalty is to their own particular obsession. Whenever opportunity arises to increase their personal power, prestige, or status, solitary Elders can work effectively together.

The Elders' longevity is less an aspect of individual biology than a reward for overwhelming efforts of will. Each ancient has outlived the extinction of their kind through obsessive drive and focused devotion upon one compelling aspect of life: philosophy, astronomy, tourism, competition, collecting exotic ephemera, or other far less innocent pastimes.

Maht Pacle—who deems himself the Obliterator—proudly boasts he is the last of his kind because he killed all the others. He hunts and destroys novel life-forms, and is only stopped from more intergalactic bloodletting after the righteous cosmic wanderer the Silver Surfer destroys all his weapons and equipment before marooning him on a lifeless world.

Elders are everlasting cosmic hobbyists. Only when a fascination pales or its pursuit is denied them,

can death come for an Elder. This happens to Matani Tivan, who, after billions of years in idyllic contemplation, loses her will to go on and perishes, leaving behind her equally long-lived husband and daughter, Carina. When he realizes the cause of her death, widower Taneleer Tivan becomes the Collector; initially preserving all life-forms against a psychically foreseen future conqueror. In time, however, he slavishly acquires objects and creatures simply to satisfy his own compulsive whims. The Collector's prophetic gifts draw him constantly to Earth and into clashes with the Avengers, before he is murdered by his long-foreseen nemesis, Korvac.

We Elders cannot die, but you can!
Grandmaster

The Soul Gem

Immensely long-lived beings like the Elders accrue rare and significant objects as a matter of course. The Infinity Stones—which utilized in combination can overrule reality—have often passed through their hands, such as the Soul Gem of the Gardener Ord Zyonz.

The least understood of the six gems, it has also briefly been the property of many unique individuals such as the High Evolutionary, the In-Betweener, Doctor Strange, Ultron/Hank Pym, Thanos, and both Adam Warlock and his future evil self, the Magus. The Soul Gem's power encompasses both rationalistic universal energies and the mystical realms of the higher consciousness. It can absorb the personalities of sentient beings it has killed and place them in a Paradise world within itself. Parasitic over time, it attaches itself to its hosts by stealing their life force. The gem currently resides with Gamora of the Guardians of the Galaxy.

Everlasting Elders

Things change after strategic genius En Dwi Gast, the Grandmaster, challenges Death to a Contest of Champions. He uses the result he has rigged to resurrect his "brother," the Collector, and seize control of the Afterlife. Although the Avengers eventually rectify the cosmic aberration, in the aftermath, Death bans all Elders from her domain. By making them truly immortal, Death plays into the hands of the Grandmaster, who all along had subtly worked for this prized result.

The fanatical immortals can also tap into a vast residual energy field created by the Big Bang which birthed the current Multiverse. Like the Power Cosmic bestowed by Galactus upon his heralds, this "Power Primordial" enables Elders to traverse space and time, survive any environment, teleport, transmute molecular matter, and manipulate a wide range of energies and radiation, all while enhancing their senses and psionic capabilities.

With access to such might, Elders often interact with Creation's preeminent entities, but have little regard for them. Grandmaster's greatest scheme is to destroy Galactus—a survivor of the previous Multiverse —thus destabilizing conceptual overlords Death and Eternity, and restarting reality with the Elders as its ultimate beings. The plan is only foiled by the timely interference of the Silver Surfer and assorted Earth heroes. ∎

Respect your Elders Although usually solitary beings, Elders will work together if it's in their mutual interests.

SINISTER SHAPE-SHIFTERS
SKRULLS

A shape-shifting warrior race originating in the Andromeda galaxy, Skrulls are a result of genetic modification by Celestials. Eons ago, Eternals, Primes, and Deviants were created from reptiles, with the genetically unstable Deviants developing body-morphing abilities and eliminating their rivals. During this turbulent period, the Deviants subdivided into two species, with the majority becoming Skrulls, a technologically advanced intergalactic trading empire. A matriarchal, magic-using minority adopted some mammalian characteristics, evolving into parasitic Dire Wraiths. Driven from Skrullos in a genocidal race-war, they founded Wraithworld in the Dark Nebula. Skrull traders expanded far beyond their galaxy until encountering the belligerent cavemen of planet Hala. Attempts to civilize these Kree led to the butchering of the Skrull envoys and theft of their technology, sparking warfare between the two species. Rapidly rediscovering their martial prowess, the shape-shifters mastered planetary infiltration, transitioning into an expansionist, militaristic conqueror race.

Skrulls are masters of science. Their physicists built the first Cosmic Cube and their biologists can modify soldiers with cyborg implants, creating Kl'rt the Super-Skrull, Power Skrull Paibok, and Warskrulls, all able to emulate other species' powers. Despite this and occasional mutations, Skrulls are considered to be evolutionarily stagnant. They are also rebellious and fanatical by nature. While most channel this passion into love for the Skrull Empire or religion, many

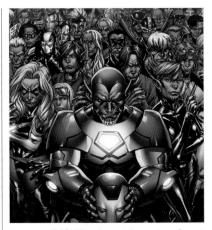

Power shift The Secret Invasion almost succeeds as the Skrulls copy the powers of Earth's Super Heroes.

are conscientious objectors and dissenters. Some become cultural pirates, scrupulously adopting and mimicking other cultures. Earth's history provides fertile inspiration, with entire planets and solar systems copying gangster-ridden Chicago of the 1920s or the 1950s Eisenhower era.

The Empire is currently in decline, ravaged by civil war following Galactus' destruction of the Imperial Fleet and throneworld Tarnax IV, and subsequent attacks by Annihilus' Annihilation Waves. ∎

SOLDIERS BLUE

KREE

Order! Order! Having defeated the Supreme Intelligence, Ronan the Accuser uses his Universal Weapon to take charge.

ON THE RECORD

ALLEGIANCES
Constantly shifting: Galactic Council, Inhumans

BASE
Northern Lobe of the Greater Magellanic Cloud, originally planet Hala

POWERS
Scientifically superior species

MISSION
Dominating the universe

STATUS REPORT
Rebuilding the Kree Empire after catastrophic invasions and internal disorder

Ambitious, inventive, and brutal, the Kree attain intergalactic dominance after Skrull traders arrange a competition between them and planet Hala's other sentient race, the telepathic Cotati plants. With advanced technology as the prize they are all relocated for one year to Earth's Moon. The primitive Kree build a magnificent city—known today as the "Blue Area"—but when the Cotati's garden is declared the winner, the Kree furiously slaughter the pacifist Skrulls. Taking the Skrulls' spaceship, the Kree master its principles, ascending from stone age to star-travel in a generation. They carve out a vast empire by absorbing defeated races into an ever-expanding sphere of influence.

Kree originate from planetary seeding by ancient Xorrians, and are further evolved from beasts to men by the godlike Progenitors. Celestials then derive Eternals and Deviants from Kree DNA, but the ferocious blue men drive all variant species from Hala. Unable to naturally evolve, Kree later conduct their own genetic trials on many worlds, including Earth where, millennia ago, they created the Terrigen-triggered Inhumans.

Led by the Supreme Intelligence—a gestalt of the empire's greatest leaders, scientists, and thinkers—Kree are experts in technological sophistication. Their arsenal includes body-modification, robotic Sentries, reality-bending Psyche-Magnetrons, multifunctional Uni-Beam weapons, hyper-spatial Omniwave Projectors, and power-boosting Nega-Bands.

Seeking to jump-start their stalled evolution, the Supreme Intelligence orchestrates many catastrophes. By allowing a Shi'ar Nega-bomb to wipe out 80 percent of the populace in Operation Galactic Storm and exploiting galactic invasions by Annihilus and the Phalanx, he pushes the Kree toward its avowed destiny: universal domination. ∎

He who does defy us shall be destroyed!
Ronan the Accuser

SPACE INVADERS
ALIENS ON EARTH

ON THE RECORD

DESIGNATION
Unregistered extraterrestrials

RESOURCES
Futuristic science, fantastical powers, guile, fanatical devotion to a greater cause

MISSION
Resource-exploitation, tourism, colonization, human eradication

STATUS REPORT
All efforts so far have been unsuccessful—even tourism

Many aliens make Earth their home or pay a flying visit. For every Spartoi, Fortisquian, or secretive Kymellian blending in or masking their presence, however, there are bigger, uninvited guests far harder to disguise, whose motives and methods are far more basic and uncompromising. The planet has constantly encountered extra-terrestrials since primeval times. Some, like the Kree or Caretakers of Arcturus, secretly shape indigenous species' development. Sadly, the

majority of aliens only have colonization or exploitation in mind. Since Pharaoh Imhotep repelled the parasitic Brood in ancient Egypt, covert planetary defense forces from the Brotherhood of the Shield to lethally punitive Men on the Wall have repulsed countless invasions from outer space or hostile dimensions. Nevertheless, some still make planetfall and cause trouble.

In ancient China, Kakarantharan shape-shifters from Maklu IV begin centuries of infiltration and subjugation. In both human and dragon form, they patiently advance their goal, even allowing one Earthling to purloin their ten rings of power to promote his own schemes as the Mandarin. Their plot only stalls because their hibernating navigator Fin Fang Foom repeatedly

Raining monsters
When Super Heroes prove insufficient to handle Leviathons, one solution is to use bigger monsters!

awakens too soon: ravaging 8th century China, the Cold War era of 1961, and the modern world.

Monstrous mash-ups
The years following World War II are particularly fraught. Humanity's discovery of atomic energy draws the attention of many hostile worlds,

Impossible Man

Most human interactions with extraterrestrials are either wondrous or scary, but there is one wholly unwelcome visitor whose intermittent appearances are something else—extraordinarily annoying.

Poppupians are a unique and powerful species who can change instantly into anything they can imagine. Thankfully, conquest and domination are not in their character, but a low threshold for boredom is. When one far-traveled individual arrives on Earth, his pranks and practical jokes cause sheer carnage. Nothing the Fantastic Four can do stops him, so they ignore his antics. Eventually, the Impossible Man leaves to seek fun elsewhere, although he has frequently returned.

The race appears to be wiped out when Galactus consumes their planet. The Devourer gets near-fatal cosmic indigestion and "Impy" simply recreates his people from his own body mass. Consequently, it is not certain that the universe is safe from further impossible aggravation.

> The time has come!! Earth is ours!
> **Diablo**

but ingenuity, luck, and Earth's few still-active superhumans foil attacks by Goom, Googam, Gormuu, Moomba, Diablo, Rommbu, and Shadow Men. They also manage to fend off representatives of myriad other minor colonial powers and solo opportunists from beyond, like liquid terror Gor-Kill. Tragically, lost opportunities abound in such times of heightened tension, and benevolent beings such as the Blip and Monstrom are also driven away. Some unlucky combatants, like lone conqueror Orrgo, are held captive: eventually serving mankind as part of S.H.I.E.L.D.'s monstrous Howling Commandos unit.

Many invaders are confined on Monster Isle: a desolate Pacific Ocean atoll near Japan. It conceals a connection to the Subterranean kingdom of Mole Man: its surface and under-Earth interior is home to numerous giant beasts, many created in ancient times by Warlord Kro from the Deviant's slave-race of "Mutates." Extraterrestrial and extradimensional incursions gradually decline as the number of Super Heroes increases, but the most ancient expansionist races—Skrulls, Shi'ar, and Kree—continue their forays, always favoring stealth and infiltration over overt assaults.

Occasionally however, old-fashioned monster raids reoccur, with Super Heroes leading the charge to repel them. The most recent is from the Leviathon Tide: a cosmic plague bedevilling many galaxies. In each case the Leviathon Mother dispatches waves of colossal, ravening beasts to crush a selected planet, preparing it as a "Desecrated Nest" for hatching new progeny. The invasion of Earth would have succeeded—despite the resistance of assorted militaries and assembled Super Heroes—but for the timely intervention of young NuHuman Kei Kawade. His power to manifest and control any monster he can draw blunts the attack. When earlier invaders Zzutak and Fin Fang Foom fall under the thrall of "Kid Kaiju," they join with Super Heroes to spearhead the counterattack that saves the world. In gratitude, the big beasts are housed with Kawade on Mu, an Inhuman locale terraformed into a new Monster Island. ■

Terror treaty Kid Kaiju and monster-hunter Elsa Bloodstone make Fin Fang Foom an offer he can't resist.

THE MAD TITAN
THANOS

ON THE RECORD

ALLEGIANCES
Black Order, Cabal, Zodiac, Infinity Watch

BASE
Chitauri Prime, *Sanctuary II*

POWERS
Enhanced strength, speed, and senses; invulnerability; flight; teleportation; telepathy; energy, matter, and magic manipulation

MISSION
Amass enough power to win favor from Death

STATUS REPORT
Dead, but still a threat to all life

Deviant child Thanos' hide-like, purple-colored skin and huge body are enough to drive his mother insane.

T hanos' parents are Earth Eternals who migrated to Saturn's moon Titan millennia ago. His father is planetary leader A'Lars. Born deformed due to a genetic abnormality known as Deviant Syndrome, Thanos' mother Sui-San tries to kill her son on sight. He survives, and after another brush with mortality, young Thanos meets the personification of Death and his

destiny is set. Abandoning the closed colony on Titan, he returns decades later leading an interstellar pirate army, and eradicates most of the planet's population. His body now modified by bionic implants, magic, and other power-enhancing techniques, Thanos targets Earth, intent on elevating himself to godhood using a reality-altering Cosmic Cube. Ultimately he is thwarted by Kree warrior Captain Mar-Vell and the Avengers.

Infatuated with conceptual entity Mistress Death, Thanos seeks to exterminate life and become a supreme being using other artifacts of power like the Infinity Gems. Failure costs him his life time and again, but he never falters, returning

as avatar and champion of Death to resume his crusade of slaughter. During his interstellar ravages, he gathers a group of disciples to carry out his schemes and embrace his nihilistic philosophies. The members of his Black Order are loyal, lethal emissaries of evil, but invariably harbor ambitions to be far more than Thanos' deputies.

An unwanted child, Thanos craves certainty, believing satisfaction only comes from total control. Despising weakness above all else, he continuously rebuilds and improves himself, striving to reshape the universe into a place that makes sense to him. Tragically, Thanos' twisted rationality is that of a death-obsessed madman.

Control freak
Despite being one of the greatest minds in existence, Thanos is intent on destruction and conquest. His heart holds great love, but only for Mistress Death. Her disdainful rejections result in his frequent resurrections to a life and reality he despises. As a consequence, Thanos ceaselessly plots to subjugate, erase, or ignore the universe around him, determined to remake an unsatisfactory reality into one

Black Order

Thanos' elite advance taskforce is brutally efficient, but not indestructible. The barbaric Corvus Glaive's atom-rending glaive-blade grants him immortality, but when he tries to form his own Black Order, Thanos compels his servant to kill himself. Glaive's wife Proxima Midnight is Thanos' most ardent acolyte, executing his orders with savage joy. He discards her for failing him, and Asgardian Death deity Hela slays Midnight with her own spear. Super-strong, sadistic, and stupid, Black Dwarf is Glaive's brother. He is killed by Ronan the Accuser. Physically weakest, Ebony Maw is a rapacious, cowardly mind-pirate with powers of mental persuasion. Psionic world-destroyer Black Swan brings arcane knowledge and ruthless cunning to the team. Lastly, psychic omnipath Supergiant now exists as a thought-wraith after being killed by Inhuman prince Maximus when she fails to destroy Earth with an antimatter bomb.

The whole team is eventually revived by the Grandmaster as his agents in an Earth-shattering competition with rival Elder of the Universe, the Challenger.

he controls. However, his hunger for conflict always betrays him.

Thanos is fixated on controlling Earth, but is constantly defeated by its native and alien defenders. During the Incursion crisis as parallel Earths crash into each other, sparking multiversal obliteration, he launches another invasion. This assault has the dual purpose of reclaiming the Infinity Gems and eliminating his son Thane, whom he sired on Earth with an Inhuman woman. Thwarted by Inhuman King Black Bolt and doomed to a "living death" by Thane, Thanos is revived and gleefully joins Namor's Cabal,

destroying alternate universes colliding with Earth. However, in the ensuing cataclysm he once again dies. Accidentally revived by Galactus, Thanos is neutralized by Black Panther and the Ultimates, before escaping capture.

Thanos' intellect and machinations have repeatedly gained him omnipotence, but his emotional flaws always sabotage his moment of triumph. A chance to break the cycle comes when he is abducted to the far future by Spirit of Vengeance: Ghost Rider and clashes with his older self—King Thanos— who rules everything that still exists. The confrontation drives the Mad Titan to escape his destiny at any cost. On returning to the present, he begins reassembling the reality-warping Infinity Gauntlet. However, when former disciple and adopted daughter Gamora attacks him, he seizes the opportunity to thwart fate, allowing her to kill him. Perhaps this time will be the last... ◼

All life is a distraction. Therefore it has no real value.
Thanos

Death duty Thanos lets nothing stand in his way to win the favor of Mistress Death—not even death itself.

ABSOLUTE POWER
THE INFINITY GAUNTLET

ON THE RECORD

COMPONENTS
Infinity Gems governing Time, Space, Reality, Power, Mind, and Soul

POWERS
Used in unison, the gems can rewrite existence

STATUS REPORT
Rebuilt by Requiem, sought after by all who know of it

The Infinity Gauntlet is a device created to use the combined power of the six Infinity Gems which, when brought together, comprise the totality of universal forces. The Time, Space, Power, Mind, Soul, and Reality Stones are first united by Thanos (pictured above) to power a cannon he built to extinguish the stars. However, his dream of universal genocide is defeated by Earth Super Heroes the Thing, Spider-Man, and the Avengers before the Mad Titan is executed by the spirit of Adam Warlock acting as the Avatar of Universal Life. Gravitating to their previous individual custodians—the Elders of the Universe—the gems are then employed in a concerted attack on Galactus and believed lost forever in a black hole. However, the cosmic artifacts are inherently attuned to universal crisis points and beings of power, and are soon back in operation.

When Thanos returns to life, he gathers the six gems, claiming they are remnants of a primal cosmic being from the time of universal creation who divided its omnipotent essence into six parts. Evidence later suggests that this might be subterfuge or misdirection on Thanos' part. Understanding their unified ability to manipulate the totality of all existence, and that they can overwhelm the Multiverse's most powerful beings

See the light
The Illuminati swear to safeguard and never use the Infinity Gems, but they are soon forced to revoke that decision.

such as Galactus, the Celestials, and Eternity, Thanos recovers the gems, constructing a glove to combine the gems' power. He then begins an assault on all life in the name of his uncaring mistress, Death. Again, Thanos is confronted and ultimately defeated by Adam Warlock and a coalition of Earth's champions, after which cosmic adjudicator the Living Tribunal decrees the gems are too dangerous to ever be combined again. As a consequence, they are split up and each one assigned a guardian in Warlock's Infinity Watch.

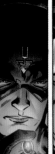

Infinity wars

Despite the prohibition, the Infinity Gauntlet is re-formed many times until it is finally destroyed when Captain America Steve Rogers uses it on behalf of Earth's Illuminati to prevent a Multiversal incursion destroying two universes set on a collision course. Although successful, the effort shatters five of the stones and causes the Time Gem to vanish altogether. Infinity Gems and variations of the Gauntlet occur in all universes, but are reality-specific, unable to function outside their own plane of origin or substantially affect each other across the totality of existence.

The crisis leads to Multiverse annihilation, with life only surviving in a pocket dimension: Doctor Doom's Battleworld. When the Multiverse is recreated, the gems revert to an unrefined state and scatter across creation. They are the subject of intense competition as numerous factions seek them. Eventually, a new wish-fulfilling Infinity Gauntlet is constructed by Thanos' former foster daughter, Gamora. Calling herself Requiem, she seeks vengeance on her father and is determined to recover

Grip on power

Individually powerful beyond compare, when the Infinity Gems are used in conjunction or unison, their force is multiplied—turning the universe into a mere plaything.

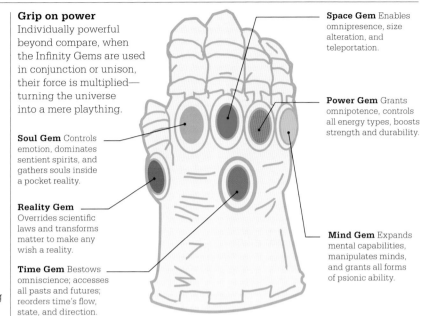

Soul Gem Controls emotion, dominates sentient spirits, and gathers souls inside a pocket reality.

Reality Gem Overrides scientific laws and transforms matter to make any wish a reality.

Time Gem Bestows omniscience; accesses all pasts and futures; reorders time's flow, state, and direction.

Space Gem Enables omnipresence, size alteration, and teleportation.

Power Gem Grants omnipotence, controls all energy types, boosts strength and durability.

Mind Gem Expands mental capabilities, manipulates minds, and grants all forms of psionic ability.

a shard of her soul from within the Soul Gem. Her deranged Infinity War sees Gamora fatally precipitate an aberrant and catastrophic rewriting of reality. The resultant Warp World consists of nightmarish amalgams of friends and foes. Finally, Asgardian god Loki's Cosmic Avengers and Adam Warlock bring her to her senses.

With reality restored, Warlock exiles Requiem, sending her on a quest to earn redemption while he attempts to end the threat of the Infinity Stones by making them self-aware. His ultimate hope is that the stones will be able to govern themselves and never again be used as the tools of greedy, ambitious, or insane individuals. ∎

Infinity Watch

Infinity Stones can be used by any life-form that experiences desire. Too dangerous to keep together or leave unguarded, they are divided up among a "Coalition of the Trustworthy" to ensure that if they are used, it is for the benefit of life. The first Infinity Watch consists of freshly resurrected Adam Warlock (Soul Gem), Gamora (Time Gem), and Pip the Troll (Space Gem), with Moondragon, Drax, and Thanos respectively safeguarding the Mind, Power, and Reality Gems.

When the team splits up, the gems fall into the care of Earth's Illuminati, until a new Multiverse demands a new Infinity Watch. Confiscating the Time Stone from Super-Skrull, Doctor Strange institutes a new roster. Warlock again holds the Soul Stone, while petty thug Turk Barrett keeps the Mind Stone. Black Widow protects the Space Stone, while the Power Stone goes to Star-Lord, and Carol Danvers watches over the Reality stone in her role as Captain Marvel.

SYMBIOTIC BONDS
VENOM

ON THE RECORD

DESIGNATION
The Klyntar

ALLEGIANCES
Agents of the Cosmos, Knull

POWERS
Genetically mimicked powers of Spider-Man, organic web generation, invisibility, extreme shape-shifting

MISSION
Protect the innocent (lethally)

STATUS REPORT
Back with Eddie Brock and making waves

As the current universe coalesced, evil god Knull created symbiotes from his own shadow to destroy his enemies: Celestials and other deities. Knull is the basis of a communal hivemind, and his amorphous, inorganic Klyntar ravage countless worlds over billions of years, until reaching Earth in the 6th century BCE. Here, Asgardian Thor severs their link to Knull. Now influenced by their hosts, symbiotes start to achieve a degree of rationality; absorbing morality and honor as well as genetic information, emotional traits, and memories.

Rebellious Klyntar then entomb Knull in an artificial world. Seeking to bury their shameful past, they form universal peacekeeping sect Agents of the Cosmos, bonding only with noble heroes. However, some Klyntar reject redemption and remain predatory: fueling and feeding on hosts' negative emotions and physiological by-products such as adrenaline and other hormones. These feral Klyntar still plague isolated planets as the ultimate apex predators. Even after being forced from a host, Klyntar always leave behind a fraction of biomass. This "codex" shares the hosts' genetic and cognitive information with the hivemind. Always replicating and amplifying the hosts' biology, symbiotes can bestow those attributes on future wearers, eventually building them into beings of godlike power with whom they can bond.

Lethal protector
When Earth's Super Heroes and Villains are abducted to an alien Battleworld by the Beyonder, Spider-Man acquires a new, programmable costume: thought-controlled, able

Dark cravings Despite trying to reform, Eddie Brock and the Klyntar feed off each other's darkest desires.

Anti-Venom

The symbiote deserts Eddie Brock when he develops cancer. He again attempts suicide, but the codex inside him reacts with lightforce energy from the villainous Mr. Negative to create a new symbiote. Anti-Venom has all his original powers, but can also heal others and destroy other symbiotes with a touch. The symbiote then bonds with Mac Gargan: formerly the villainous Scorpion. Cruel and greedy, Gargan succumbs to the Klyntar's darkest nature, killing and consuming enemies while in Norman Osborn's Dark Avengers.

The symbiote's greatest moments come when it is bonded to disabled war veteran Eugene "Flash" Thompson as part of a US military project. Agent Venom crushes evil on Earth as an Avenger, joins the Guardians of the Galaxy, and saves alien races as an Agent of the Cosmos. When the symbiote abandons him, Flash becomes a new Anti-Venom (pictured) and sacrifices his life to save Spider-Man.

to alter shape, color, and texture, and provide unlimited webbing. On returning to Earth, the wall-crawler uses the costume constantly, but as time passes, he seems perpetually tired and experiences memory lapses. He has no idea his suit is a living creature, feeding off Spidey's emotions and taking over his body while Peter Parker sleeps. Upon discovering the truth, Parker rejects it with utter revulsion. Although it has bonded to him, he escapes its clutches with the help of Reed Richards. Frustrating its attempts to reconnect, Parker leaves it to die in a church, where it attaches itself to despondent, suicidal journalist Eddie Brock: a man with an obsessive hatred of Spider-Man.

Apart, we were victims.
But together, we are Venom!
Venom

Lord of the Abyss Primal deity Knull dreams of the day his rebellious Klyntar slaves will again serve his malign will.

Welcomed at last, the traumatized symbiote establishes an unhealthy relationship with Brock. Feeding each other's hatred, they carry out a campaign of terror against Spidey as the suit duplicates and augments recorded genetic structures to make Brock a bigger, tougher, more savage Spider-Man: Venom! Eventually, Parker and Brock call a truce.

Brock's dreams of being a hero are fulfilled as he becomes a "lethal protector" delivering brutal justice to criminals. Often this means allowing the symbiote to consume the creeps it defeats. The creature causes further—inadvertent—harm when it spawns vicious, violent progeny such as Carnage. Venom's appalling offspring bonds with unrepentant psycho-killer Cletus Cassidy, a human monster even before he is merged with a blood-red bad seed, hungry for chaos and destruction.

Venom's biology is harvested and weaponized many times, such as when Life Foundation scientists create mutated symbiote mercenaries Scream, Riot, Phage, Agony, and Lasher; or when Doctor Doom produces a transformative symbiote virus to attack New York. Eventually the symbiote moves to other hosts, but after bonding with fools, monstrous villains, victims, and joining the Agents of the Cosmos with Flash Thompson, it finds Eddie Brock once again. Reunited as the real Venom but still wounded, deranged, and potentially cannibalistic, they seek to mend each other's broken psyches and find a way back to heroism. ∎

COSMIC PROTECTOR
CAPTAIN MARVEL

ON THE RECORD

REAL NAME
**Carol Susan Jane Danvers;
Car-Ell (Kree name)**

ALLEGIANCES
**Alpha Flight Space Program,
Ultimates, Avengers, Infinity
Watch, Guardians of the
Galaxy, S.H.I.E.L.D.**

BASE
**Alpha Flight Low-Orbit
Space Station; Manhattan**

POWERS
**Superhuman strength, speed,
and durability; flight; energy
manipulation; precognition**

MISSION
Forever striving to save lives

STATUS REPORT
**Expanding her remit to
cover the entire universe**

For years, US Air Force officer Carol Danvers believes she has been transformed into a multi-powered superhuman by malfunctioning Kree technology and a strange twist of fate. Only after years of turmoil and conflict as a soldier, spy, and intergalactic Super Hero does she learn that her origins are far more complex. Boston born and raised, Danvers has her eyes on the sky and her heart set on space travel. Dreaming of astronaut training, she excels at school, but leaves home to join the military when her father refuses to pay college tuition for a girl. She becomes a master pilot; closing in on her dreams after working in the USAF Intelligence Special Operations unit. Danvers' espionage success leads to her appointment as Security Officer at a NASA base where she first comes across Captain Mar-Vell. As Walter Lawson, the Kree agent has infiltrated the base to spy on human progress. When he defects to humanity, Mar-Vell's duel with Kree Colonel Yon-Rogg results in Danvers being caught in the blast of a Psyche-Magnitron.

Call of duty Danvers' life of service coincides with her great passions: fighting for justice and flying higher, further, and faster.

A true Marvel
With her memories clouded and career stalled, Danvers resigns. Becoming a journalist, she moves to New York where her arrival coincides with the debut of a new Super Hero, Ms. Marvel, who

Kamala Khan, Ms. Marvel

Born in Jersey City, Pakistani-American Kamala Khan is a smart, dutiful Muslim daughter until she is transformed by a Terrigen-cloud into a shape-shifting NuHuman. A Super Hero nerd, she has watched the uncanny events happening across the river in New York City all her life, and her favorite Super Hero is Carol Danvers— Captain Marvel.

When Khan's own amazing morphogenetic abilities kick in, she uses them to save her friends from an armed robbery, and is soon defending her city from a wave of bizarre threats as Ms. Marvel. When the universe ends and restarts, she finally meets her hero, who gives the teenager her blessing. Over months, the new kid blossoms into a mighty force for good. She briefly joins the Avengers before creating and leading a breakaway team of teenage Champions seeking fresh, less aggressive and destructive ways to solve super-problems.

bears a striking resemblance to Mar-Vell. Eventually Danvers discovers that she is Ms. Marvel, apparently genetically altered by the Kree wonder-weapon and imprinted with Mar-Vell's training, instincts, and powers. Her mind now clear and dual personalities fully integrated, she becomes an Avenger, until her powers and personality are erased by the mutant Rogue. Aided by Spider-Woman (Jessica Drew) and the X-Men, Danvers gains new abilities, tapping the infinite powers of a white hole, and leaves the galaxy.

Fighting injustice beside the Starjammers, X-Men, and Avengers on Earth and throughout space, Danvers carves out a legend as blazing human star Binary, before resettling on her birthworld. Rejoining the Avengers and later carving out a solo career under different code names—Warbird and Ms. Marvel—Danvers saves Earth and many other worlds. She also wins her greatest battle by coming to terms with the alcoholism her high-pressure life and family heritage have provoked. After months of triumphant victories against great odds, she is convinced to take the name Captain Marvel, in honor of the Kree warrior who first inspired her.

After time off-world serving with the Guardians of the Galaxy, Danvers returns to the Avengers and also takes a position with the Alpha Flight Space Program, stationed on their Low-Orbit Space Station. It is the world's first line of defense against alien incursion and Captain Marvel becomes Earth's Ambassador to the stars. Direct and uncompromising, Danvers devises the Ultimates, strategizing with the Black Panther to create a potent team to head off cosmic-level threats. However, her hard-line views on preemptive intervention bring her into contention with Tony Stark and spark a second ideological civil war among Earth's Super Heroes. While she is heartbroken at the human cost, she is unrepentant about the necessity of her actions.

Danvers' biggest shock comes after spending time with her family following her estranged father's death. Attacked by cyborg Kree Kleaners, she learns that her mother, Marie, is actually a sleeper agent of the stellar empire and called Mari-Ell. It transpires that Danvers is a human/Kree hybrid and her powers are her birthright, not a mere cosmic fluke. ■

Nobody knew the truth... my secret birthright. Not even me.
Carol Danvers

Space invaded With waves of Chitauri attacking Earth, Captain Marvel leads the Guardians of the Galaxy into battle.

CAPTAINS COURAGEOUS
MAR-VELL AND OTHER CAPTAIN MARVELS

ON THE RECORD

REAL NAME
Mar-Vell

ALLEGIANCES
Defenders, Avengers, Infinity Watch, Eternals of Titan

POWERS
Enhanced strength, speed, and durability; cosmic awareness; energy control; Nega-Bands allow space flight

MISSION
Protector of the Universe

STATUS REPORT
Dead, but his legacy lives on

When Kree soldier Mar-Vell is assigned to spy on humanity, he quickly loses his emotional detachment and goes native. Admiring his subjects, he renounces his heritage and mission to become a true Super Hero. Throughout this period, Mar-Vell is an unwitting part of the Supreme Intelligence's schemes to increase its own mental powers and kickstart the Kree's stalled evolutionary progress. The Supreme Intelligence (aka Supremor) traps Mar-Vell in the antimatter Negative Zone, bonding him with human Rick Jones via power-providing Nega-Bands. These devices tap the Zone's energies and amplify the attributes of the wearers.

Jones has been the Supreme Intelligence's tool since the Kree-Skrull war, where his latent psionic powers were first activated by the Supremor to end the conflict. The enforced partners trade places for brief periods, allowing Mar-Vell to be active in positive matter realms and across space: battling evil, thwarting Thanos' mad schemes of godhood, and becoming the cosmically aware Protector of the Universe. Ultimately, their bond is severed and the Kree defector settles on Titan with Eternal lover Elysius, before dying from combat-induced cancer.

Not fade away An honorable soldier to his core, Mar-Vell dedicates his life and soul to the safety of others.

Many heroes assume his name and mantle, such as human/Kree hybrid Carol Danvers, light-manipulating Avenger Monica Rambeau (now Spectrum), as well as alternate universe Kree warrior Noh-Varr. The most tragic successor is Skrull Khn'nr who, thanks to faulty mind-programming, dies heroically, convinced he is the true Mar-Vell.

Cosmic watchdogs

The universe is a crucial cog in a greater cosmic machine: one that needs constant monitoring and intervention. As such, all aspects of creation have special agents overseeing the process.

Descended from Eternity, Eon (pictured) is an eight-billion-year old being whose purpose is to make and advise Protectors of the Universe. Residing in an Eonverse subdimension and linked to all points in time, Eon provides wisdom, gives psychological support, and bestows Cosmic Awareness on his agents: proving knowledge and skill can always overcome sheer power. Able to resurrect the dead and reshape reality, Eon creates the light-manipulating Quantum Bands used by Mar-Vell and his Earthborn successor Wendell Vaughn aka Quasar. When Eon is seemingly killed by Oblivion's avatar, Maelstrom, Quasar is guided by, and safeguards, his daughter, Epoch, until she can fully assume Eon's role.

> It is my destiny... to attract some danger... wherever I go.
> **Mar-Vell**

Dynasty of heroes

On Titan, Elysius chooses to genetically engineer a son, Genis, by harvesting cells from herself and Mar-Vell. She artificially matures him to adulthood to protect him from Mar-Vell's enemies. With Kree training and employing the Nega-bands, Genis becomes Legacy, carrying on his father's work. During a time-warping Destiny War, he is forcibly merged with Rick Jones just as his father had been. This triggers his dormant Cosmic Awareness and Genis calls himself Captain Marvel. He also begins to go insane, thanks to the twisted influence of abstract entities Entropy and Epiphany. As his heroic deeds are cancelled out by his actions in destroying and recreating a flawed new universe, Elysius creates another child—Phyla—with Mar-Vell's DNA, to counteract him.

Elysius is unaware that on Earth, a true son already exists. Foundling Teddy Altman has been raised as human, but is in fact the result of a clandestine liaison between the Kree Captain and Skrull Princess Anelle at the height of the Kree-Skrull war. Altman is preparing to begin his own Super Hero career as the shape-shifting Young Avenger named Hulkling.

Possessing Cosmic Awareness like her brother, Phyla-Vell battles her deranged elder sibling to restore reality, exiling Genis into the time stream. Consulting with Rick Jones, Phyla becomes a new Captain Marvel, before being drawn into the extra-galactic Annihilation Wave war sparked by an invasion from the Negative Zone. When current Protector of the Universe, Quasar, is killed by Annihilus, Phyla-Vell claims his name, Quantum Bands, and role. As the crisis intensifies, Phyla-Vell also becomes avatar of abstract entity Oblivion, eventually taking the name Martyr and perishing to save

Martyr complex Phyla-Vell's pact with Oblivion compels her to turn on her allies and kill Life's Avatar Adam Warlock.

the Guardians of the Galaxy. Following countless adventures in the time stream, Genis-Vell returns to Earth and joins Super Villain penal battalion, the Thunderbolts. Dubbed Photon, he dies when his chronally super-charged body starts accelerating the age—and shortening the longevity—of the universe, forcing Thunderbolts leader Helmut Zemo to scatter Genis-Vell's body through time and the Darkforce dimension. ∎

GUARDIAN OF THE GALAXY
STAR-LORD

ON THE RECORD

REAL NAME
Peter Jason Quill

ALLEGIANCES
Guardians of the Galaxy,
Avengers, Nova Corps

BASE
Spaceship *Milano*

POWERS
Enhanced reaction time and
extended longevity from
hybrid Human/Spartoi
ancestry, element guns

MISSION
Trying to make the universe
a safer place, and earn a
buck or two in the process

STATUS REPORT
Still trying...

Peter Quill grows up poor, lonely, confused, and angry. At age ten, those resentful feelings turn to vengeful outrage when aliens blow up his home and murder his beloved mother. While fleeing, his bewilderment increases after finding a bizarre artifact in his mom's closet. It takes years for him to learn the truth. While Meredith Quill was human, the father he never knew turns out to also be alien: a warrior who crashed on Earth before repairing his ship and leaving them both behind. Raised in an orphanage, Quill develops a loathing of bullies and unfairness and determines to somehow get to space— and avenge his mother.

All efforts to join the astronaut program prove futile, however. The best Quill can do is a menial mechanics job at NASA Ops' Californian Launch Facility. Spending all his off-time in flight simulators, Quill learns fast and when he is inevitably fired, steals a captured Kree ship and blasts into space. Stranded in the void, he is rescued and enslaved by piratical Ravagers before eventually convincing leader Yondu of his worth. His loyalties are tested when the pirates capture an Earth ship. Quill saves the humans before abandoning the Ravagers to forge his own destiny. Eventually, he meets his father and learns why he and his mother were targeted so long ago. Peter Quill is a royal son: prince of the warlike Spartoi Empire and heir

Rough and ready Although a cunning strategist, Star-Lord's most effective tactics are to shoot first and strike hard.

to the title Star-Lord. He learns exactly what kind of ruthless man King J'Son of Spartax is and leaves, vowing never to be like his father.

The stars my destination

A cosmic wanderer, Star-Lord confronts injustice throughout space. Encountering powerful creatures and civilizations, he spends as much time hunted as an outlaw as a revered hero who enjoys a complicated relationship with trans-galactic peacekeepers the Nova Corps. Soon after, the cosmos is ravaged by invasion from the Negative Zone: an Annihilation Wave led by insectoid tyrant Annihilus that devastates many great empires and reduces the Novas to a few pitiful pockets of resistance. Organizing the United Front resistance movement with Nova-Prime Richard Rider, Star-Lord meets Drax the Destroyer, Gamora, Ronan the Accuser, and other powerful survivors: a collection of mighty warriors who will reshape his destiny.

After Annihilus' forces are repulsed, opportunistic technological parasites the Phalanx—led by Earth's robotic nemesis Ultron—attack the weakened Kree Empire, and Star-Lord is press-ganged by Ronan into leading a tactical strike force comprising Kaliklak warrior Bug, Earthlings Captain Universe and Mantis, Shi'ar berserker Deathcry, and two unknown and unique

I must have done something really bad in a previous life.
Peter Quill

Have spacesuit, will travel
Despite having access to weapons and tech from many civilizations, Star-Lord prefers to rely on his wits and a few tried-and-tested devices that have proved effective in the past.

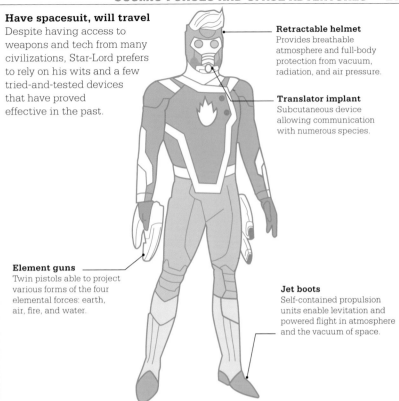

Retractable helmet
Provides breathable atmosphere and full-body protection from vacuum, radiation, and air pressure.

Translator implant
Subcutaneous device allowing communication with numerous species.

Element guns
Twin pistols able to project various forms of the four elemental forces: earth, air, fire, and water.

Jet boots
Self-contained propulsion units enable levitation and powered flight in atmosphere and the vacuum of space.

life-forms: Groot and Rocket Raccoon. Again triumphing over impossible odds, the team remain together: resolved that after two cataclysmic sneak attacks on the universe, someone needs to be ready and waiting for the inevitable next one.

Although the full roster continually changes, Star-Lord, Rocket, and Groot, plus old comrades Drax and Gamora, comprise the core of the Guardians of the Galaxy: scouring creation for trouble—and finding it. With Star-Lord notionally in command, the unit faces all manner of crises: an intergalactic War of Kings; religious slaughter by the Universal Church of Truth; invasion from a Cancerverse where there is no death; and the end of the Multiverse. Ingenuity, courage, and sheer dumb luck play equal parts in helping Star-Lord and the Guardians avert permanent Armageddon, and ensure that life goes on. ∎

On guard The Guardians of the Galaxy are unconventional heroes: outlaws and misfits protecting a universe that seems to despise them.

SHARPSHOOTING SWINDLER
ROCKET RACCOON

ON THE RECORD

ALLEGIANCES
Guardians of the Galaxy, Rocket Rangers, Halfworld

BASE
Starship *Milano*, formerly Knowhere

POWERS
Cyborg animal with enhanced strength, speed, and senses; ace pilot and tactician; weapons master

MISSION
Getting rich and protecting his friends—in that order

STATUS REPORT
Still looking for the biggest of big scores

Adventurer, thief, and reluctant hero, Rocket Raccoon was a simple animal modified by sentient robots to amuse institutionalized lunatics on the planetary asylum Halfworld. After meeting the Hulk, Rocket Raccoon is abducted by the Stranger—an Elder of the Universe obsessed with unique beings—

Did you take a double dose of naive pills today?
Rocket Raccoon

and trapped on his Labworld. Later captured by Skrulls, he becomes lost in space after encountering Earthlings Taryn O'Connell, Razorback, and She-Hulk.

Making a living however he can—generally illegally and through extreme violence—Rocket is incarcerated on Kree prison-planet Aladon Prime. Strenuously claiming he was framed, he rots there until the Empire is invaded by the Phalanx. With techno-organic life-forms subverting Kree technologies, Rocket Raccoon's unique skill set makes him crucial to the penal unit and he is offered liberty in return for going on a suicide mission. Among his fellow misfit recruits are a walking, talking

tree, Groot, and a human, Peter Quill, aka Star-Lord. Against all odds, the taskforce succeeds and (mostly) survives. In the aftermath, Rocket opts to stick with his comrades in a fluctuating team as they attempt to head off further Annihilation events. After meeting a time-traveler, he "borrows" the name of their group and starts calling his own team the Guardians of the Galaxy.

Fierce, proud, and independent, Rocket Raccoon hates appearing anything other than totally in control. His sarcastic, brusque demeanor hides a big heart and unswerving commitment to helping the downtrodden. Afflicted with a conscience—and loving a good fight—he can't help getting involved in pointless good deeds. ■

Fire away Rocket is as fast on the draw as he is with his quips, a fiery fur ball with a fully loaded mouth and armory.

ARBOREAL ALIEN

GROOT

ON THE RECORD

ALLEGIANCES
Guardians of the Galaxy

BASE
Starship *Milano*, formerly Knowhere

POWERS
Plant being with exceptional strength, durability, and plasticity; rapid growth and regeneration abilities

MISSION
Protecting his friends

STATUS REPORT
Saving the lives of the Guardians of the Galaxy

I am Groot.
Groot

Groot is an anomalous *Flora colossi* from planet Taluhnia, best known as Planet X. Lacking the innate cruelty of his fellow saplings, young Groot befriends the maintenance mammals who tend the flourishing conqueror trees. After killing one of his sadistic brethren to protect the mammals and a human laboratory subject, Groot is exiled off-world and becomes a lonely interstellar wanderer.

Eventually, Groot is captured and put into a Kree prison.

During the second Annihilation Crisis—when parasitic techno-organic Phalanx infiltrate and subjugate the Kree Empire—Groot is coerced by the warden into a unit of multipowered but expendable convicts which includes Peter Quill and Rocket Raccoon. This suicide squad is dispatched into the heart of assimilated Kree territory to destroy the Phalanx's plans to expand beyond the Kree Empire. After improbably surviving and triumphing over the Phalanx's covert leader, Ultron, the remaining prisoners stay together as the Guardians of the Galaxy. Groot and Rocket Raccoon claim they are using the team to further their get rich-quick schemes,

No, it's this way A tree of few words, tech-savvy Groot is always ready to help his buddy Rocket find his way.

but through a succession of personnel changes the unlikely heroes forge an unbreakable bond and save the universe many times.

Groot's language is extremely difficult to comprehend, but his actions never are: he cherishes life and despises senseless cruelty. He risks his life over and over again for his comrades and innocents, but is subject to the ferocious temper of all *Flora colossi*. If he considers an enemy is unworthy of life, he will kill them without an instant's hesitation. ∎

THE MOST DANGEROUS WOMAN IN THE GALAXY

GAMORA

ON THE RECORD

ALLEGIANCES
Guardians of the Galaxy, Infinity Watch, Graces United

POWERS
Bionically augmented physiology, regenerative healing factor, expert assassin and martial artist

MISSION
Revenge against Thanos

STATUS REPORT
Seeking redemption after succumbing to her darkest impulses as Requiem

After the Universal Church of Truth Inquisitors slaughter the pacifistic Zen-Whoberis for refusing to worship the Magus, ruthless plotter Thanos adopts the sole survivor. Shifting the child through time, he transforms her over decades into a living weapon through indoctrination, martial arts training, and bionic modification. Named Gamora, she becomes his agent in a scheme to kill the Magus:

Avatar of Life and foe of Death's unwanted, self-proclaimed champion, Thanos. Gamora's mission overlaps with Adam Warlock's attempts to destroy his debased future self and the two warriors become allies.

When she rebels against her "father," Thanos kills Gamora and her soul is locked in Warlock's Soul Gem until Thanos creates the Infinity Gauntlet. In response, higher beings resurrect her, Warlock, and scurrilous ally Pip the Troll, using them to oppose Thanos as an Infinity Watch to safeguard all the Infinity Gems. However, a crucial portion of her soul never escapes the Soul Gem. Following constant universal crises, Gamora leaves the Watch, wandering the stars until getting caught up in the Annihilation Wars. She finds purpose and even friends, saving lives with the Guardians of the Galaxy, but the hunger to kill her father never abates.

Obsession grips her, and when the Infinity Stones are recreated in the wake of multiversal death and rebirth, Gamora betrays the latest Infinity Watch to possess them. As Requiem, she kills friends and foes—including Thanos—and uses

the gems to reclaim her soul shard. Hoping to build a better universe, Gamora accidentally sunders all reality and creates a chaotic Warp World. Ultimately saved from herself by her Guardians of the Galaxy comrades, Gamora goes back to established reality, before being taken by Warlock on an intergalactic pilgrimage to redeem herself. ∎

Soul destroying Gamora's dreams of peace fade further away with every treacherous act Requiem commits.

GALACTIC CHAMPION
DRAX THE DESTROYER

ON THE RECORD

REAL NAME
Arthur Douglas

ALLEGIANCES
Infinity Watch, Guardians of the Galaxy, Avengers

POWERS
Great strength, speed, and durability; psionic abilities

MISSION
Killing Thanos, but recently sworn to pacifism

STATUS REPORT
Lost in another universe

Murdered by Thanos during an early reconnaissance mission to Earth, Arthur Douglas' astral essence is placed inside a new body by ascended Eternal, Kronos. Filled with mighty energies, Drax the Destroyer is hard-wired to kill Thanos. Unable to eradicate the Mad Titan, he grows frustrated as other heroes like Iron Man, Kree Captain Mar-Vell, and Adam Warlock succeed where he fails. After Thanos dies, Drax becomes an aimless cosmic nomad.

When his daughter Heather, the psychic goddess Moondragon, who is raised by Mind Priests on Titan after Douglas' death, enslaves Drax, it leads to his second demise. After Death resurrects Thanos, Kronos reactivates the Destroyer, but Drax's intellect is impaired: his mind like that of a bad-tempered child. Nevertheless, Warlock recruits him to the Infinity Watch, entrusting the Power Gem to his safekeeping. A repentant Moondragon joins, too.

The Watch disbands, and father and daughter return to Titan where Drax's mind is restored. The process is unstable and with mind and body in flux, Drax goes adventuring until arrested for killing 200,000 Skrulls. When his prison transport crashes on Earth, he dies and is reborn again,

We leave no one behind!
Drax

Green and mean Whether infinitely empowered or simply relying on muscle, Drax makes a formidable opponent.

although lacking most of his powers. Adopting human runaway Cammi Benally, he flees, but they become embroiled in the Annihilation Wars. When they are separated, Drax's search for Cammi takes him to a fateful rendezvous with other heroic outcasts and he joins the Guardians of the Galaxy. Finally doing good and making a difference, Drax commits to a vow of nonviolence before sacrificing himself on Warp World to save Gamora from the consequences of her actions as Requiem. ∎

PLANETARY POLICE
NOVA AND THE NOVA CORPS

Located in the Tranta system of Andromeda, Xandar is an ancient world of scholarly pursuits. Its inhabitants' greatest achievement is a global network of living computers, harnessing the intellects of billions of deceased citizens who have donated their brains to a unified Worldmind. It controls a limitless, primeval energy-field called the Nova Force, empowering a 500-strong planetary defense force: the Nova Corps.

When Xandar is decimated by intergalactic raider Zorr, dying Centurion Rhomann Dhey voyages to Earth, bequeathing his power to teenager Richard Rider. As Super Hero Nova the Human Rocket, Rider hones his abilities before leading an expedition of Champions back to Xandar. In the interim, the planet has shattered. Thanks to Watcher Uatu breaking his non-interference vow, survivors live under protective domes on interlinked fragments.

Hard Corps
Rider uses the Nova Force to restore their planet, but it is ravaged yet again, this time by star-pirate Nebula. Rebuilt once more, Xandar becomes base to an expanded Corps: intergalactic peacekeepers recruited from many alien species, battling piracy, aggression, and chaos throughout the universe. Extremely effective, they imprison thousands of miscreants in their holding facility the Kyln. This ends in cosmic catastrophe as insectoid tyrant

Lone rider With the Corps wiped out, Richard Rider carries the Worldmind, Nova Force, and the galaxy's destiny.

Super Nova

Nova helmets denote rank and channel Nova Force. Black ones are exclusive to elite operatives dubbed Supernovas: bestowing flight, super-strength, vacuum and radiation shielding, energy blasts, telekinesis, and trans-galactic teleportation. Donning the helmet clothes the wearer in a tailored uniform and provides language translation, strategic and tactical analysis, access to a vast library archive, auto-pilot, and holographic readings screened on a Heads-Up Display (pictured) or beamed directly into the wearer's brain.

Unlike gold helmet Nova Centurions—powered directly by the Nova Force—Supernovas are fueled by onboard generators in their headgear. Their abilities and uniforms vanish if the helmet is removed. Nova helmets are keyed to the wearer's DNA signature, activating if the assigned officer or direct family member dons it. This activates the full power-suite, and data or personal messages can be accessed.

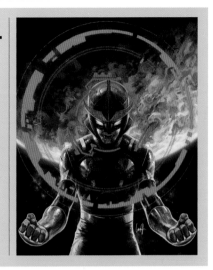

Annihilus leads an Annihilation Wave from the Negative Zone that crushes the prison, exterminates the Corps, and decimates the universe's greatest civilizations. Once more the last Centurion, Rider carries the entire Nova Force and Worldmind in his body through a series of staggering, ever-escalating battles, including conquest by techno-organic Phalanx parasites, until he ultimately sacrifices himself to prevent the incursion of an appalling living Cancerverse intent on consuming all reality.

In Rider's absence, the sentient Worldmind begins recruiting a new Corps on Earth, before transforming its selection into Novas, basing them inside living world Ego, and dubbing the mobile planetary fortress Nu-Xandar. With the Corps

Human rockets Young Sam is delighted to meet Richard Rider, but neither knows Earth's first Nova is no longer human.

depleted and scattered following the Annihilation Wave attack, many members are counted as Missing In Action. One such is Black Helmet Jesse Alexander. Schoolboy Sam Alexander discovers his missing father—a school janitor—was once a secret, cosmic-powered policeman after meeting aliens Gamora and Rocket Raccoon. When Sam dons his father's Black Helmet he is charged with a range of incredible powers and embraces a life full of adventure. Sam resolves to learn why his father disappeared and how the Nova Corps died. Through grit and luck, he survives "on-the-job" training against the Phoenix Force, Chitauri, Thanos, and others to become a New Warrior and Avenger, before becoming a mainstay of teen team the Champions. ∎

Xandar: Incident Report

After centuries of hostile encroachment and the destruction of their homeworld, the noble Xandarians form a universal peacekeeping force fielding officers from all races and species.

Billions of aggregated Xandarian brains tap and harness Nova Force.

Xandar is destroyed by Skrulls and reduced to floating globes in space.

New "cloned" Xandar becomes planetary base of Nova Corps.

Nova Corps rebuilt and stationed inside Ego as Nu-Xandar.

Xandar is razed by Luphomoid raider Zorr; however, Rhomann Dhey escapes into space.

Xandar is reconstituted by the Worldmind but eradicated again by Nebula.

Fortified Xandar destroyed by ravening Annihilation Wave insectoid horde.

SENTINEL OF THE SPACEWAYS

SILVER SURFER

ON THE RECORD

REAL NAME
Norrin Radd

ALLEGIANCES
Defenders, Annihilators, Heralds of Galactus

POWERS
Energy generation and manipulation, invulnerability, immortality, immeasurable strength and speed

MISSION
Explore the cosmos and aid the oppressed

STATUS REPORT
Once more acting as herald to Galactus

Social misfit Norrin Radd saves his indolent, hedonistic homeworld Zenn-La from destruction and in return is gifted with incredible power as a cosmic wanderer. When Galactus attacks, Radd offers the planet-devourer loyal service and is accepted. Immersed in an impermeable energy-sheath, he can now tap into a fundamental universal force dubbed the "Power

Cosmic." With a board made of this energy, Radd becomes the Silver Surfer, riding the solar winds beyond the pull of time and space.

Galactus hungers for worlds rich in life-sustaining energies—he does not distinguish between ages-old civilizations or early precursors of planetary existence. Rather than randomly scour infinite space, he has, over eons, created heralds to find them. While the Silver Surfer locates planets devoid of evolved life, other stellar scouts such as Terrax or Morg are not as altruistic, and they relish witnessing the death-throes of entire species.

Galactus' vast appetite cannot be long forestalled and, over time, he alters Silver Surfer's emotions, rendering him coldly efficient. This changes when Radd reaches Earth. His feelings reawakened by blind sculptor Alicia Masters, he rebels and joins the Fantastic Four in thwarting Galactus. His reprimand is the removal of his space-time traversing abilities. Trapped on Earth and hunted by humanity, Radd makes friends among the Super Hero community, even joining the ad-hoc association of antiheroes, the Defenders. Meanwhile, Reed Richards deduces a means to

Cosmic bonds Galactus imbues the Surfer and his board with the same Power Cosmic, binding them together.

circumvent Galactus' barrier and the skyrider becomes a universal nomad, battling intergalactic perils, clashing with Thanos, and even reconciling with Galactus to once more become his herald again. In many timelines, the Silver Surfer lives into the 31st century, acting as Protector of the Universe. ∎

CHAMPION OF LIFE

ADAM WARLOCK

For if I fail,
all life falls with me!
Adam Warlock

Grown in a human genetics laboratory by rogue research think tank the Enclave, Adam Warlock is actually a creature of divine design. A moral being created by corrupt scientists, his universal purpose is the result of ancient schemes devised by the Multiverse's great powers. Conceived as the end point of human evolution, "Him" punishes and abandons his creators to roam the stars. A second attempt goes equally awry when "Paragon" also rebels; roaming reality as ascendant being "Her."

Still evolving, Him battles Thor before falling under the influence of the High Evolutionary. Awarded the Soul Gem, Him appoints himself savior of the High Evolutionary's failing Utopian experiment Counter-Earth, which was built from cosmic detritus on the far side of the Sun. But the war against the corrupting Man-Beast costs the man-made messiah, now called Adam Warlock, his life. Retreating into a cocoon, he is reborn attuned to the universe and drawn to cosmic crisis points.

Warlock dies again battling his evil future self the Magus, and once more, beside companions Gamora and Pip the Troll as they stop Thanos from destroying the stars. Skirting

Dark mirror Although deranged and evil, the Magus is just as much an Avatar of Life as his noble counterpart, Warlock.

the boundaries of science and magic, the Mad Titan had gathered Infinity Gems in a sun-eradicating cannon, but had not realized Warlock was Life's Chosen One: the avatar of universal existence. Recalled from Paradise inside the Soul Gem, Warlock is resurrected to form an Infinity Watch to safeguard the Infinity Gems. The group polices colliding timelines, and averts repeated multiversal menaces and universal oblivion, usually alongside heroes such as the Avengers, X-Men, and Guardians of the Galaxy. It is a role Warlock is fated to play forever. ∎

ALTERNATE AND DIVER TIMELINES

WORLDS DIVERGENT

Although Prime Earth is fulcrum and forge for many universal crises, it is not unique. Flawed, divergent, or simply dissimilar iterations of the planet reoccur in every strata of reality across countless dimensional parallels. Humanity and its fellow species have no monopoly on heroism and sacrifice. Throughout time, space, and alternate dimensions, heroes and villains arise as necessity demands, breaching the walls of existence to battle where they are needed most.

Antediluvian era of Moon Boy and Devil Dinosaur.

Wolverine creates a parallel reality by traveling back in time to stop an alien invasion.

Alternate contemporary world in which all humanity possesses Terrigen-triggered super-powers.

Doomed alternate reality created by time travel, where Charles Xavier dies before founding X-Men.

A reality where Martians conquer humanity in 2000CE.

PRIMORDIAL EARTH
(EARTH-97161)

AMERICA 1870
(EARTH-1023)

EARTH X
(EARTH-9997)

AGE OF APOCALYPSE
(EARTH-295)

WAR OF THE WORLDS
(EARTH-691)

NEW WORLD 1602
(EARTH-311)

OTHER-EARTH
(EARTH-6311)

DEATHLOK
(EARTH-7484)

AGE OF ULTRON
(EARTH-61112)

Age of Marvels begins in 17th century after a time-lost Captain America lands there.

Highly advanced timeline where Earth's Dark Ages never happened.

A reality in which society collapses into anarchy in the 1980s, sparking civil war and cyborg tech.

Divergent Prime Earth timeline where Ultron exterminates humanity.

E vents in almost every universe of the Multiverse unfold in the same causal sequence and are subject to the physical laws governing the material planes. However, reality is a frighteningly fragile structure that can be readily tampered with and altered.

The ability to manipulate the inexorable flow of time is remarkably commonplace in not just higher and ascended beings, but also an ever-growing number of mortals. Described as chronokinesis, the term encompasses the power to reorder past events, travel to other times and locations, freeze the passage of time, and slow down or accelerate the progress of objects, localities, or oneself. A particularly cruel tactic involves altering the personal timeline of a person, aging or rejuvenating them against their will. Methods of meddling with time are numerous, but broadly fall into three categories: magical, scientific, and personal intervention.

Although time functions differently in higher realms, all physical events occur in a causal continuum: the real world. This region is surrounded by the timeless Limbo dimension which exists as one single, infinite, ever-changing moment. There are in fact two distinct Limbo dimensions. One—also called Otherplace—is a mystical dungeon plane with varying zones of altered time. It is inhabited by legions of demons and ruled over by potent entities such as Belasco or mutant Darkchylde Illyana Rasputin (aka Magik). In "true" Limbo, all possible moments occur simultaneously, and whether real world changes are

triggered by a spell, time machine, or psionic manipulation, all such actions cancel chronal displacement, allowing real-world change. The most notable effect is that the time-traveler disappears from one point in reality and arrives in another. As a result of being part of a Multiverse, whenever reality is disrupted by

Alternate tomorrow where Sentinels rule the US and eradicate all superhumans.

Earth as a wasteland ruled by Super Villains and their descendants.

Realm where magic and science are in equilibrium.

Potential future Earth where Martian conquerors are defeated. Home of "Tomorrow's Avengers" Guardians of the Galaxy.

DAYS OF FUTURE PAST (EARTH-811)

OLD MAN LOGAN (EARTH-807128)

STYRAKOS/ DEATH'S HEAD (EARTH-TRN234)

GUARDIANS OF THE GALAXY 3000CE (EARTH-691)

IRON MAN 2020 (EARTH-8410)

DYSTOPIA (EARTH-9200)

2099CE (EARTH-6375)

BATTLEWORLD/ CONTEST OF CHAMPIONS (EARTH TRN517)

END EARTH (EARTH-76216)

Corporations-dominated world in which Arno Stark is Iron Man.

Post-apocalyptic parallel world where Bruce Banner kills all Super Heroes and rules humanity as the Maestro.

Future reality where corporations take over and rule the world.

Nexus realm used by various higher beings to stage contests between super-beings and heroes.

Alternate future reality where the Sun expands into a red giant and humanity evolves into pure mental energy.

time alteration, a new divergent universe forms from that point. All time travel is also trans-dimensional travel. Missions to change the past, however well-meaning, are pointless and counterproductive. For every life saved or disaster averted, at least one other potentially adverse outcome exists from the moment the time traveler arrives at their destination.

Guarding the time stream

Nonetheless, constant attempts to reshape key events or steer actions into other courses can have disastrous repercussions further down—and across—the time stream; an ever-expanding domino effect to wreak havoc on the present and alter the shape of every future. To counteract this potential for holocaust, numerous organizations and self-appointed guardians have

set themselves up to police the impossible. The most powerful and least intrusive is Immortus, who rules Limbo and acts judiciously, infrequently, and only to benefit his own unknowable agenda. More prosaic and bureaucratic are the officers of the Time Variance Authority. This far-future agency is based in a Null-Time Zone, monitoring existing and new realities from the Hall of Chronometry and dispatching officers to arrest beings straying from their natural times. Their Time Courts prosecute persistent transgressors and the convicted are condemned to Time Cells: forever erased from history and locked in recurring timeloops.

Well-intentioned organizations including Earth-9500's T.O.T.E.M. (Temporal Oversight Team Eliminating Mistakes) and alien

enigma He Who Remains, are all ultimately ineffective against super-geniuses such as temporal ravager Kang the Conqueror or implacable Victor von Doom. The latter's invention, the Doomlock Chronal Variance Inhibitor, allows the Latverian tyrant to traverse the ages without creating alternate realities, while also stabilizing Doom's own timeline to prevent him from being altered by shifting events. As powerful as they are, these devices are all but helpless against those experienced in magical travel. The likes of Sorceror Supreme Stephen Strange or future mage Sise-Neg are too experienced in manipulating the metaphysical metadata of existence to be stopped by interfering busybodies, and wise enough to leave no trace of their passages through time. ∎

ANOTHER TIME, ANOTHER PLACE
MIRROR UNIVERSES

ON THE RECORD

DESIGNATION
Parallel worlds

NOTABLE EXAMPLES
**Earth-1610 (Ultimate
universe), Earth-90214 (Noir),
Earth-311 (1602), Earth-982
(MC2), Earth-9997 (Earth X),
Earth-58163 (House of M)**

STATUS REPORT
Dangerously familiar

Thanks to constant meddling with the path and progress of time, the already conflict-overloaded Multiverse grows ever-more expansive. This is true whether the infractions are simple pleasure trips by innocent chrononauts such as young Tommy Tyme, who enjoys adventures in history thanks to Merlyn's Clock of the Ages, wicked raids by bandits such as Zarrko the Tomorrow Man, or murderous assaults by invaders such as Kang the Conqueror. Whenever a time-

traveler breaches the dimension of Limbo, another divergent reality—complete with its own history and future potential—begins. By some quirk of cosmic predestination, few of these parallel streams are kinder, gentler places: most are dark, warped worlds of looming crisis, unimagined horror, and unhappy outcomes.

Windows to tomorrow Noh-Varr offers the Avengers a glimpse of many dangerous futures converging on them.

Despite the efforts of dedicated supervisors and Omniversal Guardians such as divine Merlyn and Roma, or pan-dimensional organizations such as the Captain

House (of M) proud Magic and insanity combine to turn Earth-58163 into a paradise for mutant beings.

Britain Corps and the multiversal association of super-geniuses that comprise the Council of Reeds, anarchy and decline plague the majority of divergent timelines. More a supervisory body than a task force, the Captain Britain Corps is founded by Merlyn. A legion of heroes similarly empowered by the infinite force of friction between all dimensions, the Corps is appointed to safeguard their own alternate world. However, on occasion, it has also been called upon to unite against threats to the entire matrix of realities. The Corps' citadel exists in the subdimension of Otherworld.

Time out of joint

Naturally, most of these replica realities contain versions of beings from Prime Earth, but many are radically altered by time and environment. The Multiverse-spanning Web of Life and Destiny appoints spider-heroes on countless worlds, and Iron Man and Captain America exist in multiple realties—though many are not Peter Parker, Tony Stark, or Steve Rogers.

There are more realities than there are grains of sand in the universe. With each reality, there are different truths, different falsehoods.
Uatu the Watcher

Moreover, those parallel personalities that do exist seldom resemble any hero recognizable to voyagers from established realities. Catastrophic events and attempts to change the history of Prime Earth have resulted in alarming alterations to the timeline and even more dire repercussions. When genocidal robotic tyrant Ultron eradicates most of humanity, Wolverine and the Invisible Woman go back in time to rearrange events and save the world. Although largely successful in revoking the Age of Ultron, the heroes' actions overstress the space-time continuum, creating rips and breaches that subsequently contribute to the cataclysm that ends the Seventh Cosmos.

When troubled mutant David Haller projects himself back in time to murder Magneto, he accidentally kills his own father, Charles Xavier, instead. Without X-Men, the remade world endures an Age of Apocalypse that ends with the eradication of that entire divergent timeline. An atrocity beyond comprehension, the calamity has consequences far beyond appalling loss of life, as refugees from the disaster—sadistic fiends such as Dark Beast, Holocaust, and Sugarman—escape to Prime Earth, contaminating its past with their horrific brand of mutant terrorism. ∎

See also: Ultron, Otherworld, Spider-Verse

Alternates Assemble! The heroes of Earth-9997 are familiar yet different from their Prime Earth counterparts.

TIME BANDIT
KANG THE CONQUEROR

ON THE RECORD

REAL NAME
Nathaniel Richards

POWERS
Genius intellect, strategic brilliance, control of time, futuristic weaponry

ALLEGIANCES
Council of Cross-time Kangs

MISSION
Intends to rule everything throughout eternity

STATUS REPORT
Waiting somewhere in time, ready to attack again

Sworn to rule over all and deny his future evolution into self-proclaimed guardian of time—Immortus—Kang haunts the infinite corridors of time, launching attacks on eternal enemies the Avengers and his equally despised and forever propagating other selves. A lengthy lifetime of time-travel under various guises has resulted in countless Kangs all attacking an infinitude of divergent universes, each seeking to be the sole Conqueror. This, added to the persistent threat of Kang being ultimately betrayed by his own future self, makes the villain a man who is truly at war with himself.

A descendent of time-traveling ancestor and namesake Nathaniel Richards (of 20th century Prime Earth), Kang is born in Earth-6311's 30th century: a world both utopian and insufferably dull. An early life of boredom and fascination with heroes of the past grips the brilliant youth and he resolves to have a more fulfilling existence. He rediscovers the time-travel techniques of another ancestor—Victor von Doom—and his own destiny as the greatest villain of the ages. The horrified teenager is determined to change his future by voyaging to the past. When adult Kang interferes to ensure his ultimate, and preferred, identity, the attempt goes awry, inspiring Richards, as Iron Lad, to found 21st century hero team Young Avengers. Eventually, Richards surrenders the role to stabilize the fracturing time stream and becomes the murderous Kid Immortus for a time.

Time stream tyrant With an advanced tech warsuit and access to every weapon ever built, Kang is an ever-present threat.

Journeying further back in time, Richards becomes the adult pharaoh Rama-Tut and subjugates ancient Egypt until he is driven off by the visiting Fantastic Four. He then accidentally creates a divergent reality after conquering modern Earth as the Scarlet Centurion. Defeated by a team of time-displaced Avengers, Richards flees for his home era. He overshoots and arrives in Earth's war-ravaged 40th century where he reinvents himself as Kang the Conqueror.

Voyaging back to the 20th century, Kang claims dominion of the era and clashes with the founding Avengers. Repeated defeats by these "primitives" obsess him, and further attempts to conquer the time period lead to a multitude of alternate and disparate realities, each with its own Kang. His rage is further fueled by the knowledge that at an unspecified date in his personal timeline, Kang's hunger for conflict and pride in his bloody achievements will fade, leaving only the indolent, scheming Immortus to assume his future.

Sole survivor

Kang is driven by three compulsions: to rule everything that has or will ever exist, to never weaken into ineffectual Immortus, and to utterly humiliate and destroy the Avengers. Insanely narcissistic and unsure of his own identity, Kang meddles incessantly, driven to be the

> Time means nothing to Kang, the Conqueror!
> **Kang**

Multiple mayhem The alliance of every Kang to ever exist results in acrimony and, ultimately, mass killings.

paramount conqueror of all times. Invariably, so is every Kang created by his profligate manipulations. At one point, these Kangs unite in a Council of Cross-Time Kangs, but the arrogance and ambition driving each sparks a wave of killings, until only one remains. Or so it seems: with Kang, certainty is impossible.

Kang strives to be unique and constant, repeatedly modifying his personal time stream, manipulating events, and attacking his enemies. Resolved to never surrender to his ultimate fate, he develops ever more precise control of time, recklessly slipping in between moments of history to kill his foes as babies or banish them from the time stream, heedless of the paradoxes and anomalous timelines he creates. Ultimately his mania forces the Avengers—led by an aged, future version of the Vision—to retaliate in the same manner, combining teams from different eras and abducting the infant Kang from his cradle. They are victorious, but Kang is never to be underestimated. Has he gone forever? Only time will tell. ∎

Identity crises When Nathaniel Richards rediscovers time travel, he triggers a chain of events across time that creates multiple selves, each with their own agenda.

Nathaniel Richards
30th century Earth-6311 descendent of Reed Richards and Victor von Doom, Nathaniel Richards uses time travel to satisfy his need for action.

Iron Lad
After meeting his evil future self, 16-year-old Richards travels back in time to found the Young Avengers and prompt the reformation of the disbanded adult team.

Kid Immortus
Failing to save Young Avengers teammate Stature, Iron Lad accepts his destiny. Turning to evil, he clashes with Doctor Doom and Annihilus before retiring to master his powers.

Rama-Tut
An aggressive, conquest-hungry adult, Nathaniel Richards builds a chronal chariot called the Sphinx to become the overlord of ancient Egypt.

Scarlet Centurion
Defeated in Egypt, Richards becomes a malign schemer, creating and controlling an alternate Earth until a team of time-stranded Avengers oust him.

Kang the Conqueror
Accidentally arriving in the 40th century, Richards remakes himself as supreme war-maker and rapacious marauder of time-zones and divergent realities.

Immortus
Richards' far flung future self is a conniving, sedentary guardian of the time stream, whose true motives cannot be determined or trusted.

TIME-TRAVELING SOLDIER
CABLE

ON THE RECORD

REAL NAME
Nathaniel Christopher Charles Summers

ALLEGIANCES
X-Force, X-Men, Clan Askani, Six Pack

POWERS
Telepathy, telekinesis, and teleportation; future tech and armaments; cyborg enhancements; time travel

MISSION
Protecting the past to save the future

STATUS REPORT
Taking life one day at a time

The result of a bitter feud between mutant tyrant Apocalypse and genetic outlaw Mister Sinister, Cable is born to a life of struggle: a time-roving soldier in a never-ending battle to defend life. His father is X-Man Scott "Cyclops" Summers and his mother a clone of Jean Grey—created by Sinister to preserve the genetic potential of two of Earth's mightiest mutants. Sinister abducts the couple's infant child Nathan and experiments on him until he is rescued by Scott's team, X-Factor. Nathan is infected with a techno-organic virus by Apocalypse and is only saved by traveling 2,000 years into the future with the help of freedom fighter Sister Askani. Here he learns to use his telekinetic abilities to keep the virus at bay and becomes a resistance leader in the struggle against Apocalypse, who has conquered the world in the millennia since Nathan's birth.

After decades of combat, including attempts to destroy Apocalypse and his successors through surgical strikes into the past, veteran warrior Nathan—now calling himself Cable—infiltrates the 20th Century in a lengthy covert campaign to stop his archenemy and Cable's own cloned "brother," Stryfe. The evil doppelgänger is determined to ensure Apocalypse's dominance, and Cable spends decades fighting him, establishing himself as a mercenary with specialist task force Six Pack. In the process, Cable sells future tech to businesses, inadvertently fueling the super-weapons arms race. Finally, fully engaged with his past, he commandeers mutant leader Charles Xavier's youthful New Mutants, training them as a paramilitary X-Force.

Cable attempts to build a relationship with his father, Cyclops, and becomes an ally of the X-Men. After mutants are decimated on "M-Day," he hides their prospective messiah, Hope Summers, in the time stream. Here he trains her to be another warrior in his tireless efforts to safeguard humans and mutantkind from all perils—and themselves. ■

Teen idol Cable trained mutant savior Hope Summers to be smart, tough, and ruthless: ready for any future foe.

TOMORROW'S AVENGERS
31ST CENTURY GUARDIANS OF THE GALAXY

ON THE RECORD

REAL NAME
Guardians of the Galaxy

NOTABLE MEMBERS
Vance Astro, Charlie-27, Martinex, Yondu, Starhawk (Stakar/Aleta) Geena Drake

ALLEGIANCES
Galactic Guardians, Defenders, Avengers

MISSION
Liberating the oppressed

STATUS REPORT
Traversing space and time righting wrongs

A millennium from now on Earth-691, 1,000-year-old Earthman Vance Astro, genetically modified humans Charlie-27 and Martinex T'Naga, and Centaurian Yondu Udonta unite. Their mission is to free Earth—and most of known space—from enslavement by the ancient, all-conquering alien species the Badoon. As the struggle grows, they are joined by male/female Arcturan godling Stakar and Aleta, who share the body of time-bending enigma Starhawk. Assisted by present-day Super Heroes, their campaign eventually succeeds and the stellar warriors enlist new allies, such as Mercurian Nikki and human precognitive Geena Drake, to bring liberty and stability to the rest of the future galaxy.

Dubbed "Tomorrow's Avengers," many of these 31st century Guardians of the Galaxy's exploits include time travel, where they encounter and ally themselves with modern heroes such as the Defenders, Thor, Avengers, Black Panther T'Challa, and the Thing. They are the first heroes to defeat the multiversal cyborg tyrant Korvac as he repeatedly attempts to become the universe's supreme being.

The Guardians' struggles also take them across the parallel realities of the Multiverse. After battling beside a time-lost "Thor Corps"—consisting of Beta Ray Bill, Eric "Thunderstrike" Masterson, and Dargo Ktor, the 26th century Thor of Earth-8710—the Guardians are drawn into a temporal anomaly where they encounter and team up with Prime Earth Guardians of the Galaxy Groot, Rocket Raccoon, and Drax the Destroyer.

This unlikely alliance then clashes with a third Guradians team: a hitherto unrecorded squad from the 11th century, also dedicated to preserving creation and ensuring universal peace. The massed heroes battle Hermetikus—the founding first Guardian—and prevent his dreams of dominating all creation, before returning to their own eras. ∎

Generation games Guardians from three millennia can only save this galaxy after they stop battling each other.

THE WEB OF LIFE
SPIDER-VERSE

ON THE RECORD

DESIGNATION
Web-Warriors

ALLEGIANCES
Web of Life and Destiny

BASE
Loomworld (Earth-001)

POWERS
**Various arachnid abilities/
devices, precognitive senses,
enhanced physiology, tactile
adhesion, web generation**

MISSION
**Preserving life throughout
the Multiverse**

STATUS REPORT
**Recovering from relentless
attacks across all realities**

The infinite Multiverse has
countless Earths, and on
almost all of them life is
championed by spider-powered
individuals, connected by a
transcendental psychic network
called the Web of Life and Destiny.
Earth-001 is the heart of this
construct, the Loomworld from
where a benign Master Weaver
oversees mystic Spider-Totems and
Spider-Avatars, dispensing power
to select individuals across all
realities. Spider-Totems are said
to "let the Spider in," but how the
recipients manifest powers or
employ them varies greatly:
as many beneficiaries use these
"gifts" for personal gain as for the
betterment of their world.

The multiversal system
is corrupted and almost
destroyed when vampiric
Totem-Eaters the Inheritors
conquer Loomworld: forcing
the Master Weaver to open
other realities to their
remorseless predation.
So great is the Inheritors'
greed that they seek to
devour any totem-empowered
prey (such as Black Panther
T'Challa or M'Baku the White
Gorilla), but the essence of
Spiders is their greatest
delicacy. After turning the
heart of life's grand design
into a charnel house of past
feasts, the Inheritors are

Cutting the cord A repentant,
reformed Inheritor Karn becomes
the new Master Weaver.

ultimately defeated and cosmic
order restored by a coalition of
arachnoid champions from
embattled realities—several from
Prime Earth. In the aftermath,
cross-dimensional teams of Spider
Heroes band together as Web
-Warriors policing those Earths
deprived of arachnoid defenders
by the Inheritors.

On Prime Earth, the totemic
power of arachnids is strong:

manifesting as a wealth of spider-themed and empowered Super Heroes. When Inheritor Morlun stalks the world he is repulsed not once, but many times. Although Peter Parker is the most significant of these webbed wonders, there are many others, the vast majority of them female, such as Spider-Women Jessica Drew and Mattie Franklin, Spider-Girl Anya Corazon, or organic web-spinner Cindy Moon, aka Silk. The Web of Life and Destiny is the conduit for a unique warning system dubbed "spider-sense" and also fuels the precognitive ability of psychic savant Cassandra Webb (Madame Web). On her death, she passes on her burdensome gifts to former Spider-Woman Julia Carpenter.

A worldwide web

So great is the allure of Prime Earth, that spider-champions of divergent realities and timelines are drawn into action there. Time-displaced Miguel O'Hara temporarily makes Manhattan his home after being plucked from his own era—2099 on Earth-TRN588—while young Miles Morales becomes a permanent resident when portions of his home universe on Earth-1610 are subsumed into Prime Earth's reality. Likewise, the spidery destiny of Peter Parker and his close circle of friends and enemies reoccurs in many universes. ■

See also: Spider-Man, Spider-Woman, Other lives

I'm a Spider-Woman too, Jess. We all are!
Gwen Stacy

Web of alternate lives

The Web of Life and Destiny knits all worlds together, with transdimensional strands carrying power to its countless arachnid agents and even bringing Web-Warriors together when necessity demands.

Peter Porker/Spider-Ham (Earth-8311) Spider bitten by a radioactive scientist, he transforms into a humanoid pig while retaining his arachnoid abilities.

Gwen Stacy/Ghost-Spider (Earth-65) Bitten by a radioactive spider, she battles to honor the memory of her dead friend and neighbor, Peter Parker.

Miguel O'Hara/Spider-Man 2099 (Earth-TRN588) Genetically altered hero with spider DNA who fights injustice in two separate eras.

May Reilly/Lady Spider (Earth-803) Super-genius inventor builds a spider suit and simulates spider powers with steam punk technology.

Ai Apaec/Decapitator (Prime Earth) Cannibalistic Peruvian Spider-god genetically transformed by Norman Osborn into a member of his Dark Avengers.

May "Mayday" Parker/Spider-Woman (Earth-982) Second generation Super Hero, her spider-powers manifest at the age of 15, similar to those of her father, Peter Parker.

Adriana Soria/Spider-Queen (Prime Earth) Mutated by radioactive Super-Soldier Serum and contact with Venom turns her into a giant, ravening monster.

Mary Jane Parker/Spinneret (Earth-18119) Uses high-tech bio-suit and Klyntar symbiote to mimic the biological spider-powers of her husband and daughter.

Mattie Franklin/Spider-Woman (Prime Earth) Accidentally granted spider-powers, she impersonates Spider-Man before finding her own hero persona.

Annie Parker/Spiderling (Earth-18119) Inherits spider-powers from Peter Parker and develops potent psychic link to Web of Life as the Patternmaker.

Cassandra Webb/Madame Web (Prime Earth) Psychic intelligence gatherer who casts a precognitive web of intrigue until she is murdered.

Anya Corazon/Spider-Girl (Prime Earth) Collateral damage in a war between clans, she develops spider-powers, fights for justice, and joins the Web-Warriors.

Julia Carpenter/Spider-Woman (Prime Earth) US Intelligence operative and West Coast Avenger takes on the role of a new Madame Web.

OTHER LIVES
MILES MORALES AND OTHER SPIDER-HEROES

ON THE RECORD

REAL NAME
Miles Morales

ALLEGIANCES
Avengers, Champions, The Ultimates

BASE
New York City

POWERS
Super-strength, speed, and reflexes; tactile adhesion; precognitive senses; bio-electric stings and webbing

MISSION
Living up to his idols and ideals

STATUS REPORT
Making his new world a better place

Spider-Man is a great hero not just on Earth, but across the Multiverse, where minute differences multiply and where divergent worlds produce web-warriors who appear familiar and are yet vastly different. On many of these embattled planets the Web of Life and Destiny's Spider-totems select iterations of the same arachnid hero over and over again.

On Earth-1610—Prime Earth's closest parallel—Peter Parker becomes a valiant Spider-Man after being bitten by a spider altered in the labs of wealthy industrialist Norman Osborn. Although always feeling out of his depth, the noble teenager repeatedly saves the planet and its most insignificant individuals indiscriminately and tirelessly, until murdered by his greatest enemies. Inspired by the hero's death and empowered by the same genetically modified spider venom, young Miles Morales then takes up Parker's responsibilities as Spider-Man. Still little more than a child, Morales faces a host of deadly adversaries, espionage and intrigue, staggering cosmic crises, the unfolding mystery of his constantly evolving powers, and the daily drudgery of coping with a secret identity while attending a boarding school.

On Earth-311, the age of Super Heroes came in the year 1602 and Peter Parquagh's arachnid powers serve the cause of liberty in a newly discovered, British colonized America, until he is murdered by the Inheritor Morlun. On Earth-8311, a spider is transformed into a pig to

Ham-fisted Tentacles of evil prove no match for the totemic Spider-power of Web-Warriors like Peter Porker.

battle evil as Peter Porker, the spectacular Spider-Ham, while Earths-18119 and -982 are both protected by a Peter Parker much like Prime Earth's. On the first, he battles beside his wife and daughter with Mary Jane as tech-suited Spinneret and Annie as arachnid-powered Spiderling. On Earth-982, his career ends in injury and his daughter May "Mayday" Parker strives in his stead, firstly as teen hero Spider-Girl and then as the sensational Spider-Woman.

Spider-Man 2099

In a number of alternate timelines—most notably Earths-928 and TRN588—a third Age of Marvels opens in the dystopian future of 2099. This is a world ruled by ruthless corporations where freedom is a perk of wealth, and everyone else works to climb to the top of the financial pile. When brilliant geneticist Miguel O'Hara tries to quit his job at Alchemax, his boss Tyler Stone (and, unknown to O'Hara, his biological father) addicts him to super-narcotic Rapture to ensure his services.

Desperate, O'Hara seeks to modify his DNA to escape enslavement, but his assistant sabotages the experiment and O'Hara is molecularly remade with spider genes.

Now a human spider, O'Hara battles alongside many other newly emergent Super Heroes against the corporate dictatorship. He then travels back in time— and to Prime Earth—where he becomes a contemporary scientific colleague of Peter Parker and crime-fighting ally of Spider-Man.

Ultimate Spider-Man

This pattern repeats across the web of the Multiverse until Time Runs Out and the Seventh Cosmos is destroyed in a cascade of Earths crashing into each other. The last to be extinguished are Prime Earth and Earth-1610, home to the dark, uncompromising defenders dubbed the Ultimates. Thanks to the intervention of Super Heroes, the last remnants of life are saved from eternal subjugation on Doctor Doom's Battleworld: a waystation constructed beyond the Multiverse, and cobbled together from fragments of several disparate realities and alternate timelines. With Doom the God defeated, a brand new Multiverse is reborn and restored as the Eighth Cosmos begins.

For the restored masses—on Prime Earth and across time and space—it is business as usual: simply the day after Earth's heroes have once again defeated more unknowable foes and narrowly

Sparky spider As well as producing threads of bio-electricity, Morales can deliver a mean venom punch.

> I'm Spider-Man. Well... one of them.
> **Miles Morales**

averted yet another catastrophe. However, that is not the case for Miles Morales, who now lives— and has always lived—on this world, with his friends and family fully restored to life. Even more amazing is that Peter Parker is also alive and still fighting the good fight as Spider-Man, sharing the same secret: that they come from different, dead worlds. Encouraged by Parker to continue his career as the other male web-slinging wall-crawler, Morales quickly establishes a name for himself as a lone hero, as a trainee Avenger, and eventually in a team of idealistic and dedicated young Super Heroes: the Champions. ■

SOMEPLACE STRANGE
WEIRDWORLD AND OTHERWORLDLY REALMS

ON THE RECORD

NAME
Weirdworld

LOCATION
Transdimensionally fixed in geostationary Earth orbit

RESOURCES
Untapped magic, myriad realms and kingdoms locked in precarious proximity

STATUS REPORT
Supposedly unreachable, it somehow abducts the unwary from Earth

Although separated by dimensional walls, the Superflow, and powerful cosmic mechanisms, all alternate realities are connected by the Web of Life and Destiny. Thus, they frequently impinge upon each as the walls of reality gradually erode or are willfully compromised. Some prove far more accessible than others, regularly affecting and endangering the inhabitants of Prime Earth. Others are only future possibilities, like the divergent tomorrow of the

Femizons, which deposits wondrous warrior Thundra in a world where mere men are deemed women's equals, or overlapping planes like Xemu's bellicose "5th Dimension." The latter is in fact Earth-6212, geographically intersecting with a region of Long Island and sharing the same physical laws as Prime Earth.

Polemachus is one of the more radical Earth-adjacent alternates, a barbaric planet warmed not by a sun, but through unstable energy rings encircling it. Atomic tests on Earth damage the rings and Polemachus' supreme warlord Arkon the Magnificent (pictured above left) repeatedly battles the X-Men and Avengers as he attempts to destroy Earth to preserve his

Weird and wondrous
Goleta the Wizardslayer had never met such a trouble-attracting newcomer as Earth girl Rebecca Rodriguez.

homeworld. Polemachus is erased when the Multiverse is eradicated, but its living remnants are absorbed by Doctor Doom's Battleworld before being consigned to the dimensional maelstrom that is Weirdworld when the Eighth Cosmos comes into being.

Interdimensional Council of Reeds

Certain individuals reoccur with unnerving regularity across the Multiverse, albeit altered by local events and environments. Doppelgängers of Captain America, Peter Parker, and Tony Stark abound, but perhaps the most significant duplicated personality is Reed Richards. The super-genius exists in almost every alternate Earth and, thanks to his innate intellect, all variations ultimately congregate as an Interdimensional Council of Reeds, resolved to fix the problems of the Multiverse.

The Reed of Prime Earth varies significantly from most in that he alone knew his father (time-traveler Nathaniel Richards) and combines a need to solve crises with humanity and empathy. When misuse of each reality's Infinity Gauntlet leads the Council into war with the Celestial star gods of Earth-4280, many of their number are killed and Reed Richards of Prime Earth returns to his home dimension. In the rebirth of life following the creation of the Eighth Cosmos, a new, more conciliatory Council of Reeds has formed.

Fantasy islands

Originally a distant realm of elves, wizards, and magical creatures far removed from Earth in space and time, Weirdworld is shattered and haphazardly reassembled after the destruction of the Seventh Cosmos. As a part of Battleworld, it becomes a repository for numerous mystical realities struggling to survive.

> Welcome to Weirdworld. Run!
> **Arkon the Magnificent**

When Doom is defeated and the Multiverse reborn, Weirdworld remains impaired and fragmented: fixed beyond human detection in a pocket dimension transecting the Bermuda Triangle above Prime Earth. Here magic and science duel for dominance with minor realms such as Crystallium, and Morgan Le

Living hell Nova Richard Rider was doomed to battle the Cancerverse for all time until it mysteriously let him go.

Fay's magical kingdom constantly warring even as the amalgamated Realm seemingly gathers up ever more inhabited dimensional detritus and unlucky travelers from Earth.

Others worlds are fully products of different laws, such as the universe containing Earth-8311, where a planetary Anthropomorphic Field imbalance precludes the evolution of humans, and the population consists of animal doppelgängers of Prime Earth heroes and villains. The most appalling divergence of all is the Cancerverse, home to Earth-10011. Here, due to the interference of Elder deities, the Many-Angled Ones,

Death has no dominion. No life can end here, and the realm exists as a corrupted amalgam of greed and hunger eager to spread across and absorb the rest of the Multiverse.

Prime Earth has long been the focus of transdimensional gatherings and temporal deviations. This may be because the planet is home to a cosmic phenomenon known as the Nexus of Reality. The Nexus is a pan-dimensional gateway that provides a path to all possible realities across time and space, and even realities between realities. Its origins are unknown and its purpose unclear. However, the potential for cataclysm and chaos is huge. The Nexus has brought infection-spreading zombies to Prime Earth, summoned demons from hell, and even been weaponized by the Thunderbolts as a method of rapidly deploying its super-powered operatives. Although free-moving, this unique locus is generally located near the swampland near Citrusville, Florida, guarded by—and occasionally within—the tragic and monstrous mix of magic and perverted science known as the Man-Thing. ∎

See also: Parallel lives, Death

BACK FROM THE DEAD
ZOMBIVERSE

ON THE RECORD

DESIGNATION
Collective Super Consciousness

LOCATION
Currently Earth-2149

POWERS
Propagates by infecting live hosts with insatiable hunger

MISSION
Consume all life

STATUS REPORT
Crusade temporarily halted by superhumans from Prime Earth

Caught in a timeloop, undead Super Hero Sentry arrives from his own future, bringing a terrible plague that eradicates everything. As zombies, victims transmit an anaerobic virus via bodily fluids, instantly infecting new hosts with ravening hunger, but without affecting cognition. With all their former abilities intact, the zombies join a viral super consciousness. It propagates with efficiency, targeting superhumans.

In days, Earth-2149 is devastated by zombies. The virus seems self-defeating; eating itself out of resources with incredible speed. However, the dead go dormant when supplies diminish, and if fresh victims arrive, their rapacious cravings return. When the Silver Surfer visits Earth, his defeat leads to Galactus being consumed by Zombie Iron Man, Spider-Man, Luke Cage, Giant-Man, Colonel America, Wolverine, and the Hulk. Now imbued with Cosmic Power, they head into space, and within 40 years the entire universe is dead. Eventually, the Sentry plunges through time to begin the cycle of doom anew.

Back on Earth-2149, dimensional travelers from Earth-1610 have opened up further possibilities: other life-filled realms in which to advance the virus' Hunger Gospel. Total disaster is only averted by an ultra-specialized agency on Prime Earth. Having experienced many cross-dimensional disasters, Prime Earth has created the Alternate Reality Monitoring and Operational Response Agency (A.R.M.O.R). The team is a UN-mandated research task force: first responders to all incidences of trans-reality conflict. They guard against contamination

Bite club Nobody, not even Super Heroes, are immune to the rampant zombie virus plaguing Earth.

from extradimensional agents and address time stream disruptions. Making Zombiverse breaches their prime concern, Director Charles Little Sky (aka Portal) deploys unique but expendable operatives such as living vampire Michael Morbius, Machine Man Aaron Stack, and interdimensional migrant Howard the Duck as A.R.M.O.R.'s key away team to stop the plague spreading, whatever the cost. ∎

ANOTHER BRITAIN

OTHERWORLD

ON THE RECORD

DESIGNATION
Mystical Realm: collective British unconscious

PURPOSE
Final sanctuary for all things mythical, ethereal, and otherworldly

MISSION
Preserving all that is good, holy, and natural

STATUS REPORT
Ever changing and forever imperiled

The Sword will be drawn again.
Soul of Avalon

Some places and people are special, as are their spiritual shadows and reflections. For centuries, the British Isles house numerous tribes of humans, gods, and heroes. As millennia pass, the Isles develop a distinct metaphysical mantle, cloaking the region in a subdimension mirroring the United Kingdom's physical geography, and inhabited by fairies, giants, and other creatures considered by many on Earth to be mere folklore.

A contradictory place of serenity and strife, Otherworld is made up of twin kingdoms. Noble Camelot (pictured above) and its mighty champions reside in Avalon, as does the Starlight Citadel: palace of Omniversal Guardian Roma, her father Merlyn, and the base of the multidimensional Captain Britain Corps. It is also home to the Green Chapel, a mystic barometer of Earthly ecological health and hallowed bastion of the Green Knight and his Knights of Pendragon. Avalon holds precious and powerful artifacts: the Holy Grail, soul-challenging Siege Perilous, the Amulet of Right—which transforms Brian Braddock into Prime Earth's Captain Britain—and the Sword of Might, which remakes Kelsey Leigh into

Lionheart. Sister island Tír na nÓg safeguards Celtic tradition as home to the Tuatha de Danaan pantheon.

Otherworld is the collective British unconscious and seat of all magic. As the soul of a living nation, it changes and grows, such as when modern divinities birthed by the 18th century Industrial Revolution win themselves—through war and diplomacy—a separate kingdom of bleak Manchester Gods. Before Christianity, access to other universes was frequent: voyagers merely slipped through mist, forest sunshine, or calm waterways. ∎

Deus ex machines Trickster god Loki negotiates between Otherworld leaders and the industrial Manchester gods.

FUTURE GLADIATOR
KILLRAVEN

ON THE RECORD

REAL NAME
Jonathan Raven

ALLEGIANCES
**Freemen, Avengers,
X-51's Heralds**

ORIGIN POINT
**Post-Martian invasion:
Earth-691; Earth-2120**

POWERS
**Peak athlete, trained
gladiator, psychic access to
all human knowledge**

MISSION
**Personal survival and
human liberty**

STATUS REPORT
**Roaming in the Multiverse
saving lives**

There are critical moments in history across infinite realities that radically define the way in which each reality progresses. During Prime Earth's World War I, a Martian invasion is repulsed by Allied Super Heroes. However, in at least two other Earth realities—Earth-691 and Earth-2120—follow-up invasions by the aliens as the 20th century draws to a close are devastatingly successful. The Martians obliterate Earth's superhuman defenders in shattering blitzkrieg attacks before decimating humanity in nuclear fire.

With flesh-eating Martians ruling—and gradually consuming—the survivors, young Jonathan Raven is singled out by human collaborator Keeper Whitman. Ostensibly training him as a gladiator, Whitman augments the boy's body, making him stronger, faster, and tougher than normal humans. He also alters Raven's brain: creating an ability to tap Martian minds and implanting all human knowledge into his subconscious. Whitman's true goal is the invaders' destruction. Reaching maturity, unbeatable gladiator "Kill Raven" rebels in the arena, slaying his first Martian master before gathering an army of similarly trained warriors and mutants. Calling themselves the Freemen, they strike repeatedly and by the middle of the 21st century their Earth is free.

At one point during the struggle, Killraven encounters time-traveling hero Spider-Man and is drawn out of his universe into trans-dimensional adventures: battling Kang the Conqueror beside the Avengers, and becoming a Herald of robotic doomsayer X-51, the Machine Man of Earth-9997. The latter chooses Killraven and other solitary heroes from alternate Earths such as Iron Man (Earth-8410), Wolverine (Earth-811), and Hyperion (Earth-1121), to warn the Multiverse of a threat posed by Celestial star gods. Briefly institutionalized on Prime Earth, Killraven escapes back to his own reality to fulfill his destiny and win the War of the Worlds. ■

Mars attacks Resistance fighter Killraven uses his gladiatorial skills to fight the coldly rational alien invaders.

THE DEMOLISHER

DEATHLOK

ON THE RECORD

REAL NAME
Luther Manning

ALLEGIANCES
US Army, Project Alpha-Mech

ORIGIN POINT
**1980s US Civil War
on Earth-7484**

POWERS
**Cybernetically enhanced
intellect and physicality**

MISSION
**Killing the madmen who
turned him into a weapon**

STATUS REPORT
**Adrift in the time stream,
looking for peace**

I n alternate timeline Earth-7484,
the US descends into dystopian
anarchy in the 1980s. During
war games, Army Colonel Luther
Manning is fatally wounded, but
astonishingly regains consciousness
in 1990. He has been rebuilt by
deranged, warmongering CIA agents
Simon and Harlan Ryker, instigators
of Project: Alpha-Mech. Manning's

brain, nervous system, and remaining
organs are sealed inside a steel
exoskeleton and interfaced with
a sentient battle computer.

Code named Deathlok the
Demolisher, he is programmed by his
mad superiors to be a remorseless
killing machine. However, his
dormant mind and indomitable will
override his programming, and he
destroys the Rykers' operation and
their insane plan to become gods by
assimilating with Earth's computer
network. Soon after, the Demolisher
saves Prime Earth's Spider-Man when
the time-lost hero lands in Earth-
7484's war-torn US, before being
catapulted through time himself.

With his personal timeline
compromised, the Demolisher
is drawn to Prime Earth by Super
Villains Mentallo and the Fixer,
and reprogrammed to attack the
American President. Impounded by
S.H.I.E.L.D., the Demolisher falls into
the hands of conglomerate Roxxon's
Nth Command, led by Henry Akai
(aka Timestream). Akai uses an
army of cyborgs from divergent
timelines to change history, and
transforms Earth-616's Luther
Manning into a Deathlok to combat
Akai's archenemy, rebel cyborg
Michael Collins. When this Manning

Death shock The demolisher's life after
death involves killing people he doesn't
know for reasons he doesn't understand.

dies during battle, Earth-7484's
Demolisher reboots and he joins
the fight against Timestream's
forces. With Akai's defeat, all
time-displaced cyborg warriors—
including the Demolisher—are
drawn back to their original realities.

Somewhere in another time
and place, the Demolisher remains
locked in his deadly cyborg frame,
still fighting the good fight. It is all
he has left to "live" for. ∎

ABOVE AND BEYOND
THE ULTIMATES

ON THE RECORD

FOUNDING MEMBERS
Captain Marvel (Carol Danvers), Black Panther (T'Challa), Blue Marvel (Adam Brashear), America Chavez, Spectrum (Monica Rambeau), Anti-Man (Conner Sims), Galactus

MISSION
Learn everything, anticipate everything, fix everything

STATUS REPORT
Returned to active duty after a lengthy sabbatical

After countering successive Multiverse-endangering crises involving all of Earth's Super Heroes and most of the planet's extraterrestrial allies, Captain Marvel is determined to avoid future disaster. Consulting with fellow Avenger Black Panther, a radical solution is adopted: cosmic triage and crisis intervention. The two heroes gather a mighty team of troubleshooters to anticipate universal threats, assess potential permanent solutions, and execute them preemptively.

Physicist Adam Brashear is sought for his cutting-edge knowledge and the might he wields as Blue Marvel. Monica Rambeau, aka Spectrum, controls light and having led the Avengers and Nextwave, combines vast powers with strategic brilliance. The final recruit is America Chavez, a unique hero from the magic-infused Utopian Parallel. Having saved hundreds of realities in her self-proclaimed role as Paramedic of the Multiverse, the dimension-hopping Chavez readily joins the Ultimates as the Universe's "Big Picture" team.

Planet-devouring Galactus is their first target. Their solution to his

Cube route Thanos underestimates the Paramedic of the Multiverse in his failed quest for the Cosmic Cube.

overwhelming threat is to overfeed him, evolving him from a creature hungry for life energy into a benign Lifebringer turning dead rocks into hospitable worlds. Former antimatter villain Conner Sims joins them as Galactus' new herald, reuniting the team following an acrimonious split during the second superhuman civil war. With Galactus, they embark on extraordinary missions: liberating shackled universal avatar Eternity; exposing the oldest sentience in all Creations; battling counterparts from expired realities, as well as taking on reality's highest beings. When Galactus reverts to his world-ravaging state, the Ultimates return to defend Earth from Chitauri attack and plan for the next mission. ■

We're the Ultimates. The Ultimate team, to solve the ultimate problems.
Captain Marvel

MENDING THE MULTIVERSE

EXILES

ON THE RECORD

FOUNDING MEMBERS
Blink (Clarice Ferguson, Earth-295), Nocturne (TJ Wagner, Earth-2182), Thunderbird (John Proudstar, Earth-1100), Magnus (Magnus Lehnsherr, Earth-27), Mimic (Calvin Rankin, Earth-12), Morph (Kevin Sidney, Earth-1081)

MISSION
Repairing fractured realities

STATUS REPORT
Constantly deceived, but resolved to fix the problems and learn the truth

Part of a greater Omniverse, the Multiverse comprises countless realms: a very fragile construct held together by capricious events and key individuals. Any change to time or circumstance can snowball into cataclysmic consequences, dooming entire realities to corruption or worse. In response, agencies from within or beyond the Multiverse—who harbor hidden agendas and seek to maintain a specific status quo—often employ individuals from within the crisis zones to mitigate the damage and rectify problems. One such task force is the Exiles, a team largely, but not exclusively, comprised of mutant heroes and villains.

Continuously replaced with members from various Earths, the Exiles work for the Timebreakers. These pacifistic insectoids attempt to repair damage they had themselves caused by meddling with the vast crystalline palace the Panoptichron, from where the Timebreakers monitor the Omniverse from outside its bounds. Initially led by teleporter Blink, the Exiles craft surgical adjustments to many timelines. After hundreds of missions, the Timebreakers' mismanagement almost sparks total multiversal Armageddon when Omniversal overlords Merlyn and Roma wage war for control of the mystic sanctuary Otherworld. In the ensuing conflict, several mortal heroes are used as cannon fodder by both sides before peace is restored.

After this realities-shaking event, Sabretooth (Earth-295) takes charge of a new lineup of Exiles (pictured above left) fixing chaotic

Front and center Blink returns to action as the leader of the latest Exiles team whose mission parameters remain unchanged: do or die!

timelines. Basing themselves in the Panoptichron and picking their own assignments, these Exiles are all too aware that prolonged exposure to the crystal matrix will result in them being absorbed by it. Regardless, they valiantly carry on their missions. Sometime later, when a Time Eater begins devouring realities, the Unseen (Nick Fury of Prime Earth) recruits Blink and forms a brand new squad of Exiles, despite the Watchers forbidding his interference. ■

THE END OF EVERYTHING

TIME RUNS OUT

T he cosmos is a universal system that explosively comes into existence and grows, before contracting to die and start anew: a never-ceasing cycle. The current iteration is different: rather than a gradual decline, the Seventh Cosmos ends early because of a malfunction in the divine machinery that underpins it. When the Superflow fails, alternate universes begin crashing into each other with the Earth of each as the critical contact point. Despite the efforts of Super Heroes on every world and ancient alien overseers, such as

We're out of time. It's over. All is lost.
Black Panther

the Builders, the process escalates and soon few existences remain. At the instant when "Time Runs Out," Prime Earth's Doctor Doom uses the power of the Beyonders to combine living fragments of several universes into a vast Battleworld over which he rules as its god.

A timeless place of constant conflict in disparate Warzones, the dark dream ends when Reed Richards and a lifeboat of Super Heroes is uncovered. They had escaped the end of the Seventh Cosmos by removing themselves

Existential Doom Reality's last heroes face a living nightmare: Doom is god... and he hates them!

from reality. Their efforts on Battleworld result in Richards using the Molecule Man's power to end the constant Secret Wars and form a new cosmos, practically unchanged from what had existed before. However, there are differences. Heroes such as Miles Morales of Earth-1610 is seamlessly integrated into the new Prime Earth and most who had died are reborn with no knowledge of what has happened.

Many powerful individuals do remember what has transpired and change accordingly; the most notable being Doom. Experiencing the utter failure of ultimate omnipotence, the world's most dangerous man seeks to redeem himself as a new Iron Man. ■

REPEAT CYCLE
GWEN(POOL) AND THE ART OF MULTIVERSAL MAINTENANCE

ON THE RECORD

REAL NAME
Gwen Poole

ALLEGIANCES
M.O.D.O.K. (Mercenary Organization Dedicated Only to Killing)

POWERS
Able to step outside reality and read it like a comic book: total knowledge of all Super Hero and Villain secrets

MISSION
Having fun and being important

STATUS REPORT
On hiatus from (some) reality

Multiversal existence always periodically ends. However, the latest cosmic annihilation is immediately followed by the formation of a new, fully mature Multiverse—the Eighth Cosmos—rather than one that has gradually evolved and expanded after a Big Bang event. This iteration only exhibits certain minute alterations in the natural laws governing its physical state to distinguish it from its predecessor. Moreover, the rebirth is known to a few survivors of the previous existence, while the governing multiversal abstract beings seem to carry on their ascribed roles from the seventh iteration. How this will affect the future remains uncertain.

One possible herald of that uncertainty principle is the advent of siblings apparently from beyond the accepted boundaries of reality. Gwen Poole is an ordinary young woman in her own origin dimension (Earth-TRN565) who plays games and reads lots of comic books. When a scientific accident deposits her on Prime Earth she realizes that it is populated with all her favorite characters and that she knows all their secrets. Worried over her continued existence if those beyond stop "reading her," she becomes costumed mercenary and villain Gwenpool, killing with impunity while using a true sociopath's excuse: her victims don't really exist.

Also claiming to come from a greater reality, where multiversal life is perceived as a series of mass-market entertainments, is Gwen's brother Teddy. His main concern is getting home and away from this insane region of constant danger. The notion that Gwen is delusional ends after she resolves to become a hero and reinterprets her awareness of higher realms. She develops the ability to slip outside Prime Earth's space/time borders and manipulate the regions beyond existence: the all-encompassing "Gutter." ∎

Gutter snipe
Gwen can step outside reality, manipulating all the people and things left within it.

GLOSSARY

Abstract entities (also abstract or conceptual beings)
Sentient forces of immeasurable power, often associated with a fundamental metaphysical aspect of existence, such as justice, infinity, or death.

Adamantium
An artificially created alloy of iron ore; most impervious substance on Earth—used to create Captain America's shield.

Alternate Earth
A world resembling Earth in physical characteristics, natural phenomena, life-forms, and, to some extent, history. It exists in an equivalent space to Earth's in an alternative universe.

Alternate or parallel universe
A continuum superficially resembling Earth's that coexists separately in the Multiverse.

Android
An artificial being designed to resemble a human as closely as possible.

Annihilation Wave
A devastating invasion by a near-infinite army of rapacious insectoids from the Negative Zone that shattered many intergalactic civilizations.

Antimatter
Matter composed of particles that are counterparts of the particles composing positive matter. When positive matter meets antimatter, both are destroyed and converted to energy.

Bioelectricity
Generation of electricity by living organisms. Electrophysiology permits plants, insects, and animals to glow or produce electrical discharges.

Bionic
Artificial simulation or enhancement of biological processes or capabilities. A cyborg can possess bionic limbs or organs, whereas an android's body is entirely bionic.

Biosphere
The regions of a planet in which living organisms can exist.

Celestials
Godlike unknowable aliens who predate the Multiverse and are devoted to experimenting with life on many worlds. Their missions to these planets are known as "hosts."

Clairvoyance
The ability to see into the future, past, and/or present outside the scope of ordinary perception.

Clone
A genetically identical organism created from the DNA (deoxyribonucleic acid) of another organism.

Cosmic awareness
Enhanced consciousness that provides a sense of oneness with the cosmos, enabling the mind to access information beyond the range and capacity of the physical senses.

Cosmic beings
Creatures of immense power, who are usually immortal and often have cosmic parentage.

Cosmic Cube
Energy matrixes that alter reality at the behest of a holder, the cubes are, in actuality, incubators for new cosmic or abstract beings.

Cosmic power (also Power Cosmic)
Vast energy derived from extraterrestrial sources that most sentient races cannot control. Utilized by entities such as Galactus, the Silver Surfer, and Warlock. Cosmic power wielders can control matter and energy, teleport objects across space and time, create force fields and interdimensional portals.

Cosmos
Totality of existence between a Big Bang and a Big Crunch. Every known cosmos has also been sentient.

Chronokinesis
The ability to mentally manipulate time.

Cybernetics
Study of biological (e.g., human nervous system) or artificial (e.g., electronics) communications systems. The term also refers to synthesizing mind and machine, and detecting thoughts in organic brains and translating them into biomechanical responses.

Cyborg
A living organism significantly modified, augmented, or altered by cybernetic and mechanical devices.

Death
(1) Cessation of life functions in a living being, causing life essence (also known as consciousness, spirit, or soul) to leave the physical body. Certain life essences briefly exist after death as an astral presence. An astral presence whose physical form has died is called a ghost. (2) Abstract embodiment of the process of death; a higher being of the Multiverse.

Demon
A generic term for predatory and parasitic supernatural beings dependent on the physical life-forces of living beings or their metaphysical essences such as souls.

Deviants
Evolutionary offshoot of humanity created through the Celestials' experiments. Deviants tend to look monstrous and have no set phenotype (physical characteristics common to all members).

Dimension (also known as realm)
A discrete region of reality containing space, matter, and energy. The universe is the dimension that Earth shares with other planets, stars, and galaxies. Earth-like dimensions possess physical characteristics and natural laws similar to that of Earth. Alien dimensions differ in their physical

properties and laws, while mystical dimensions are primarily governed by the arcane tenets of magic.

Dimensional travel
The process of leaving one universe and entering another, achieved by physical, psychic, psionic, or magical means.

Divergence
The process by which a single reality splits into two identical realities at a specific point in time when an event triggers two separate chains of causality in different realities. Divergence mirrors the "many worlds" theory of quantum mechanics.

Doppelgänger
A ghostly double of a living person. Commonly, "doppelgänger" refers to any duplicate or lookalike of a person, often referred to as an "evil twin."

Electroplasm
A substance comprised of living unstable molecules, whose source and properties remain largely unknown.

Enigma Force
A mystical energy field permeating and generated by the Microverse to preserve and protect all life. An aspect of the Enigma Force randomly and repeatedly empowers distressed beings in various realms with reality-bending Uni-power, transforming them into the Enigma Force's avatar, Captain Universe.

Entropy
(1) Universal tendency for energy in a closed system to equalize. On a macro scale, entropy represents the inevitable degradation of matter and energy to an inert state unable to sustain life.
(2) An abstract being, son of Eternity.

Eternals
Evolutionary offshoot of many races created through experiments by Celestials. Eternals have extended life spans, are virtually indestructible, and possess superhuman physical and energy manipulating powers.

Extradimensional
Of or having to do with a dimension other than that of the Prime Earth.

Extraterrestrial
(1) A living organism from a world in this dimension other than Earth;
(2) Of or having to do with a world in this dimension other than Earth.

Gamma radiation
High-energy electromagnetic radiation, which in large doses is lethal to most—but not all—living organisms.

Gods
Hugely powerful beings with extended lifespans frequently worshipped by sections of humanity. Most gods now reside extradimensionally, but may have lived on Earth in ancient times.

Heart-Shaped Herb
A unique plant found only in Wakanda that grants users with enhanced strength, senses, speed, reflexes, durability, stamina, and advanced healing abilities.

Hellfire (also soulfire)
Mystical energy similar to ordinary fire and capable of burning physical objects through heat, but also traumatizing souls of living beings.

Homo sapiens
Baseline primate species to which modern human beings belong.

Homo superior (see Mutants)

Homo mermanus
Evolutionary offshoot of Homo sapiens possessing gills and the ability to breathe and live underwater.

Incursions
The cataclysmic phenomena known as incursions result from an unprecedented contraction in the Multiverse. This, in turn, caused universes throughout the Multiverse to collide, with the point of impact being each universe's respective Earth. Incursion is the name given to the period of time in which two Earths approach collision—eight hours.

Infinity Stones (also Infinity Gems)
Vastly powerful primal artifacts able to circumvent universal natural laws. The individual gems grant the ability to override specific universal functions, such as time, space, or reality.

Inhumans
Humans purposefully altered at a genetic level by exposure to Terrigen Crystals or Mist.

Interdimensional
The space between two universes, each of which exists in its own dimension.

Iron Fist
Combat champion of transdimensional city K'un-Lun, a position attained by defeating all challengers in ritual combat and by slaying the immortal, resurrecting dragon Shou Lao the Undying.

Kaiju (origin Japanese)
The term literally translates as a "strange creature." In English, it has come to mean "giant monster."

Life-form
Any organism or entity that can be considered "alive," regardless of whether it conforms to current understandings of biology and physics.

Limbo
A unique dimension existing outside the timestream. Reality in Limbo is a single, ever-changing moment where all that ever was, is, and could be, coexist. Human beings within Limbo do not age or die. Limbo is a conduit to the timestream and enables time travel.

Man on the Wall
A term describing a succession of self-appointed human guardians who secretly eradicate alien and magical threats and/or beings they judge to be inimical to human life and development.

Metamorph (also Polymorph)
An organism capable of altering its shape and appearance in whole or in part, including the ability to add or subtract mass.

Microverse
A parallel universe that is accessible by compressing one's mass sufficiently to enter this universe through an artificially created nexus. Microverses were once mistakenly thought to exist within atoms.

Micro-world
A world existing within the Microverse. Once erroneously believed to exist on subatomic particles.

Mutagenic
Ability of a substance or other trigger to make genetic level changes within a living organism.

Mutant (also Homo superior)
A being with physical characteristic(s) not possessed by either parent. In many cases, this is known as an X-Gene, which, when triggered, enables the being to access abilities previously unavailable to their species.

Mystery men
Unsanctioned crime fighters who hide their identities and operate covertly in America from the 1920s to the 1950s.

Multiverse
A grouping of separate universes.

Nega-bands
Power-enhancing wrist bands designed by the Kree Supreme Intelligence (aka Supremor) to match the Quantum Bands used by the Protector of the Universe. Nega-bands draw their energy from the antimatter Negative Zone and the wearer's own willpower and psionic reserves.

Negative Zone
A universe composed of antimatter that exists in another dimension.

Nexus
A point in a dimension offering access to other dimensions or time periods.

Ten Realms
Interlinked pocket dimensions connected by the energy field known as Yggdrasil.

NuHumans
A term that refers to humans that possess dormant Inhuman genes who mutate and gain extraordinary powers after uncontrolled exposure to Terrigen Crystals or Mist.

Omnipotent
Generic term describing beings who possess incalculable levels of power.

Omniverse
Meta-reality encompassing and extending beyond the accessible universes, multiverses, and greater realms of Underspace and Overspace.

Overspace
A higher dimensional region beyond tangible reality where metaphysical entities such as Eternity, Infinity, and Death can interact with physical beings. This plane of existence is often reached through physical expansion.

Phoenix Force
Primordial cosmic manifestation of creation, destruction, and life's potential. It is also the nexus of all multiversal psionic energy.

Pocket dimension (also pocket realm or pocket universe)
A dimension with a finite and relatively limited amount of space, too small to be considered a separate dimension.

Precognition
The ability to perceive events before they occur. Achieved by mentally scanning various alternate futures, rather than using deduction based on current knowledge.

Primordial Power (also Power Primordial)
Near-infinite force comprised of residual energies generated by most recent Big Bang. A precursor to the Power Cosmic, it is almost exclusively tapped by Elders of the Universe.

Project: Rebirth (also Project: Super Soldier; Operation: Rebirth)
Top secret US Army program, begun during World War II to develop Super-Soldiers through biochemical processes.

Psionic
Term used to describe the psychic manipulation of matter and energy or perceive events via mental contact. Also refers to mechanical means of stimulating a sentient being's natural "psi" abilities. Abbreviated to psi only when describing the powers.

Pym Particles
A theoretical subatomic particle discovered by Dr. Hank Pym that enables size changing. The Pym Particles work by shifting matter into the Kosmos Dimension when shrinking or accruing matter from it when enlarging.

Quantum Bands
Energy bands created by the cosmic entity Eon for her Protectors of the Universe. Gaining energy from the Quantum Zone—the source of all multiversal energy—the Bands allow wearers to control the electromagnetic spectrum and "quantum jump" vast interstellar distances.

Reality
The unified totality of space/time that Earth shares with other stellar bodies such as galaxies, all operating under uniform physical laws and connected to other associated dimensions, such as Asgard, Dark Dimension, or Negative Zone. Separate, alternate realities exist with varying degrees of similarity.

Reality warping
Ability to alter reality, matter, and energy; manifest a person's thoughts or desires; bend time and space; travel across timelines; manipulate the laws of physics; and destroy virtually anything. Regarded as the ultimate super-power.

Red Room
A secret Soviet Cold War program devised to create super-agents through physical training, chemical enhancement, and psychological conditioning. The program was divided on gender grounds, one dedicated to training female agents as Black Widows, the other to producing male Wolf Spiders.

Reincarnation
The process of returning to life after having died, usually as a soul reborn in a new body.

Resurrection
When a departed soul is given renewed life in the deceased's original body.

Robot
Artificial life-form constructed from mechanical components.

Sentient
Possessing intelligence near or above the human level. Often includes self-awareness, problem-solving, and tool use, but not necessarily sanity.

Singularity
A point or region where the normal rules of physics don't apply. Normally found only in a black hole, it is a concentration of matter so dense that space and time are infinitely distorted by gravitational forces.

Soul
A living or once-living being's life essence, consciousness, or spirit.

Space warp (also Stargate)
A natural or artificially created nexus that leads from one point in space through hyperspace into another point in space.

Super-powered (also superhuman)
Possessing abilities and capabilities beyond those of baseline Homo sapiens.

Super-Soldier Serum
General term used to describe a number of processes designed to enhance human physical and mental potential. Constituent elements can include chemical and hormonal stimulants and mutagens, as well as radiation such as Dr. Abraham Esrkine's still-classified "Vita-Rays."

Superflow
Barrier medium composed of informational space that separates parallel universes in the Multiverse. The Superflow acts as a conduit that enables telepathy while feeding dreams and sparking inspiration.

Synthezoid
Artificial being whose physiology and functions mimic those of human beings as closely as possible.

Telekinesis
Psionic ability to move or manipulate matter without physically touching it, especially over long distances.

Telepathy
The psionic ability to send or receive thoughts directly into or from other minds. A person who possesses this ability is called a telepath.

Teleportation
Ability via psionic or artificial means to transport oneself, people, or objects from one point in space to another without physically traveling. A person who possesses this ability is usually called a teleporter.

**Terrigen Crystals
(also Terrigen Mist)**
Crystalline mineral possessing mutagenic properties affecting certain dormant genes implanted in early humanity. Processed into a gaseous form, Terrigen Mist was used for millennia to transform Inhumans into powered individuals.

The Hand
An international order of ninja assassins and criminals utilizing magic and necromancy, and sponsored by a primordial demon called "The Beast."

Time
Multiverse-wide phenomenon ordering events and preventing all reality from happening at once.

Time stream
Multiverse-wide phenomenon that keeps all reality flowing in the same direction, toward entropy. The time stream is not a literal place.

Underspace
An infinite higher dimensional region beneath tangible reality, subatomic realms, and the Microverse, generally reached by extreme physical contraction and compression.

Universe (also Earthspace)
A single dimension constituting all of the space/time Prime Earth shares with other planets, stars, and galaxies.

Unstable molecules
Synthetic material discovered by Reed Richards that instantly adapts to varied environments. The material's unstable molecular structure enables it to be highly resilient to drastic changes in heat, cold, pressure, and density, and resistant to dirt. As such it is ideal for Super Hero costumes.

Uru
An extradimensional metal that is malleable yet extremely hard when tempered. Uru also has the capacity to harness and enhance magical energy. Thor Odinson's mighty hammer Mjölnir is forged from Uru.

Vampire
A demonic creature who survives by feeding upon the blood of the living, typically humans. Vampirism is extremely infectious and sometimes a single bite can transform a human into a vampire. The origin of most vampires can be traced to a spell written by Elder God Chthon in the Book of the Darkhold.

Vibranium
Extraterrestrial mineral that can absorb all forms of vibration, from sound waves to concussive impacts. On Earth there are two known forms: Vibranium is found in the African kingdom of Wakanda, while the metal-dissolving form known as "Anti-Metal" is located in the Savage Land.

Weapon X program
A succession of covert US and Canadian government programs established to create super-agents through extreme physical enhancement and psychological conditioning.

Web of Life and Destiny
A psionic construct that connects alternate universes through a Master Weaver who disburses arachnoid abilities to deserving individuals and facilitates transdimensional travel along its strands.

Werewolf
A human being who transforms into a humanoid wolf or wolflike creature, usually on nights of the full moon. The transformation can be either attributed to the supernatural phenomenon known as lycanthropy or attained through long-forgotten scientific processes.

INDEX

E

F

G

H

I